Finding the Lost Year

Finding the Lost Year

WHAT HAPPENED WHEN LITTLE ROCK
CLOSED ITS PUBLIC SCHOOLS

Sondra Gordy

THE UNIVERSITY OF ARKANSAS PRESS

FAYETTEVILLE

2009

Copyright © 2009 by The University of Arkansas Press

All rights reserved
Manufactured in the United States of America

ISBN: 978-1-55728-900-1 (cloth)
ISBN: 978-1-68226-169-9 (paper)
eISBN: 978-1-61075-152-0

25 24 23 22 21   5 4 3 2 1

Text design by Ellen Beeler

⊗ The paper used in this publication meets the minimum requirements of the American National Standard for Permanence of Paper for Printed Library Materials Z39.48-1984.

Library of Congress Cataloging-in-Publication Data

Gordy, Sondra Hercher.
Finding the lost year : what happened when Little Rock closed its public schools? / Sondra Gordy.
    p. cm.
Includes bibliographical references and index.
ISBN 978-1-55728-900-1 (cloth : alk. paper)
    1. School integration—Arkansas—Little Rock. 2. Public schools—Arkansas—Little Rock. 3. Discrimination in education—Arkansas—Little Rock. 4. African Americans—Education—Arkansas—Little Rock. 5. African American students—Arkansas—Little Rock. 6. Little Rock (Ark.)—Race relations. 7. Central High School (Little Rock, Ark.). I. Title.
LC214.23.L56G67 2009
379.2'63097677309045—dc22

2009001522

for Dr. C. Fred Williams
mentor and colleague
who always believed in this project

and for
Sandra Hubbard
documentary filmmaker and
Lost Year classmate who inspired me
to tell the unknown stories of the 1958–59 school year

CONTENTS

ACKNOWLEDGMENTS

This book would not have been written without the advice and generous kindness of friends, colleagues, and those who were once strangers.

Because the research for this book began over thirteen years ago, citing each individual who helped me along the way is impossible, but to each of you I am grateful. For the many Lost Year participants who granted me interviews, thank you for allowing me to tell your story. For all those at the University of Arkansas Special Collections, the University of Central Arkansas Archives, and the University of Arkansas at Little Rock Archives, I am appreciative of your responses to my many requests for help.

A number of institutions provided funding for the research for this book, as well as the research and production of the sixty-minute documentary entitled *The Lost Year:* the Arkansas Council for the Humanities, the National Endowment for the Humanities, the Fred Darragh Foundation, and the President's Fund at the University of Central Arkansas. Funding for the Web site www.thelostyear.com came from the Bridge Fund at the Arkansas Community Foundation.

To all those at the University of Arkansas Press, I am grateful for your patience and fine work.

INTRODUCTION

Before the Lost Year

*None of that happened to you. Why offer memories you
do not have? Remembering can be painful, even frightening.
But it can also swell your heart and open your mind.*
—*Toni Morrison,* Remember: The Journey to School Integration

September 1957 lives in the minds of many Americans as a time of disgrace for citizens and high school students in Little Rock, Arkansas. Many writers and historians have documented the initial story of the Little Rock Central High desegregation crisis. Images of shouting segregationists and tales of miscreant classmates play out in the black and white images of the day: Governor Orval Faubus calls out the Arkansas National Guard to block the entry of nine black high school students into a white student population of almost two thousand, as American viewers and audiences worldwide watch through the new medium of television. Within three weeks, U.S. president Dwight Eisenhower sends the 101st Airborne Division to trump Faubus's authority with that of the federal government, while preserving order and giving protected entry to the Little Rock Nine.[1]

Important as the story of September 1957 and the following months is in the history of both civil rights and public education, the complicated period that followed actually reveals more about the nature of a community in crisis. An extensive and ongoing literature regarding Little Rock's reaction to the *Brown I* and *Brown II* decisions makes the 1957–58 Little Rock desegregation crisis the single most studied event in Arkansas history.[2] Authors have examined the crisis at Central High through a wide variety of lenses over a fifty-year period, producing a wealth of literature that informs this study. Often these examinations, whether personal memoir or rigorous analysis, concentrate on the media-rich period that ended with the graduation of Ernest Green, the first and only senior among the Little Rock Nine.

The purpose of this work is twofold. Its premise is that the Little Rock school crisis did not end when Principal Jess Matthews handed a Central High diploma to the school's first black graduate in May 1958. This book captures the details of the second year of confrontation, a time known as the Lost Year of 1958–59, when all Little Rock public high schools stood closed—locking out 3,665 black and white students. Its emphasis allows an examination of the period between the first federal enforcement of the *Brown* decision for "desegregation" in Little Rock and the later push for broader "integration" brought by *Swann v. Charlotte-Mecklenburg* (1971), with its use of busing. More narrowly, it examines a more neglected period between Little Rock's desegregation by *Brown* and its first use of pupil assignment laws in the 1959–60 school year. Little Rock school officials employed such laws when they allowed just a few black students to enter Central High and Hall High in 1959, after the Supreme Court's affirmation of pupil placement in *Shuttleworth v. Birmingham Board of Education* (1958). Even more specifically, this book details the community background of *Cooper v. Aaron* (1958), a landmark case that author Tony Freyer has recently declared a "catalyst for overcoming defiance." The *Cooper* ruling of September 12, 1958, marks the very beginning of closed schools in Little Rock, when Governor Faubus again used state law to delay a federal court ruling. Freyer looks back, fifty years later, to label this complicated case one that "enable[d] the Supreme Court for the first time to affirm *Brown* on the basis of judicial supremacy underpinning U.S. constitutional democracy."[3]

Second, this work examines the complicated period of the Lost Year through the eyes and words of the black and white displaced students and teachers, those victims most affected by Little Rock's closed public schools. It is intended to bring out of the shadows of history many nonelite participants whose stories have truly been "lost" and to portray the dramatic second year of crisis as one of personal loss and often courage. This is, in a way, a community study, examining how a people came to grips with the necessity of change and how they adjusted to the demands of a far-reaching cultural shift. It is based on interviews with more than twenty black and white teachers and more than fifty former students in both the black and the white communities.

As a historical work, this book's focus is narrow, but it argues more broadly for a different interpretation of two crucial votes cast by Little Rock citizens during the Lost Year. It questions recent interpretations of both the September 1958 referendum called for by Arkansas Act 4, regarding school closure, and the recall vote on May 25, 1959, which removed the extreme segregationist Little Rock School District (LRSD) board members. This study revisits Numan Bartley's 1969 interpretation of the September vote, which finds that the closure-of-the-school vote cannot be seen as a true referendum by Little Rock citizens and parents, because "Governor Faubus and the segregationists assured the voters that private segregated schools would promptly replace the public schools."[4] This goes against the recent interpretation by John Kirk, who refers to "the so-called 'Lost Year' of 1958–59" by saying, "It must be remembered that it was the predominantly white electorate that voted to keep the schools closed rather than integrate them." Kirk continues: "That electorate presumably included the parents of many of the white children who were left without an education. In that sense, the year was less lost than tossed—given away."[5] This book argues that to discount the immediate and long-term consequences of closed public schools on almost four thousand students because of their parents' beliefs or actions is absurd.

Regarding the May 25, 1959, recall vote, this study returns to the earliest reporting of that vote to argue against more recent interpretations. Elizabeth Jacoway interprets the STOP victory of May 25, 1959, quite narrowly. Jacoway views this removal by recall vote of the three extreme segregationists through the comments of several members of the community, such as the retained school board member Everett Tucker, who said that he did not think the community had suddenly decided to be in favor of integration. Though Jacoway quotes a newspaper headline from New York declaring "Faubus Loses" and acknowledges that the vote was a "devastating blow for Orval Faubus," she stresses that the "STOP victory did not usher in a golden era of advancement for Little Rock's black citizens." She also insists, "It was the black vote that won the election."[6] This book argues that the May 25, 1958, recall vote demonstrates three things. First, the vote reveals the continuation of an existing coalition of upper-class white voters and black voters that can be traced back to at least 1950. Second, the vote was based on race, not just on the issue of "opening the schools." Third, the recall results handed Little Rock's white leadership a victory that could have been used to move forward with desegregation on a greater scale, had white leaders not squandered the results in what historian Ben Johnson calls a pattern of "evasion and delay."[7]

The dramatic events of September 1957 routinely overshadow the complicated, confusing, frustrating, and more tedious events of the Lost Year, a tendency reflected in the extensive writing that has emerged from the Little Rock desegregation crisis. A considerable literature regarding Little Rock's reaction to the *Brown I* and *Brown II* decisions began soon after the 1957–58 school year, instigating the long historiography of Central High desegregation. The first collection of memoirs of the crisis was followed by broad studies of school desegregation and civil rights, which together make up much of the literature on Little Rock's experience. One of the first personal accounts was by Virgil Blossom, the superintendent of Little Rock public schools at the time of the crisis. As a primary participant in events, he penned his recollections to defend his role as a gradualist. He records that with the help of his LRSD board, he attempted to comply with federal authority, while state authority and individual extremists worked against his plan for desegregation. He concludes that desegregation's failure can be blamed on the "vacillation of political leaders at state and federal levels" trying to avoid responsibility for enforcement and also on the actions of well-organized segregationists determined to "prevent a showdown on their own home-grounds."[8] More recently, Jacoway, in her monumental and detailed analysis of the crisis, *Turn Away Thy Son: The Crisis That Shocked the Nation,* and in her article "Richard C. Butler and the Little Rock School Board: The Quest to Maintain 'Educational Quality,'" comes closest to defending Blossom's and the school board's gradualist approach.[9] Jacoway's expansive, meticulous study of the two-year period lays out the drama through a focus on the actions of pivotal players, many of whom were white leaders in the dispute. By organizing each chapter around these people, many of whom were friends and relatives of her family in Little Rock, she presents an in-depth analysis of each individual's actions within the broader, complicated story of desegregation, political maneuvering, racial conflict, legal confusion, and social chaos. She carefully fleshes out these human stories, even for those characters commonly blamed for causing the conflict. Jacoway agrees with recent scholarship that stresses fear of miscegenation as an underlying basis for white hysteria regarding wholesale racial integration. Surprisingly to many, she portrays Orval Faubus as less an avowed segregationist seeking ongoing political power than a racial moderate seeking to avert violence within the context of the political reality of the day.

In an earlier work Jacoway describes the community's white elite businessmen as "taken by surprise" by the response of segregationists after the business community carefully orchestrated the region's economic progress after World War II. Though these business leaders had reformed city government, worked to lure industry, and secured a federal air base in Jacksonville, Arkansas, the explosive response to desegregation convinced them that economic progress demanded that the community finally make some progress in race relations.[10] An early critic of the actions of Blossom and the school board was George C. Iggers, a white professor at the all-black Philander Smith College in Little Rock. This German Jew, an active member of the local chapter of the National Association for the Advancement of Colored People (NAACP), wrote unfavorably about both Blossom and the school board's delaying tactics.[11] More recently, historian John Kirk has also written critically of Blossom, the school board, and Little Rock's white businessmen in their failure to successfully move forward with racial integration.[12] Kirk's 2002 *Redefining the Color Line: Black Activism in Little Rock, Arkansas 1940–1970* speaks from the perspective of the black community before, during, and after the Central High crisis. Kirk includes chapters on the *Brown* decision, as well as on the Little Rock School Crisis, written from the point of view of local and national NAACP leaders and, to a lesser degree, the Little Rock Nine. He argues that whites' efforts to respond with only minimum compliance to important court rulings on desegregation amounted to just another form of resistance—if not massive resistance—to school desegregation. He stresses the importance of local civil rights leaders and, in his more recent work, *Beyond Little Rock: The Origins and Legacies of the Central High Crisis,* broadens his study.[13] Also critical of the white school leaders is historian Karen Anderson, who criticizes the LRSD board in two areas. Anderson finds that the school leadership asked the courts for delays in integration, while limiting the number of blacks admitted into formerly white schools, in order to maintain what they identified as "education quality." She also argues that the board's failure to enforce stricter disciplinary policies in the 1957–58 school year was an attempt to prevent making "martyrs to the segregationist cause."[14]

One of the earliest historians to examine Little Rock within a broader survey of southern resistance to desegregation was Numan Bartley in 1969.[15] His early study focuses on Arkansas and the other ten states of the former Confederacy that enacted legislation to prevent or hamper enforcement of school desegregation. Examining the topic of massive resistance, Bartley places Arkansas on the periphery of the Deep South, showing how it appeared to mimic states such as Virginia, which had inaugurated massive resistance in 1955 with the "Southern Manifesto." Bartley's work, published over ten years after the crisis, contains an extensive bibliography on Little Rock and Arkansas that demonstrates the wealth of information published within a very short time frame. Among the many periodicals and newspapers he references, Bartley gives special praise to the perceptive coverage of political and racial events in the *Arkansas Gazette* and in the editorials of the *Memphis Commercial Appeal*. Indeed, in his 1969 work, Bartley cites fourteen monographs directly related to Arkansas. Bartley first recommends Corrine Silverman's noninterpretive narrative *The Little Rock Story,* as well as the collection of documents and readings compiled early on by Wilson Record and Jane Cassels Record.[16] Four works that Bartlett mentions concentrate on the role of the church in the controversy, some openly critical of religious and political leaders. Colbert Cartwright, a Little Rock activist minister, wrote articles entitled "Lessons from Little Rock," and "The Improbable Demagogue of Little Rock.[17] The Episcopal bishop Robert R. Brown published *Bigger Than Little Rock* in 1958, a larger work that concentrates on the role of the church in the crisis. Brown covers, firsthand, events leading to the crisis and describes the ineffectiveness of Little Rock ministers in influencing events.[18] Thomas Pettigrew and Ernest Q. Campbell, Harvard sociologists, wrote *Christians in Racial Crisis: A Study of Little Rock's Ministry, Including Statements on Desegregation and Race Relations by the Leading Religious Denominations of the United* States in 1959.[19] In this sociological work, Pettigrew and Campbell use specific examples of Southern churchmen speaking up quietly for school desegregation but also highlight the fissure in some denominations over race relations. They find that most of the community's denominational clergymen viewed racial integration as morally right and desired to do something about it, but many failed when faced with the dilemma of their opposite-thinking laity and the power within their churches' institutional structure.[20] Not a clergyman himself, but one of the rare laymen to head the Southern Baptist Convention, veteran congressman Brooks Hays was affected by politics as well as religion. His memoir of the crisis, *A Southern Moderate Speaks,* published in 1959, explains his concern with race relations and his efforts to better them during his political career. Hays's work provides evidence of the political consequences that could befall a moderate in Little Rock at the hands of segregationists. After signing the Southern Manifesto with all the other members of Arkansas's congressional delegation, Hays later attempted to broker an agreement between Governor Orval Faubus and President Dwight Eisenhower at the beginning of the 1957 crisis. Hays lost his congressional seat to segregationist Dale Alford by a shocking margin in a short write-in campaign in November 1959.[21] Alford and his wife also wrote their own version of the Central High crisis, from the point of view of segregationists.[22]

More recently, David Chappell's *A Stone of Hope: Prophetic Religion and the Death of Jim Crow* examines various aspects of religion and the southern civil rights movement. Chappell focuses on liberalism and its failure in the 1930s, the spiritual courage of blacks working for political change, and the weakness of some enemies of civil rights.[23] Carolyn Gray LaMaster has focused on the Jewish response to desegregation in Little Rock, highlighting many in that community who were active in the cause.[24] Additionally, Irving Spitzberg's *Racial Politics in Little Rock 1954–1964* traces the involvement of many in the Little Rock Jewish community who acted during the desegregation crisis, especially during the STOP campaign.[25] Mark Newman, in "The Arkansas Baptist State Convention and Desegregation 1954–1968," finds that the desegregation crisis in Little Rock and the growing worldwide awareness of American racism eventually led Baptists to relinquish their support of segregation, finding that it went against their historical commitment to missions around the world.[26] Jane Dailey's most recent work, "Sex, Segregation, and the Sacred after Brown," argues that historians have underestimated religion's role in both supporting and dismantling civil rights for blacks.[27] Dailey finds that both the black community and the white community, with its opponents and supporters of desegregation, have used religion to support their own views.

Numan Bartley's seminal work, *The Rise of Massive Resistance,* also examines works from a political point of view, focusing on voting patterns, the one-party system, and the nature of politics in Arkansas. He cites the work of V. O. Key, in *Southern Politics in State and Nation,* Key's section on Arkansas entitled "Pure One Party Politics."[28] The weaknesses of the one-party system are also explored in Boyd Alexander Drummond's dissertation, which traces the state's politics from the 1930s until the time of desegregation.[29]

Since Bartley's 1969 work, the literature on the Crisis Year has not diminished. Other personal accounts by key participants emerged soon after Blossom's account. Daisy Bates, the state chair of the Arkansas NAACP, published her personal life story, recounting events at Central High.[30] While Bates's book has been long honored as a source of the local NAACP point of view, Grif Stockley's recent biography of Bates dispels some of her personal information as untrue, while continuing to honor Bates's courageous work, assigning her even greater regard.[31]

Governor Orval Faubus waited until the 1980s to write his version of events in Little Rock, but his work disappointed scholars, in that he simply linked together newspaper headlines, text, and some political cartoons, adding running commentary.[32] More recently, Roy Reed, an *Arkansas Gazette* reporter of the period and later a correspondent for the *New York Times,* published *Faubus: The Life and Times of an American Prodigal,* providing a fuller treatment of Faubus's life that casts him more as a politician than as a leader.[33] Another participant in the drama of Little Rock was Elizabeth Huckaby, the vice principal for girls at Central High during the crisis and beyond. Huckaby waited until her retirement from teaching to publish *Crisis at Central High,* using her personal memorabilia, her diary, and school records to fashion an inside chronology of events within the school during the first year of integration. Subsequently, a made-for-television adaptation of the same name received broad acceptance. More importantly, Huckaby's collection of school and personal records, housed at the University of Arkansas, remains a fund of valuable primary source materials for scholars.[34] Her personal diary of the 1959 calendar year is housed in Little Rock.[35] Another Central High faculty member, librarian Lola Dunnavant, maintained a diary (later edited) that describes the 1957–58 and 1958–59 school years from her point of view as a segregationist.[36] In addition, Central High School's vice principal for boys, J. O. Powell, wrote an unpublished manuscript that stresses his personal frustration with most other members of the LSRD administration.[37]

Soon after the 1957–58 school year ended, events transpired over the summer to bring about the Lost Year of 1958–59. This period of closed high schools in the city extended the crisis for another year. The most helpful summary of political events during this period is a short work by Henry M. Alexander called *The Little Rock Recall Election,* which records voting patterns in the important election of May 1958.[38]

In the summer of 1958, Governor Orval Faubus led the Arkansas General Assembly to pass a series of state laws to once again counter mandates from the federal courts regarding desegregation. One group that arose almost immediately after school closure and worked to open the closed high schools was the Women's Emergency Committee to Open Schools (WEC), headed by city matriarch Adolphine Fletcher Terry. A summary of the racially charged environment was self-published by a president of the organization as early as 1972. This memoir, by Vivion Brewer, was published posthumously in 1999 as *The Embattled Ladies of Little Rock.* Brewer tells the story of the Lost Year from her perspective as an activist working against both racial and gender biases.[39] Sara Murphy's more recent *Breaking the Silence: Little Rock's Women Emergency Committee to Open Our Schools 1958–63* adds to the literature of personal experience in the WEC, extending the story to the development of the Panel of American Women, a multiracial, multiethnic group that worked for healing from 1963 to 1972. Both Brewer and Murphy portray the WEC as more than a group of women trying to open the schools, from their perspectives as racial liberals who were embarrassed by the political behavior of Faubus and the segregationists but constrained by 1950s gender roles.[40] The voices of such Lost Year moderates, who worked to open the closed high schools, reveal that period as the first opportunity participants had to take their community back from the segregationists. Lorraine Gates also highlights the significance of gender in "Power from the Pedestal: The Women's Emergency Committee and the Little Rock School Crisis." Gates includes the few 1980s sources that even mention the work of the WEC, quoting Irving Spitzberg to contrast the delayed action of the white community's male leadership to the actions of these white women.[41]

Irving Spitzberg, a Lost Year classmate from Hall High, had published his *Racial Politics in Little Rock 1954–1964* nine years earlier. Spitzberg centers his study around the creation of the STOP campaign for the recall election in May 1959, coining the term *burgher elite* for the civic leaders who finally emerged after the two-year crisis. Raised within the Jewish community and connected by family to the WEC, Spitzberg led the student STOP movement in the spring of 1959, which positioned him to work with and for those "burghers" he came to honor in his writing.[42] Shorter works such as Neil McMillen's 1971 article "The White Citizens' Council and Resistance to School Desegregation in Arkansas" focuses on the entire period of desegregation through the lens of the white segregationists, highlighting both Hoxie, Arkansas, and great detail regarding Little Rock.[43] David Chappell also writes of the white community but focuses on whites who helped blacks gain civil rights in Little Rock and three other southern cities in *Inside Agitators: White Southerners in the Civil Rights Movement.* Chappell finds that black success often came to those who exploited the divisions in the white community. In his article "Diversity within a Racial Group: White People in Little Rock 1957–1959," Chappell divides whites into three distinct groups based on racial views and finds that their differences grew during the crisis.[44] Historian Graeme Cope has also written of whites in Little Rock but has focused on segregationist students, as well as male and female adults. Cope's article "A Thorn in the Side" describes in meticulous detail the Mother's League of Central High, while "Honest White People of the Middle and Lower Classes" focuses on the Capital Citizens' Council. "'Marginal Youngsters' and 'Hoodlums of Both Sexes'? Student Segregationists during the Little Rock School Crisis" describes segregationist students. All three of Cope's articles were published in the *Arkansas Historical Quarterly.*[45]

Tony Freyer's recent work, in *Little Rock on Trial:* Cooper v. Aaron *and School Desegregation,* explores the court case initiated by parents of black children in Little Rock in 1956 against the Little Rock School District, tracing its complicated legal manifestations into a significant turning point in the U.S. civil rights struggles that he says reaffirmed the U.S. constitutional democracy based on judicial supremacy. This supplements Freyer's earlier *Little Rock Crisis: A Constitutional Interpretation* (1984) and "The Past as Future: The Little Rock Crisis and the Constitution" (1997).[46]

While this list of sources on the Central High desegregation crisis is incomplete, no previous author has concentrated a study on the displaced students and teachers of the 1958–59 Lost Year. This book endeavors to tell that story through the multiple voices of these individuals, recorded in recent interviews but also in personal diaries and documents from the period. It is intended to show the school crisis as a community crisis, leading to extensive personal and family disruptions; to demonstrate how Little Rock's leaders responded or failed to respond to the task of forming a racially integrated society; and finally to recognize the long-term consequences of forcing young people to craft their views on race and desegregation within such a racially charged environment. In short, this work gives voice to those affected by the neglected Lost Year, which marked the beginning of Little Rock's failed public policy in meaningful desegregation and its loss of public community.

To understand the Lost Year, one needs to recall the rudiments of the first year of desegregation in Little Rock. Following is an annotated timeline of the 1957–58 crisis, providing factual background and insight to allow the reader to understand more fully the Lost Year that followed.[47]

MAY 17, 1954. The dramatic events in Little Rock, described above, would come in response to the 1954 U.S. Supreme Court decision *Brown v. Board of Education of Topeka, Kansas,* which mandates a change in public education across the country. Racial segregation is no longer acceptable or legal based upon the Fourteenth Amendment to the U.S. Constitution.

MAY 1954. Superintendent Virgil Blossom and the Little Rock School District (LRSD) board announce their intention to comply with the *Brown* decision, but only after the courts have outlined an implementation decree.

MAY 24, 1955. The LRSD board adopts a phased plan of integration called the Blossom Plan. After several changes, the Blossom Plan would develop into a quite limited approach that would begin only at Central High in 1957, after the construction of two new high schools for the growing urban population of Little Rock. One of the new high schools, Hall High, would be for whites only, in the well-to-do western edges of Little Rock. The other, Horace Mann High in eastern Little Rock, would become a blacks-only high school.

MAY 31, 1955. The U.S. Supreme Court issues its *Brown II* implementation order, directing school districts across America to proceed with desegregation with "all deliberate speed." Chief Justice Earl Warren writes the Court's unanimous decision, which in reality sets no specific deadlines. Southern school boards interpret this decision as a chance for delay.

JANUARY 23, 1956. Twenty-seven black students in Little Rock attempt to enroll for the second semester at Central High, Little Rock Technical High, Forest Heights Junior High, and Forest Park Elementary School. They are refused enrollment by the LRSD Board of Education.

FEBRUARY 8, 1956. Twelve black parents, on behalf of thirty-three black students, file a federal lawsuit called *Aaron v. Cooper* asking for immediate desegregation of Little Rock schools. The case uses the names of William Cooper, president of the LRSD board, and John Aaron, the first listed black student. The suit is sponsored by the National Association for the Advancement of Colored People (NAACP). In its varied forms, this case would extend integration in Little Rock and across the South.

MARCH 11, 1956. All eight of Arkansas's U.S. senators and congressmen demonstrate resistance by joining other southern legislators in signing the "Southern Manifesto"—a document that denounces the U.S. Supreme Court's decision on desegregation and encourages the southern states to resist it. They are joined by ninety-two other southern members of Congress.

APRIL 6, 1956 (FRIDAY). Horace Mann High School for blacks opens on McAlmont, replacing overcrowded Dunbar High, which becomes a junior high for blacks.

AUGUST 28, 1956. U.S. district court judge John E. Miller upholds the LRSD board's gradual desegregation plan in the case of *Aaron v. Cooper.*

NOVEMBER 6, 1956. Orval Faubus wins reelection for a second term as governor after defeating the Democratic candidate Jim Johnson in the summer primary and the Republican Roy Mitchell in the November general election.

MARCH 27, 1957. Central High School hosts Ninth Grade Night as an orientation, and Superintendent Virgil Blossom welcomes future sophomores and their parents to the school. He had agreed to discuss desegregation and the plans of the LRSD, but he speaks for five minutes and does not mention desegregation.

APRIL 29, 1957. An appeal of *Aaron v. Cooper* to a federal appellate court results in the upholding of the LRSD board's gradual desegregation plan. Judge John Miller had approved this plan at a lower level in federal district court the previous August.

JUNE 27, 1957. Members of the Capital Citizens' Council, Reverend Wesley Pruden, and the lawyer Amis Guthridge submit a set of public questions to the LRSD board regarding plans for the social interaction of black and white students. They also inquire about opportunities for white and black students to attend segregated schools should their schools be integrated. This follows letters from the same organization to Governor Faubus asking that white and black students attend segregated schools.

JULY 27, 1957. The LRSD board responds to the questions of the Capital Citizens' Council, saying that providing only separate schools for whites and blacks will violate the court order to proceed with integration. It assures the public, however, that social interaction of the races will not occur and uses this opportunity to explain that the only Little Rock high school to be integrated is Central.

AUGUST 1957. A variety of constituents file a series of suits in federal and chancery courts to either delay integration or declare some state segregation laws unconstitutional. Mrs. Clyde Thomason, the secretary of the newly formed Mothers' League of Little Rock Central High School, files one such suit. The Mother's League is a segregationist group supported by the Capital Citizens' Council. The League wishes to prevent integration at the high school, where some of the women have children.

AUGUST 23, 1957. Preregistration of students for all Little Rock schools begins. High school students pick up schedules, textbook lists, and an instruction sheet with first-day directions and school rules. Administrators at Central High expect as many as twenty black students whom higher school authorities might assign to their building, but no black students appear on this day.

AUGUST 26–27, 1957. Preregistration at Central High continues, with sixty new students coming from Scott High School in Scott, Arkansas. The Pulaski County superintendent agrees to transport and pay tuition for these rural students so they might have more academic offerings than the small rural high school can provide. Some students are Japanese Americans who live and work on a produce farm near Scott.

AUGUST 27, 1957. Several black students attempt to enroll at Central High but are turned away by the registrar, who tells them they must go to the superintendent's office to obtain transfers for registration. Neither of the vice principals nor principal Jess Matthews sees the students.

AUGUST 29, 1957. U.S. district court judge John E. Miller withdraws from the pending desegregation case and allows Judge Ronald Davies from North Dakota to replace him in federal court, surprising both Superintendent Blossom and Governor Orval Faubus. Judge Murray Reed in the Chancery Court grants an injunction against integration in the case filed by Mrs. Thomason of the Mothers' League of Central High.

AUGUST 30, 1957. Federal district court judge Ronald Davies orders integration to proceed the following Tuesday.

SEPTEMBER 2, 1957. Labor Day is the final day of summer vacation for all Little Rock students. Governor Faubus speaks on local television that evening, announcing that he has called out the Arkansas National Guard to preserve order at Central High. He says that the state militia will act not as segregationists or integrationists, but as "soldiers called to active duty to carry out their assigned tasks."

SEPTEMBER 3, 1957. Hall High opens for whites in western Little Rock on a segregated basis.

SEPTEMBER 3, 1957. Teachers and white students attend Central High despite armed guards around its perimeter. National Guard lines prevent black janitors, maids, and cafeteria cooks from entering. No black students appear, as Superintendent Blossom has requested that they stay away for their own safety.

SEPTEMBER 3, 1957. The LRSD board petitions the federal district court, asking for instructions. The board maintains that in light of the governor's actions in calling out the Arkansas National Guard, the board should be exempt from any charge of contempt; it asks that "no Negro students attempt to attend Central or any white high school until this dilemma is legally resolved."

SEPTEMBER 4, 1957. Two hundred seventy Arkansas National Guard troops maintain a perimeter around Central High, turning away all the black students who attempt entry. Elizabeth Eckford, age fifteen and arriving alone, is twice turned back by soldiers. She walks two blocks and waits for a bus to take her home. Taunting her throughout are approximately two hundred shouting adults. Lieutenant Colonel Marion Johnson, the troop commander, turns away other black students who come expecting to enter Central High. Johnson says that he is acting under Governor Faubus's order to keep them out.

SEPTEMBER 7, 1957. Federal district court judge Ronald Davies, at a hearing on the school board's petition for a temporary suspension of the integration order of September 3, denies its petition. He is critical of the board's actions, saying, "The testimony and arguments this morning were, in my opinion, as anemic as the petition itself."

SEPTEMBER 14, 1957. Governor Orval Faubus, accompanied by Congressman Brooks Hays, meets with President Eisenhower at Newport, Rhode Island. Eisenhower's statement includes these words: "The governor stated his intention to respect the decision of the U.S. District Court and to give his full cooperation in carrying out his responsibilities in respect to these decisions." Faubus's statement, after this conference, includes the following: "When I assure the President, as I have already done, that I expect to accept the decisions of the court, I entertain the hope that the Department of Justice and the federal judiciary will act with understanding and patience in discharging their duties."

SEPTEMBER 16, 1957. An Associated Press report in the *Arkansas Gazette* describes an interview with black students who are "marking time" until the Central High dispute is settled. Included among student names is sophomore Jane Hill. Her name will also appear in Elizabeth Huckaby's book *Crisis at Central High,* as Huckaby gathers class assignments for the black students waiting to enter the school.

SEPTEMBER 20, 1957. The federal district court enjoins the governor and the National Guard from further interference at Central High. The same evening, Governor Faubus orders the National Guard troops away from Central High, ending his seventeen-day military encounter with federal authority. He leaves for the Southern Governor's Conference in Sea Island, Georgia.

SEPTEMBER 23, 1957 ("BLACK MONDAY"). Eight black students enter Central High under protection of the local police and state troopers armed with riot guns and tear gas. The crowd outside becomes very threatening and attacks three out-of-state news reporters. Three and one-half hours after their entrance, school authorities and police remove the black students through a side door and speed away in police cars. Reporters describe the crowds outside as "hysterical."

SEPTEMBER 23, 1957. President Dwight Eisenhower denounces the "disgraceful occurrences" at Little Rock and threatens to use "whatever force may be necessary to enforce the law and the federal court order." He issues a cease, desist, and disperse directive.

SEPTEMBER 24, 1957. President Eisenhower, informed of another mob at Central High after his cease-and-desist directive, federalizes the Arkansas National Guard, thus removing it from Governor Faubus's authority, and orders federal troops into Little Rock. One thousand members of the 327th Airborne Battle Group of the 101st Airborne Division are flown from Fort Campbell, Kentucky, to Little Rock. The president speaks to the nation over radio and television the same evening.

SEPTEMBER 25, 1957. The Little Rock Nine attend classes at Central High under the protection of the 101st. They arrive after a full school assembly where General Edwin Walker warns students not to interfere with carrying out the orders of the federal court. The first bomb scare, where school authorities respond with a fire drill, occurs that afternoon. It is the first of many to come.

SEPTEMBER 26, 1957. Vice principals at Central bar from class the eighty boys and girls who signed out and left school on Wednesday, when the 101st escorted the blacks into school. Administrators require a conference with school authorities before returning to the building.

OCTOBER 1, 1957. Federalized National Guard troops begin to take over responsibility from the 101st. School administrators ask them to "stay as much as possible in the background," a technique that Vice Principal Elizabeth Huckaby describes as "an error in judgment."

Rumors of a student walkout are circulating.

OCTOBER 3, 1957. Elizabeth Huckaby, alone, faces down a large group of white students who are confronting the Little Rock Nine outside the building, while other administrators and military officers attend a closed meeting in the principal's office. The student walkout planned for nine A.M. materializes, but many seniors, scheduled for college entrance exams, do not participate. Approximately 150 students walk out, some returning to the building by a side door. Those who remain outside go across the street and burn a black effigy. Huckaby collects seventy names, and school authorities suspend all of these students, pending conferences with their parents and Superintendent Blossom.

OCTOBER 7, 1957. The sixth week of school and third of integration begins. A new system of assigning two guards per black student begins for their individual protection.

OCTOBER 7, 1957. Appealing to segregationist fears, Faubus announces that members of the 101st Airborne Division troops invaded the girls' dressing rooms at Central High. Federal government spokespersons deny this charge.

NOVEMBER 18, 1957. The federalized Arkansas National Guard remains in charge at Central High as the 101st Airborne troops leave the city.

DECEMBER 17, 1957. The LRSD board suspends Minnijean Brown for six days for retaliating against white students and dumping a bowl of chili on their heads. The board readmits Brown on January 13, 1958.

JANUARY 10, 1958. Darlene Holloway, a white girl, is suspended after a shoving incident involving Elizabeth Eckford.

FEBRUARY 6, 1958. The LRSD board again suspends Minnijean Brown, along with Lester Judkins Jr., who poured soup on her in the cafeteria. Brown has also called Frankie Ann Gregg "white trash" after Gregg hit Brown with a purse.

FEBRUARY 16, 1958. The LRSD board publishes as an advertisement a school board statement on disciplinary policy, saying that it must provide an educational program and that if this means unruly students must be expelled, it will expel them.

FEBRUARY 17, 1958. The LRSD board suspends three white students and expels Minnijean Brown for the remainder of the year. The board charges one white student, Billy Ferguson, with pushing Gloria Ray down a flight of stairs. It suspends Howard Cooper and Sammie Dean Parker for wearing "One Down and Eight to Go" cards. These printed badges refer to Brown's expulsion.

FEBRUARY 20, 1958. Using a form of the *Aaron v. Cooper* case, the LRSD board files for a delay of two and one-half years in further desegregating Little Rock. The school board asks to be relieved of the burden of desegregation until the U.S. Supreme Court better defines "all deliberate speed," as specified in *Brown II* (1955).

FEBRUARY 26, 1958. Sammie Dean Parker, a suspended student from Central High, and her mother physically attack Elizabeth Huckaby at a conference in Superintendent Virgil Blossom's office.

MARCH 4, 1958. Amis Guthridge, a lawyer for the Capital Citizens' Council, offers a platform to suspended student Sammie Dean Parker to appear on a live thirty-minute television program, allowing her to say that her expulsion from Little Rock Central was unjust and was used as an example to other white students.

MARCH 12, 1958. The LRSD board allows Sammie Dean Parker to reenter Central High for the remainder of the school year after she agrees in writing that she will abide by the school's rules of conduct. Some historians have said that the LRSD board and Superintendent Blossom feared creating white martyrs in the community.

MAY 5, 1958. It is announced in New York that the *Arkansas Gazette* has received an unprecedented two Pulitzer Prizes, one the Gold Medal and another for editorial writing.

MAY 25, 1958. Baccalaureate services are held at Quigley Stadium for graduates of Central High.

MAY 27, 1958. At Quigley Stadium, Central High School graduates 602 seniors, including the first black, Ernest Green.

ONE

The Summer of Relief Turns to Anxiety

Here we go again.
—Diary of Elizabeth Huckaby, August 18, 1958

LITTLE ROCK, MAY 27–SEPTEMBER 12, 1958

MAY 27. Central High graduation.

JUNE 3. Federal district court hearing regarding requested two-and-one-half-year delay in further integration by the LRSD board.

JUNE 3. Public dinner and celebration of Pulitzer Prizes won by the Arkansas Gazette.

JUNE 21. Federal district court judge Harry J. Lemley grants a delay to the LRSD board.

JULY 29. Governor Orval Faubus wins the Democratic nomination for his third term as governor. Brooks Hays wins the Democratic nomination for his ninth term in Congress.

AUGUST 18. The Eighth Circuit Court overturns the Lemley ruling.

AUGUST 21. Chief Judge Archibald Gardner stays the Lemley ruling, segregating Little Rock high schools until the Supreme Court rules.

AUGUST 26. Faubus calls an extraordinary session of the Arkansas General Assembly to pass state laws forestalling further desegregation.

AUGUST 26. The U.S. Supreme Court agrees to hear the Little Rock case.

AUGUST 26. The LRSD board delays the opening of all schools from September 2 to September 8.

AUGUST 29. The Arkansas General Assembly adjourns after passing sixteen bills, including Acts 4, 5, and 9.

AUGUST 29. The U.S. Supreme Court announces it will consider the basic question of Little Rock integration.

SEPTEMBER 1. The LRSD board delays the opening of all four Little Rock high schools until September 15 and announces that all other public schools are to open on September 4.

SEPTEMBER 12. The U.S. Supreme Court announces its unanimous decision that Little Rock must proceed with the Blossom Plan for integration.

SEPTEMBER 12. Faubus signs fifteen bills into state law and announces the closure of all Little Rock high schools on Monday, September 15.

Elizabeth Huckaby, the vice principal for girls at Little Rock Central High School, spent most of Tuesday, May 27, 1958, preparing for that evening's graduation ceremony. Though a teacher at the school since 1930, she had never worried more about a commencement ceremony. Her diary entry for that day reflected this anxiety: "Tenseness all day about Commencement."[1] Ernest Green was to receive his diploma that evening, the only senior among the Little Rock Nine. He and his eight black classmates had desegregated Little Rock Central High School nine months before. In midafternoon, Huckaby attended a faculty meeting regarding final grades and then left for Quigley Stadium's football field to help work on the elaborate system of labeling every chair with the name of a graduate. The plan included alternating rows of boys and girls in alphabetical order to build an enormous V, with blue caps and gowns for the boys and white caps and gowns for the girls. The students themselves had rehearsed their parts and cleaned out their lockers and were now at home with family and friends, preparing for this ceremony so rich with the traditions of both this particular school and American education. Huckaby planned one strategy to guard against minor disruptions during the ceremony. She and fellow teacher/school nurse Marian Carpenter would sit in chairs on the circular track, at eye level with the students. From there they knew they could identify any senior by row and seat assignment, should any graduate choose to toss an egg at Ernest Green, as rumored.[2]

The FBI had made much more elaborate preparations for safety, searching the upper windows of houses overlooking the stadium for possible sniper positions. The stadium itself would have uniformed police everywhere, and local plainclothesmen as well as FBI officials planned to be in place that evening. On this Tuesday afternoon, representatives from the military and the local police, Principal Jess Matthews, and Superintendent Virgil Blossom held a final conference on the field.[3] The fear of disruptions or even violence had risen to new heights after the baccalaureate ceremony for graduating seniors, held two days before. This traditional Sunday-afternoon religious service had gone off smoothly, even with approximately "twenty Negro spectators waiting to escort Ernest Green after the ceremony."[4] Only as Green's family and friends exited the stadium did a white Central High senior, Curtis E. Stover, spit on one of the young black girls in Ernest's group. Police immediately took Stover into custody, despite the screams of his mother, whose behavior worsened at the police station. This parental demonstration echoed the actions of some other white parents throughout the long 1957–58 school year, but police still charged Stover with disturbing the peace.[5] Although the baccalaureate ceremony had been open to the public, school officials now decided to limit the graduation ceremony to eight tickets per graduate.

These preparations for commencement by school administrators, local police, the military, and the FBI served Central High and the planners well, the ceremony taking place without incident. Ernest Green was number 203 among the 602 graduates that evening, but number 1 among black graduates of Central High School. Martin Luther King Jr. was in the audience, having spoken that morning at a commencement ceremony in Pine Bluff, at the all-black Arkansas Agricultural, Mechanical and Normal College. This civil rights leader, known for his connection to the Montgomery bus boycott, rode away from the ceremony in a taxi with the new graduate.[6]

In retirement, Elizabeth Huckaby published her memoir *Crisis at Central High,* which chronicles daily events during the first year of racial desegregation in Little Rock. She ends her book with a description of the relief she felt after the tense but peaceful school graduation ceremony on that Tuesday evening in May 1958. She describes how she and other teachers at Little Rock Central were "delighted with the success of graduation, ebullient with the lifting of the tensions of the year."[7] For the first time in over nine months, Huckaby and the entire community of Little Rock gave a collective sigh of relief: Central High had successfully completed a school year—a year that stands as an icon in the history of civil rights in America, marking a battle waged between state and federal authority.

For Ernest Green to safely enter the front doors of Central High on September 25, 1957, he, with his eight black classmates, had needed the protection of the 101st Airborne Division of the U.S. Army. Television crews had broadcast worldwide the photographed image of the students' entry into the school, and similar images had appeared on the front pages of hundreds of newspapers across the nation and the world. But in May 1958, many teachers, parents, and students were rejoicing. Huckaby's ninety-one teaching colleagues had met their classes daily, from September 1957 to May 1958, despite crowds of protesters, walkouts by students, and soldiers in the hallways. When frequent bomb scares forced the evacuation of the building, when parents repeatedly removed their children from the premises after false radio reports of violence, and when members of the press continued to circle the school to report this story of desegregation, teachers struggled to maintain a sense of normalcy for their students. Constantly vigilant for disruptions and even violence, they did their jobs, completed an academic year, and graduated a class of over six hundred students.[8]

In her personal diary, Huckaby wrote late the night of graduation: "No demonstration against Ernest Green. Almost everyone in a gay mood about school—glad for the success of graduation, release from tension of the year."[9] This entry contrasts sharply with those Huckaby penned on the days leading up to graduation. She had written to her brother Bill on May 4, twenty-two days before school was to end, that harassment of the black students was rising.[10] Her journal echoed this sentiment as final exams and the end of the school year approached: "extra guards at school—trailing Negroes again for today and Monday."[11] Several of the young women among the Little Rock Nine had taken refuge in Huckaby's office earlier that day. One, Elizabeth Eckford, had no exams and was not in the building. Gloria Ray reported that some students had tried to block her entry through a doorway but that military guards had interfered on her behalf. Later, someone had tossed eggs her way but hit a white classmate instead. Because of final exams, students were coming and going constantly, following their testing schedules. Perhaps because the students' schedules were not routine, Huckaby felt unease: "many teachers [were] 'on edge' because of rumors"; "Carlotta, Gloria, and Jefferson signed out at 2:00 P.M."[12] Because of the tensions and rumors during these last few days of the school year, the remaining black students left the building at the end of this final day of classes under the watchful eye of Vice Principal J. O. Powell. Now these tense days were over, and graduation marked Huckaby's relief.

The day after graduation, Huckaby and other faculty returned to school, where they held a party for retiring and departing teachers. Huckaby had never been so ready for summer vacation, and later, as she tried to work on some paperwork and administrative tasks, she "was not able to settle down to it much."[13] The following day she left to accompany her husband, Glen, on a fishing trip to Lake Ouachita. Glen was a retired junior high principal, and he and Elizabeth spent much of their time together fishing or hunting. Over the years, he had taught her to hunt squirrel, duck, and other game.[14]

Huckaby's diary entries for the week after graduation describe mundane activities, as she returned to her summer administrative duties at school. One entry, however, does hint at an exciting upcoming evening: one week to the day after Central High's commencement ceremony, Huckaby recorded that she had called her brother Bill, a music librarian in New York, to ask if he wanted to fly into Little Rock for a reception and dinner at the Marion Hotel honoring the *Arkansas Gazette* and its editor and owner, J. N. Heiskell. The announcement of the two Pulitzer Prizes awarded to the *Gazette* had been made on May 5, stating, "The *Arkansas Gazette* was the first newspaper in the 41 year history of the journalistic awards to win the Pulitzer Gold Medal and the editorial writing prize in the same year."[15] Seventy-six-year-old Adolphine Fletcher Terry would organize the festivities. The wife of former congressman David D. Terry, and the sister of Arkansas's only other Pulitzer Prize winner at the time, poet John Gould Fletcher, Adolphine Terry had been a political and social force in the Little Rock community for years. Nonetheless, she met a cool reception for her planned celebration when she contacted several men in the business community, the Chamber of Commerce, and the Arkansas Industrial Development Commission. Eventually, however, she found forty volunteers to help her with the evening's details.[16] After years of service to her city and state, and as a strong supporter of the *Arkansas Gazette*'s moderate stance during the preceding school year, Terry surmised that if such a dinner were a success, it would show the *Gazette* "that a large group of moderates in the city approved of the stance the newspaper had taken."[17]

Elizabeth Huckaby and other moderates wished to celebrate the awards and the newspaper, which had lost 18 percent of its circulation and one million dollars in revenue from segregationist boycotts. At the time, Little Rock's other daily newspaper, the *Arkansas Democrat*, more often took a conservative approach to its coverage of the desegregation crisis and never suffered from such boycotts. The *Arkansas State Press,* the black-owned newspaper of L. C. Bates and Daisy Bates, eventually went out of business in 1959 as a result of segregationist threats to white-owned businesses that advertised in the paper.[18]

Huckaby's brother arrived from New York on Monday afternoon, the day before the dinner. On Tuesday morning, Huckaby's husband dropped her off at the Federal Building, where she was to appear in court as a witness for the Little Rock School Board. Lawyers for the School Board had called her and other teachers from Central to testify in its case requesting a two-and-one-half year delay in the board's plan for integration. The irony of the opening court session and the evening's celebration taking place on the same day would later become painfully clear.

That evening, the Huckabys gathered friends and family and attended the celebration of the newspaper's receipt of the Pulitzer for meritorious public service, along with an estimated 925 people, the largest crowd ever assembled in the Marion Hotel. Heiskell and his son-in-law Hugh H. Patterson Jr. won a prize for publishing, and Harry S. Ashmore, the paper's executive editor, won an individual prize for his editorials encouraging the community to abide by the U.S. Supreme Court's decision outlawing school segregation.[19] Huckaby's journal describes the excitement at the reception in the Continental Room prior to the dinner. Huckaby was pleased to be in the company of her family, including her father, a retired Presbyterian minister, and many of their friends. She describes those attending the gathering as "all the stability of the community."[20] She writes that Winthrop Rockefeller "presided graciously" over the ceremony and that Ralph McGill, editor of the *Atlanta Constitution,* gave an "excellent talk."[21] McGill's talk described the history of the Pulitzer Prize and provided a biography of its founder, but most of McGill's speech was devoted to attacking "spineless newspapers who [were] almost neurotically sensitive to criticism"—unlike the *Arkansas Gazette.* McGill credited the *Gazette* with demonstrating integrity and facing its responsibilities, saying that it "had brought honor to the city, the state, and the newspaper profession" during this first year of desegregation at Central High School.[22]

These two ceremonies, the graduation and the dinner, marked the end of a difficult year. Now there could be personal celebration and closure. Both events affirmed Huckaby's personal beliefs, and she stayed up the evening of the dinner until one A.M., visiting at her home with her brother and like-minded friends. Late evenings were quite unusual for this fifty-three-year-old woman, who was up at five A.M. the following morning to bid farewell to one of her houseguests. On this Wednesday morning, though school was officially out for summer, her administrative duties called for her to be back at Central High by eight-thirty A.M. so that she could complete attendance records and work on the annual report. Vice principal for girls at the school since 1946, and an English teacher there since 1930, she was used to rising early. But this morning she headed back to bed for a little more sleep until she received a harassing phone call from an unknown woman at six A.M. Huckaby was accustomed to such annoyances, since her name and those of Principal Jess Matthews and Vice Principal J. O. Powell were often in the news. Many in Little Rock who were opposed to desegregation of the public schools might easily link her name to the more moderate in the community: she had served as one of the top three administrators at the troubled school during the previous tumultuous year, and her name had appeared in print many times. Segregationists labeled her an enemy because of her support for racial integration and for the Little Rock Nine, particularly the six girls who were directly under her administrative direction. In February 1958, in a well-publicized confrontation at the superintendent's office, a segregationist student had threatened and physically attacked her.[23]

Perhaps today's phone call was a reaction to a photo on page 2 of the morning *Gazette*, which pictured teacher Margaret Reiman and Huckaby leaving the courtroom of federal district court judge Harry Lemley the day before. Observing the formality of the 1950s, Huckaby had dressed in her blue shantung dress and worn a hat for her testimony at the nine-thirty A.M. hearing. The court case was related to a requested delay in integration by the Little Rock School District and provides a retrospective of the legal maneuverings before and during the 1957 crisis.

Even before the Supreme Court ruled that segregated schools were unconstitutional on May 17, 1954, in *Brown v. Board of Education of Topeka*, some in Little Rock had worked on a plan for desegregation. As early as 1952, the Education Committee of the local branch of the NAACP had recommended that the LRSD board experiment with the admission of selected black students from the existing Dunbar High to specific courses at the all-white Little Rock Senior High. George Iggers, a white professor at the all-black Philander Smith College and a leader in the Little Rock NAACP from 1952 to 1956, had written a report published by the interracial Little Rock Committee on Schools, which, according to Iggers, had received "serious attention in both the black and white communities."

Plans to negotiate with the LRSD board and the current superintendent, Harry A. Little, fell through, however, when the press got wind of the meeting. The board canceled, fearing public reaction.[24] Iggers stresses that the local chapter of the NAACP initiated the earliest overtures toward integration in Little Rock's schools. He points out that some believed—and incorrectly reported—that the national office of the NAACP had chosen Little Rock as a testing ground, pressing the organization's local branch to file litigation as part of a "Southwide strategy to secure compliance with the Supreme Court's decision of 1954 and 1955."[25] Instead, according to Iggers, the national office had counseled the local branch *against* an early legal suit targeting desegregation.[26]

Soon after the Supreme Court's 1954 decision in *Brown*, the new superintendent, Virgil Blossom, and the LRSD board met with the executive board of the Little Rock NAACP. It was then that Blossom outlined the original "Blossom Plan," under which integration would begin at the high school level and move to the junior high schools the following year and still later to the elementary schools. At this point, Blossom promised to draw up a set of city school zones designed for the assignment of pupils regardless of race—something he called "color blind attendance zones."[27] According to the Blossom Plan, integration would begin after the completed construction of two new high school buildings, probably in 1956. Blossom explained his proposed timing for desegregation—a full three years after the *Brown* decision—by arguing the need for additional school facilities for Little Rock's growing population. Since World War II, Little Rock had grown more than any other area of the state, due to in-migration and the postwar baby boom. New school facilities were needed across the district, but the greatest need was at Dunbar, which housed black junior high, high school, and college students.[28] A new building in the eastern part of the city—subsequently named Horace Mann High—and Hall High—to be built for the whites in the city's western upper-class suburbs—would supplement the two existing high school facilities. Blossom originally planned to integrate both of the new high schools. Further, Little Rock High School (later Central High), located in the racially mixed neighborhood of the central city, was to be integrated, while Little Rock Technical High, a vocational school for white boys, was not. The Blossom Plan also called for a delay in Little Rock desegregation until the U.S. Supreme Court had issued its implementation decree, to follow *Brown I*. To those who hoped that such a decree would bring quick compliance with desegregation, the *Brown II* decision of May 31, 1955, was more than a disappointment: the U.S. Supreme Court's implementation order encouraged school boards to integrate with "all deliberate speed" but did not explain or describe what full compliance might be; nor did it give a definite deadline for desegregation. Because of the high court's hedging, school administrators across the South and segregationists everywhere were emboldened to oppose integration, to defy it completely, or certainly to delay it further.[29]

Almost immediately, Blossom and the board modified their integration plan, creating a new voluntary transfer plan in which no student had to attend high school in his or her zone but could apply for attendance in another. They then announced that only black teachers were to be assigned to Horace Mann High in eastern Little Rock and only white teachers to the three remaining schools, including Hall High in the elite western suburbs. They moved the starting date for integration to 1957 or 1958. They abolished Dunbar Junior College for blacks (located within the existing Dunbar High School) but denied blacks entry into the all-white Little Rock Junior College, which was at that time under the board's authority. They planned that Dunbar would serve as a black junior high and, most disturbing to blacks, announced that when Horace Mann opened, it would be a segregated black high school.[30]

The local NAACP and some parents of black students in Little Rock were dissatisfied with this slow start to school integration, suffering a loss of faith in Superintendent Blossom and the school board. They had earlier considered a lawsuit, but with the announcement declaring Horace Mann as all-black school, rather than one in a "color-blind zone," they decided to act. On January 23, 1956, parents of thirty-three black students appeared with their children at various high schools and junior high schools and attempted to register in the white schools. After being refused admission, as expected, they applied to the local NAACP branch for legal aid. Thelma Aaron and other parents then filed a class-action suit to force the LRSD to comply more rapidly with the Supreme Court's 1954 *Brown* decision. Claiming that authorities had not made a "prompt and reasonable start toward full compliance," they were disappointed when the federal district court ruled in August 1956 that the school board should simply follow the outlined plan and begin desegregation in fall 1957 at the high school level. Judge John E. Miller endorsed the school board's limited and modified plan and failed to grant the plaintiffs any injunctive relief. The court did, however, retain jurisdiction over the case to guarantee the "effectuation of the plan."[31]

By May 1957, the Central High attendance area included 1,712 whites and 200 blacks. Horace Mann had 328 whites and 607 blacks. The school that would be named Hall had 700 whites and 4 blacks. But with the transfer rule established by Blossom and the LRSD, these figures became meaningless.[32] According to Iggers, the school board and Blossom had "fundamentally revised the court-approved Blossom Plan again" in the summer, ignoring their own voluntary transfer plan, and assigned all the black students, except nine, to Horace Mann High.[33] Over 50 black students living in the Central zone had applied to attend that school but were assigned to Mann, while all white students living in the Horace Mann zone were assigned to Central. That the Blossom Plan had become a token one that met the letter of the law more than its spirit goes without saying. Allowing a very limited number of blacks to join a white student population of 2,000 at Central High in 1957 demonstrated Blossom's and the board's breach of faith with the NAACP.[34] This same bad faith extended to Blossom's and his board's interactions with Governor Orval Faubus.

Faubus's biographer Roy Reed aptly describes the uneasy dance that Superintendent Blossom and Governor Faubus engaged in throughout the summer of 1957. Reed documents the relationship between Faubus and Blossom and his LRSD Board as one of competing agendas, attempted cooperation, and finally efforts to publicly blame the other side for all failures. As early as June 1957, the attorney Archie House, representing the superintendent and the board, and Arthur Caldwell, from the Justice Department, had paid a private visit to federal judge John E. Miller. House and Caldwell, fearing the rising rhetoric and hostility from white segregationists, asked Miller what might be done to chasten the Capital Citizens' Council (CCC). The emergence and strength of public segregationist groups had been rising in Arkansas since *Brown I,* and Miller now suggested that "if they believed" that the CCC "was conspiring to prevent his order from being carried out"—that is, to oppose the token integration of Central High in September 1957—then "someone should ask for an injunction."[35] House insisted that Blossom and the board would not do that. House then made a second trip to Fort Smith, this time with Blossom, to tell Miller about the behavior of the segregationists and the CCC. Blossom and the board, with rumors of violence rising in the community, were growing more anxious about their plan for token integration in September 1957.[36] Wayne Upton, a lawyer who served as the LRSD board president, visited with Miller in early August, when Miller suggested that "someone of standing, not a radical segregationist, might file a suit in a state court to test the state's anti-integrationist measures." If the state court enjoined the school board from proceeding with desegregation, "Miller would consider suspending the board's plan until the matter was litigated."[37] Within two days, Blossom and Upton joined Faubus for breakfast, agreeing that a lawsuit was a good idea. As Reed says, "This was the great game at its most dangerous." Faubus was "surrounded by watchful opponents."[38] Mrs. Clyde Thomason, a member of the Mothers' League of Central High (an arm of the White Citizen's Council), filed the lawsuit, demanding that Chancellor Murray Reed enforce the state anti-integration laws and stop the desegregation of Central High. In his memoirs, Faubus asserts that he, Blossom, and Upton were all involved in getting the lawsuit filed.[39] But the dance between Blossom and Faubus was stopped short by Judge Miller, who suddenly removed himself from the scheme by calling his superiors in the judiciary and asking to be relieved of the case. Roy Reed reports that the case was then temporarily assigned to the no-nonsense federal judge Ronald N. Davies, from Fargo, North Dakota.[40] Davies ended the charade and ordered Central High to be desegregated. Miller, then, had figuratively pulled the rug out from under the dancing couple's feet.[41] Blossom and the board, across the divide from the governor, called each other liars and began the blame game. Faubus called out the National Guard on the evening of Labor Day, in 1957, to prevent the violence he insisted would occur at Central High and to block the entry of the Little Rock Nine. When he did so, he not only sealed his political future, with segregationist support, but also handed Blossom and his board their scapegoat. They and the "high collared businessmen of the Little Rock establishment," Reed says, "still looking down their noses at the hillbilly governor, needling, demanding, cajoling," had tricked him into "saving their necks without risking their own."[42]

By the summer of 1958, in the courtroom of Harry J. Lemley, Blossom and his board were now requesting a delay in their own token integration plan. They had decided to follow this course of action in the spring of 1958, even before the first year of integration had been completed, but the hearing was scheduled to begin one week after graduation. Blossom and the school board wished to stress the difficulty of carrying on a program of education in a climate of extreme vocal public resistance. And they planned to lay as much blame as possible for the previous year of integration chaos at the feet of Faubus and the segregationists. The day before the hearing, school attorneys rehearsed their witnesses in the superintendent's office, giving them questions that they could expect to be asked on the stand. As a vice principal at Central High School, Elizabeth Huckaby was expected to serve as a witness for the LRSD.[43]

On June 3, 1958, Huckaby testified in a small courtroom, crowded with approximately 150 people, before Judge Harry Lemley's federal district court. She described the audience as consisting "mostly [of] the NAACP and the Mothers League," a segregationist group of white women.[44] Thursday's *Arkansas Gazette* described the scene similarly: "The crowd by its own choice was rigidly segregated. Negroes sat on one side of the courtroom and white persons, most of which have been identified with the segregationist movement, occupied the other."[45] Huckaby was one of nine school officials to describe, this first day, how "integration at Central High had created chaos and tension, disrupted the educational program and put a financial burden on the school district." The combined testimony prompted the *Gazette* to report the first day's coverage with the headline, "School Officials Describe Chaos in Central High."[46]

Huckaby's court appearance marked the closure of her brief celebration and the opening of another battle in Little Rock. Her presence at the morning's testimony and the evening's festivities left her straddling a sea change. This hearing, where she was the first person called to testify for the Little Rock School Board, was only the first of three events that summer that would move Little Rock back from the racial integration it had begun just ten months before. Huckaby had hoped the summer could bring a few months of rest and healing to her community's racial wound. Instead, the wound deepened with the court case, the nomination of Orval Faubus for a third term as governor, and an extraordinary session of the Arkansas General Assembly. On this one day, Huckaby was part of the historical events that marked the closure of the 1957 Central High crisis and opened the lesser-known events of the Lost Year. The token plan of racial integration that had begun in September 1957 was now in jeopardy, and all the efforts of students and teachers to make it a success might be for naught. These three events—the requested delay, Faubus's nomination, and the calling of an extraordinary session of the Assembly—set the stage for a school year even more peculiar than the one that had just ended.

■ ■ ■

For three days, from June 3 to June 5, 1958, school board attorneys Richard Butler and A. F. House and NAACP lawyers Thurgood Marshall of New York, Wiley Branton of Pine Bluff, and Ulysses Simpson Tate of Dallas examined and cross-examined their witnesses. The headline from the *Gazette* article describing this second day of testimony seemed to explain why the board had requested this delay in integrating Central High: "Waiting for the Next Governor, School Board President Tells Court."[47] President Wayne Upton said that he and the board thought that Governor Faubus might be out of office if they were granted the two-and-one-half-year delay, and he cited the governor's recent statements threatening to call out troops for a second year to forestall court-mandated desegregation. The board's limited plan of desegregation, from September 1957, had been met with Faubus's summons of the Arkansas National Guard to prevent the Little Rock Nine's entry into Central High. The board, therefore, clearly blamed the governor for first organizing formal resistance against the Blossom Plan. Asking for something other than a repeat of the governor's action the previous fall, the board placed the blame for stubborn resistance on Faubus.

Almost all the testimony over this three-day period pointed to past difficulties within Central High and the frustrations the board felt as a result of "total opposition from the executive, legislative, and judicial branches of state government." Superintendent Blossom stated that this opposition "put school officials in an almost untenable position." He described the "total opposition" of the state, arguing that "the executive branch placed troops around the school, the legislature passed four acts to impede integration and the judiciary has not aided any in enforcement. Instead of aid, we have opposition."[48]

Blossom and the board attorneys wanted two things in testimony from their teachers and administrators: they wanted them, first, to paint a picture that showed how the quality of the school's educational program had suffered during the previous year and, second, to demonstrate that the atmosphere surrounding the community's acceptance of racial desegregation had become more hostile than before. As testimony from board witnesses progressed, a third issue emerged: Upton stated that he thought it was primarily the responsibility of agencies other than the school board to seek indictments against persons interfering with the integration plan.[49]

Blossom later described the Little Rock City Police's arrest of about fifty persons for disturbances at the school in September 1957. He lamented that some were fined and others turned loose and that all the fines were later suspended. He also implied that the federal courts had fallen down on the job by not prosecuting the persons responsible for the mob violence outside the school when Faubus called out the National Guard to prevent admission of the Little Rock Nine. Blossom contended that federal authority had failed again when President Eisenhower sent in the U.S. Army and when the Justice Department refused to prosecute outsiders. Blossom believed that

Faubus's calling out of the National Guard had encouraged many in the community to think that they simply did not have to follow the plan for integration.[50] In his 1959 book, Blossom asserts that a change in the community attitude had prompted the board to ask the courts for the delay in integration, questioning whether the board could "continue its program of gradual integration . . . in view of vastly hardened segregationist resistance."[51] Blossom stresses that by the summer of 1958, public opinion had shifted away from supporting a gradual integration plan, which the community had mildly supported the summer before. Now, after a year of integration enforced by federal troops at Central High, the community "had become antagonistic" and lost all sense of proportion, seeing everything through the lens of integration.[52] Repeatedly—both in his book and on the stand that June day—Blossom referred to the requested two-and-one-half-year delay as a "cooling off period." Historian John Kirk argues that Blossom and the board's minimal compliance fed the forces of massive resistance within the community, actually encouraging more resistance.[53] The board's request for a delay in its token plan for integration demonstrated its failure to take a moral stand on desegregation and its intention to continue its policy of minimum compliance.

Huckaby was joined in testimony on June 3, 1958, by J. O. Powell, the Central High vice principal for boys. Each echoed the other's recollections and conclusions, and both blamed problems within the school on outside agitators and advocated stronger action by authorities beyond the school. Powell said, "I am convinced that if the ringleaders had been removed by juvenile authorities or police action of some kind, we would have had a much smoother school year." In cross-examination of Powell, NAACP attorney Wiley Branton asked, hypothetically, whether suspending student leaders of disruptions in the school for longer periods—until the end of the year—would have improved the atmosphere. Powell answered, "I have a very affirmative view on that."[54]

Huckaby also testified that she had been concerned with the safety of the "Negro" students until the final day of school, because they were the ones under attack. She suggested that she was "glad" to deal with integration problems if the court directed the school to continue the plan but countered, "I hope if it does the Court also directs that organized groups be restrained."[55] The board members saw a delay of integration as the solution to upcoming difficulties, based on their experiences of the previous year. Unlike Huckaby, they were not "glad" to deal with integration problems.

Exactly what Huckaby felt is evident in her diary. Two days later, she made it clear that she was not wholly supportive of the school board's requested delay: "Board hopeful for postponement. (I'm not—not even what I want!)"[56] Huckaby and the teachers had worked hard to implement the plan the board had proposed, with some teachers much more supportive of integration than others. The crisis had presented opportunities for many to be morally courageous; some rose to the challenge, and others did not. Over time and throughout recorded history, some heroes have emerged—and some of them have never been recognized. Inside Central High, along with the Little Rock Nine, other heroes worked daily to follow the directives of the U.S. Supreme Court, to follow the plan outlined by the board, and to bring their personal moral compass to bear on the situation.

If Huckaby was personally opposed to the delay in integration, Vice Principal Powell was equally opposed. He stated that the school year would have run "much smoother if the ringleaders who had caused the trouble had been removed from the school." This was countered by Upton's assertion that "had the Board tried to operate with an 'iron fist' it would have created more trouble than it would have prevented." The day's total testimony came down to a single issue—disruption of the educational process—but Powell's opinion veered away from the school board's on whether enough had been done to maintain discipline within the school.[57] At school the next day, Huckaby recorded how Powell felt about his testimony: "J.O. said he was making a list of duties for his probable successor. He was referring to the fact that his testimony had been at variance with that of others at the court proceedings."[58]

For reasons that are unclear, Principal Jess Matthews was not included among the board's witnesses. Huckaby reports that he was to be "out of town and unavailable for subpoena." Although "he didn't much like avoiding the issue . . . he was willing to abide by the decision of the lawyers and Mr. Blossom. (He went fishing Sunday and didn't get home till Tuesday evening.)"[59] Huckaby also notes that Matthews "felt like a heel" for not being allowed to testify.[60] J. O. Powell's unpublished manuscript also documents the many disruptions by troublesome students during the 1957–58 school year, indicating the strong frustration he felt with Jess Matthews for what he considered his superior's failure to punish the repeat troublemakers at Central High during the 1957–58 year. Powell's view was that the lawyers did not want Matthews to testify and be put on the spot regarding the record of expulsions and suspensions. Later, during cross-examination, Thurgood Marshall questioned Superintendent Blossom on this very issue.[61]

Huckaby and Powell were not among Little Rock's elite. They were middle-class teachers/administrators who had been in the trenches at Central High every day of the crisis year. They had continually fought to implement the *Brown* decision and were willing to go back and do so again. However, their testimony and memoirs indicate that they needed and would have welcomed assistance from any agency that might better police the agitators. Each believed that teaching and learning had been disrupted in Central High. Unlike Blossom and the school board, and unlike those forces of massive resistance outside their spheres, Huckaby and Powell would come to represent a small but growing minority of Little Rock citizens who acted for a brief and remarkable moment in the spring of 1959 as champions of public education for all children and supporters of moderation in a tension-filled environment.

On the second day of testimony, cross-examination by NAACP lawyers included pointed questions for everyone, particularly for Superintendent Blossom, who took the stand for three hours of the four-and-one-half-hour session. Thurgood Marshall asked Blossom if his request for a delay in integration was designed to seek more time to solicit public opinion favoring integration. Later, when Blossom brought up issues of the expense of additional guards and personnel, Marshall asked, "Do you think that it is reasonable for you to ask the Court to deny people their constitutional rights just because it's going to cost you money otherwise?" Marshall queried Blossom about how many students had been punished inside the school. Blossom reported that two hundred had been suspended and "several" expelled. When asked further about the number expelled, Blossom listed three names. While suspension was temporary, expulsion prevented a student from ever enrolling again. Thus, during the entire year of difficulties inside Central High, the school board and administration had barred only three of two thousand students.[62]

Blossom's testimony listed reason after reason for the requested thirty-month delay; he recounted events from the previous year, including the administration's preparation for racial integration, the effect of the governor's use of state troops to bar black students from the school, and every occurrence during the first month of desegregation. In each example, he stressed the school authorities' concern "for the safety of all children" in the face of the "hardening of resistance" by the community against integration at Central High.[63]

Blossom and board president Upton were frustrated, but this was no new frustration. The U.S. federal courts had ordered them in 1956 to proceed with desegregation in Little Rock according to the limited Blossom plan. But voters had an opposite approach, passing anti-integration state laws to forestall or oppose federal rulings as early as November 1956, when they approved a constitutional amendment, an initiated act, and a resolution—all to thwart federal court authority.[64] This is indeed evidence of growing public resistance in Arkansas.

Most of the NAACP's strategy during the June 1958 hearing relied on the testimony of two expert witnesses from New York, both educators. The third day's newspaper headline summed up these educators' opinions: "Board Was Too Lenient in Dealing with Trouble, N.Y. Educators Declare." Dr. David Slaten, the superintendent at Long Beach, Long Island, New York, responded to NAACP attorney Branton's question: "What would be the effect of a delay in integration?" "Nothing in the evidence," Slaten replied, "leads me to conclude that the situation would improve with the passing of time."[65] The logic of the NAACP and that of the school board were at loggerheads. Thurgood Marshall pointed out that Superintendent Blossom and the board had never considered seeking injunctive relief against persons causing trouble at Central High, stressing that the only relief the board had sought was to delay its own plan for gradual integration. Blossom admitted that his board had not sought injunctive relief, a technique used successfully by the school board in Hoxie, Arkansas, in 1955.[66] When Blossom said that Little Rock had not considered such a move, Marshall's subsequent question and Blossom's reply represented everything that was at issue in this hearing. Marshall asked, "Couldn't that be part of the reason the community has lost faith in the law?" Blossom answered, "No, we would have had more trouble if we had done the things you have suggested."[67] The NAACP and black parents believed that the school board had not done everything possible to implement its own plan for desegregation. The school board, on the other hand, believed that the proper response to what they perceived as rising resistance was delay and forceful intervention by some other entity.

The requested delay played into the hands of segregationists and helped lead to the Lost Year. As historian Karen Anderson convincingly argues, the board took a minimalist approach to desegregation, hoping to maintain its standing with white elites and the business leadership. Board members were less concerned with straining relationships with blacks and thus failed to "offer public support for desegregation on moral grounds."[68] By returning to court for delays, and by allowing a token number of approved black children into Central High and other white schools in later years, the board attempted to placate the most ardent segregationists, while appealing to moderates with their rhetoric of "maintaining educational quality." Anderson argues that the board's failure to enforce strict disciplinary policies at Central High in 1957–58 was an attempt to avoid creating "martyrs" to the segregationist cause.[69]

Judge Lemley closed his hearings at the end of Thursday, June 5, 1958, promising to return a ruling in a few weeks. No matter how Lemley ruled, his decision was almost certain to engender an appeal. Appeals of cases through the federal courts usually take months or more, but if the appealing side asks the higher court for a stay of the lower court's ruling and that stay is granted, then all conditions going into the court remain the same until the final part of the appeals process is completed. The summer months of 1958 were to be filled with such tactical maneuvers by both the NAACP and the LRSD board. Each ruling seemed to say either "yes" or "no" to the delay of integration, but each decision of a higher court, if stayed, reverted to a previous ruling, leaving the citizens of Little Rock in a quandary regarding whether schools would reopen and whether those schools would be racially integrated or segregated.

Lemley's ruling and the timing of his ruling were significant not only for the school board and students but for voters. In July 1958, Democratic candidates for governor were running for the party's nomination. In the South and in Arkansas, a one-party state, the Democratic nominee for an office was, in effect, the winner. A ruling by Lemley to delay integration could be to Governor Faubus's advantage. Faubus was running for a near-unprecedented third term against two lesser-known Democrats—Chris Finkbeiner, a Little Rock meatpacker, and Chancellor Lee Ward, a judge from Paragould. If the Lemley court granted a delay, Faubus and the many segregationists who supported him could conclude that their defiant stance during the Crisis Year had earned them relief from the *Brown* decision, or certainly a delay. If Lemley ruled to postpone further desegregation requested by the board, the segregationists' harassment, vocal opposition, and bad behavior would have apparently won over not only the school board but the courts.

Faubus opened his campaign headquarters on West Markham Street fairly late, on June 19, 1958, for the vote, scheduled for July 29. Arnold Sikes, Faubus's executive secretary, and J. Orville Cheney, the state revenue commissioner, headed his short campaign, which focused almost entirely on the segregation-integration conflict.[70]

As Faubus revved up his campaign for a third term, the school board awaited the court's judgment. Blossom and the board blamed, first, the governor and, second, other segregationists for stalling their gradual arrangement for school integration. Three days of their testimony laid the blame at his feet. The last thing they wished was for Faubus to gain his third term as governor. Yet their own testimony played out in his favor. Now the public knew what had happened inside Central High in 1957–58, information the board had carefully suppressed to that point.

During the 1957 school year, school administrators had encouraged teachers within Central High to keep quiet about events inside the school. Howard Bell, a biology teacher at Central High, wrote in the summer of 1959 that "we were advised almost daily throughout the school year to be quiet on the integration controversy as a policy, leaving its solution to the community. As a group we followed our instructions like good soldiers whether we agreed with them or not."[71] During that first school year, teachers were never quoted by any news sources; coverage of events inside Central's walls relied more on rumors than on fact or official comment. But daily headlines from the current hearings exposed the carefully suppressed chaos and tensions inside Central High. Now the public knew about the bomb threats; the small fires in the hallways; the damage to school property; and the physical intimidation that had taken a heavy toll on the school staff, the students, and the educational environment. If Blossom found the community's acceptance of integration dwindling and resistance mounting, it was his own testimony that played into its growing disapproval—and into the governor's hands. Voting in the Democratic primary was less than eight weeks away. The school board's token plan for desegregation, its sought-for delay, and its failure to respond assertively to student and outside resistance now exposed its own ambivalence about pursuing meaningful integration.

■ ■ ■

Blossom and the board, opposing Faubus's reelection as governor, were handed an opportunity to speak out publicly against him before the upcoming vote. The June 20, 1958, issue of *U.S. News and World Report* included an exclusive and copyrighted interview with Faubus giving his version of all the events of the previous school year, including those leading up to the September 1957 crisis at Central High. Faubus justified all of his actions under the guise of ensuring the safety of the children and the public, claiming that he had prevented impending violence. Immediately, the board responded. While its members had previously "refrained from taking part in continuous public controversy," they now said they were publicly responding to Faubus because he had chosen to speak out in a magazine with a national circulation.[72] The *Gazette* headline "School Board Rips Governor's Version of Crisis at CHS," on June 18, 1958, was followed by a point- by-point summary of the board members' and Blossom's contradictions of Faubus's history. Faubus's words had exposed their behind-the-scenes maneuvering and bad faith, and they were striking back. At this moment, they chose to release to the public all statements Blossom made to the FBI in September 1957, which challenged Faubus on all the essential points of his version. Most fundamental to their rebuttal was their declaration that the governor, prior to the September 1957 integration, had refused "to issue a statement urging compliance with the federal court order." Also troubling to the board was Faubus's failure to speak out for law and order during the public gatherings outside Central High.[73] Only school board member Dale Alford countered these released statements, issuing a prepared statement saying that he had opposed their actions, which, he asserted, were not in the interest of "the school children of Little Rock."[74] Alford continued to distance himself from the remaining board members and by October was formulating plans to pursue higher office.

On June 21, 1958, just fifteen days after the hearings ended, and only three days after the public exchange between the board and Faubus, federal judge Harry J. Lemley granted the board permission to delay its federal court-approved plan for gradual integration. In his thirty-five-page opinion, Lemley accepted fully the board's arguments. Attorney Wiley Branton, the Arkansas lawyer for the NAACP, filed notice of an appeal by noon of the same day. Additionally, Branton filed a notice of *supersedeas,* which asked that the Lemley ruling be stayed pending completion of the appeal.[75] The Lemley decision would allow Little Rock's schools to open on a segregated basis in the fall of 1958, but if the Lemley decision were stayed until higher courts could rule, then the existing plan for integration would remain in force. Because of the NAACP appeal, higher courts agreed to hear the case. Event number one leading to the Lost Year had just transpired: the federal district court had approved the LRSD board's request for a delay, and the case was now climbing up the ladder of federal court jurisdiction.

Elizabeth Huckaby kept complete records in her diary about both her personal life and community events. But on June 22, 1958, when Judge Lemley's decision made the front page of the Sunday-morning papers, Huckaby made no mention of it. Though she faithfully read the daily news-papers, that Sunday she kept to her regular ritual of going to the home of her elderly parents on Scott Street to take her father to church, then staying with her mother to cook their Sunday dinner. She was deep into her summer freedom. Her administrative duties from the previous year were over by this time in June, and perhaps that is why she makes no mention of the ruling in her diary. Perhaps, too, she knew the judgment would be appealed. Or maybe she failed to mention it because she did not agree with the school board's request for the postponement of racial integration after the efforts so many had exerted the previous school year. Huckaby's upbringing had instilled in her a desire to look past issues of race. "Prejudice simply wasn't in any of our patterns of thinking," she said, crediting her parents with raising her and her four siblings to hold this view. Against the increasing volume of discontent, a few voices of moderation were being silently recorded in secret places.

Though her diary failed to mention the ruling, Huckaby's letter to her brother Bill, written the same day, does describe the situation. Huckaby remarks that Lemley's ruling had left her with "mixed feelings." She feared a repetition of the previous year as "unthinkable" and lamented a lack of leadership around which "sensible people [could] rally." She doubted that in two and one half years the situation could become any better, and she worried that it could become worse, "unless the Citizens' Council and Mother's League get slapped down." She mentioned that the need in Little Rock was for leadership, a quality she said was lacking.[76]

Like the many other teachers and students in Little Rock, Huckaby carried on with her normal summer activities. Her social life, which she indicated had been greatly hampered during the preceding school year, was back in full swing. On Saturday, the day before the Lemley court ruling, she had attended the wedding of Susie Blossom, the daughter of Superintendent Blossom, along with some of her teaching colleagues. By Sunday afternoon, she was helping to plan another party, this one to be held in her own home, for bride Terry Marshall, the daughter of a friend. She had already devoted her first days of freedom from school to cleaning out closets and drawers and working around the house and yard with her husband, Glen. He was a few years her senior, and they were to celebrate their twenty-fifth anniversary this summer. They had never had children, but this granted them time to enjoy their mutual love of sports. One sport that Glen did not share with Elizabeth was golf: as a retiree, he played frequently when she worked or when she was busy with her own activities. During a normal summer the couple took a fishing trip or two, as they had this May.[77]

In July, the couple took a ten-day road trip to visit relatives in the Southeast, going as far as Tallahassee, Florida, with stops in other states along their route. They returned to Little Rock late Saturday night, on July 26, just days before the summer primary. With them was Clara, Elizabeth's sister, who had joined them from New York for most of their journey and who planned to stay in their home to visit with her parents across town. The Tuesday after their return was Glen's birthday, as well as Election Day. After rising early to bake Glen's birthday cake, Elizabeth drove Clara to visit with their parents and take her father to vote. They had to obtain an absentee ballot for her mother, who was unable to go to the polls. That evening Elizabeth cooked dinner for Glen and Clara and welcomed her teaching friend Sybil Hefley and Sybil's husband for a visit. After the Hefleys left at nine P.M., the Huckabys turned on the radio for an update on voting. Elizabeth penned few words about the results in her dairy: "News too bad so we turned it off." The following morning she wrote, "Up at 6. Faubus's victory complete, unprecedented."[78]

On July 29, in the Democratic primary, Faubus left his two opponents for governor far behind. The total vote was the highest ever recorded for a single candidate in a preferential primary.[79] The dominant issue of the campaign had been racial integration, despite efforts by his opponents, Finkbeiner and Ward, to focus attention on other topics. When the final tally was counted, Faubus carried seventy-five out of seventy-five counties and became the second man in Arkansas history to earn a third term for governor. His reelection—or more accurately, his renomination—was clearly a referendum on his actions of the previous year. Voters across the state supported him and supported his stand for state's rights over federal authority. Faubus had stood up to what he called "integration by force and by bayonet point."[80] And most Arkansas voters stood right there with him.

Though the state and all its counties supported Faubus, an examination of certain precinct records in the city of Little Rock reveals a rising number of voters turning against Faubus in 1958. These precincts were the predominantly black districts (1B, 1C, 1E, 2D, 2E, 3C) and the upper-class white precincts (4E, 5D, 5E, 5F, 5G). In each of these areas, separated by race and class, Faubus received fewer votes than the combined numbers for his two opponents, Finkbeiner and Ward.[81] These two disparate groups thus registered their disapproval of Faubus's actions at Central High the previous fall, foreshadowing a later vote of Little Rock residents, in May 1959. Both race and class were factors for those who opposed the popular governor, and he carried Little Rock by only 430 votes. After Faubus's first term, his opponent in the summer primary of 1956 was Jim Johnston, the articulate segregationist who stood further to the right on race and rhetoric than the governor. In this vote, all predominantly black and upper-class white precincts supported Faubus—showing that when given a choice between two "segregationists," they would choose the more moderate of the two. For those who suspect that the city's upper-class whites and the black community never supported Faubus, precinct numbers from previous gubernatorial primary races show a mixed record. In the summer of 1954, Faubus had opposed incumbent Governor Francis Cherry. Five of the predominantly black precincts chose Cherry over Faubus, but two precincts supported the political newcomer. In the wealthy white areas of western Little Rock, there was resounding support for Cherry over the hillbilly candidate from Madison County, pointing toward the class differences that Faubus often cited when he called persons from the more affluent western precincts "the silk-stockings brigade."[82]

Though Huckaby's diary revealed her frustration over Faubus's nomination, she did find one "bright spot" in the headlines: "Hays returned to Congress over Guthridge."[83] This reference was to Congressman Brooks Hays, who was nominated for his ninth term despite the fact that he was considered the most moderate of any of Arkansas's delegates or even of all the South's representatives to Congress. In this Democratic primary, Hays had defeated Amis Guthridge, an attorney for the Capital Citizens' Council, a vocal segregationist group. Though Faubus was assured of his third term as governor, central Arkansas voters had shown support for a moderate in Congress.

It was now the end of July. Two crucial events triggering the Lost Year were now in place—the requested delay by the school board and Faubus's mandate from the voters. Orval Faubus then wasted little time in bringing about the third event. Some believed Faubus would call a special session of the Arkansas General Assembly should he need to mount state forces another time against federal court jurisdiction. The morning after his primary win, his photo on the front page of the *Arkansas Gazette* showed a grinning governor flashing the "V" for victory sign under the headline, "Faubus Sweeps to Third Term; Landslide Margin Tops 2 to 1."[84] Assured of his position, he could now rest until the courts made further rulings regarding the appeal the NAACP had lodged. He had a little time before he needed to act.

One task that Elizabeth Huckaby had begun during her summer away from school was to organize all the clippings, school bulletins, and collected materials from the previous school year so that she could write "the story" of the tumultuous 1957–58 school year. She realized that school records and reports and incidental materials should be saved, and she had already suggested to Principal Matthews that all such items might be deposited with Little Rock Junior College. She understood the significance of Little Rock's crisis and wanted to make an accurate accounting of events, as a participant in them. Unlike many public versions, hers would recount the daily events of the previous school year from within Central High and from the perspective of those most affected by them—students and teachers. The powerbrokers in the community had their public versions, but she, as one teacher, could preserve for history the private stories fresh in her memory. Huckaby, one small player in what seemed monumental events, knew that her truth needed to be recorded so that it might one day empower other small players in the drama of Little Rock.[85]

The very first day of her summer—the first morning she did not have to report to school—she wrote, "Started work on Little Rock story, using [my] journal as guide . . . a big job—perhaps I won't get it done, but I'll start."[86] On Tuesday, June 16, she wrote that she had "pasted up clippings from February–March. Found myself wakeful." Two days later, after their fishing trip, Glen objected to her "paperwork," insisting that she "take it easy."[87] The memories, tensions, and anxieties of the previous school year were coming back too vividly to suit Elizabeth's husband, who gently voiced his objections to her work. The following day, he went off to the golf course in the afternoon, and Elizabeth chose that time to work further on her "clippings on integration." But Glen did not find a partner at the course: "He came back before three . . . and caught me at it." Elizabeth doesn't again mention her husband's objections, and on June 28 she recorded that she had written "an introduction or preface, and a dedication for my story."[88]

The mundane events of the summer filled her days, and she wrote in her dairy of the weather, visits with friends, the wedding of a close friend, and her houseguest Helen Marshall. Then on Tuesday, August 18, she noted her awareness that her vacation was ending: the following day, Wednesday, was to be her first day back for administrative duties at Central High. She wrote that she "took pleasure in not going anywhere, doing anything, since I must start on round tomorrow."[89] She spent the day working on "the story" of the previous school year, until four P.M. She didn't turn on the radio until a friend called to tell her that the Eighth Circuit Court had ruled. She wrote: "Judge Lemley reversed. Faubus, will call session. Here we go again."[90] The fact that the appeals court in St. Louis would set aside the Lemley delay was exactly what she had wanted when she testified in June— to proceed with gradual desegregation at Central High. What she did not want was for her governor to call an extraordinary session of the state's General Assembly to once again fashion state laws that might thwart federal authority.

At school on this first day back for administrators and staff, Earnestine Opie, the registrar, asked Huckaby to go over the schedules of the returning seven black students: Opie had arranged for two or more of the black students to be together in class whenever possible.[91] School personnel were assuming that integration would continue this year at Central High because the Eighth Circuit Court had ruled the day before that Lemley's delay was overturned. Early in the day, Principal Jess Matthews asked Huckaby how she was doing. Huckaby wrote, "I had to report, 'Fine—except for headaches, stomachaches, and moist palms due to renewed crisis."[92] Now her husband, Glen, could quit worrying about how her memories of the previous year had made her restless and uneasy whenever she worked on her "story." Impending challenges were about to create new anxieties and confusion.

The seven judges of the Eighth Circuit Court of Appeals in St. Louis, after hearing the NAACP's appeal of the Lemley decision, ruled six to seven to overturn the delay. But the one dissenting judge, Chief Judge Archibald Gardner, was to come into play on the side of the Little Rock School Board. The board, which had asked for and won the delay at the lower court level, said it would appeal the Eighth Circuit Court case to the Supreme Court and ask that the Eighth Circuit stay its mandate or set it aside until the Supreme Court could rule on the matter. Chief Justice Gardner, the dissenting vote in the St. Louis court, granted the stay three days later, on Thursday, August 21. The result was to reinstate the Lemley delay, setting aside the Eighth Circuit Court's reversal until the Supreme Court could hear the case. Judge Gardner's ruling meant that Little Rock's schools would now open on a segregated basis for the 1958–59 school year. Any black students planning to enter Central High, including the seven remaining of the original Little Rock Nine, would have to instead return to their segregated black high school, Horace Mann. The Supreme Court, in summer recess, was not scheduled to open its annual session until the first Monday in October. During this very confusing week, Huckaby planned the schedule for teachers and prepared for the seven black students, whose status kept changing by court order. She noted in her diary on Wednesday, August 20, that President Eisenhower had threatened to send troops again and that Faubus had made public statements challenging the president. Would Central High be on the national stage again? There was confusion over whether black students would be attending classes. The *Arkansas Democrat* noted on

Thursday, August 21, that the seven black students were expected to register the next day.

On Friday, 975 students came to Central High to pick up schedules. Huckaby recorded that television cameras had been in place in front of the school before noon, but no black students came that Friday. Did the remaining members of the Little Rock Nine know of the Eighth Circuit Court's stay and of the most recent decision that they were not to be allowed in the same white school they had all attended the previous year? All high school students in Little Rock were probably confused regarding the status of Central High. They may not have been as anxious as Huckaby, who wrote: "A restless night. I had thought relief from tension would make me sleep, but had a hard time going to sleep, then rolled and tossed, and waked early."[93] The Little Rock School Board, satisfied with Gardner's stay, publicly announced that all Little Rock schools would open on a segregated basis on September 2, 1958.[94]

■ ■ ■

To counter the work of the Little Rock School Board, Thurgood Marshall took over the Little Rock case as chief counsel for the NAACP. After the Gardner stay, Marshall sent a special petition to Supreme Court justice Charles Whittaker, asking him to set aside the Gardner stay. Marshall realized that each of the nine Supreme Court justices served one or more of the twelve federal circuit courts. Whittaker was assigned to the Eighth Circuit Court in St. Louis, and it was to Whittaker that Marshall now appealed with an additional request. This one asked him to stay the Lemley decision itself. Either way, if Whittaker would grant one of the NAACP requests, Central High would open on an integrated basis.

Not trusting any decision by the federal courts, Governor Faubus set about pursuing his backup plan. He had made his stand against integrating public schools by federal court order a year before, and he was going to do everything possible to forestall any order to proceed with integrating Central High this second year. The *Arkansas Democrat* announced on Saturday, August 23, and the *Arkansas Gazette* announced the next day, Faubus's call for an extraordinary session of the Arkansas General Assembly. No matter what happened in the court system, now buoyed by his recent overwhelming nomination for a third term as governor, Faubus was preparing six pieces of legislation to hand to the state's 135 senators and representatives when they arrived in Little Rock for the Tuesday, August 26, opening of the Sixty-first General Assembly Special Session. Radio and television coverage of Governor Faubus's address to the joint meeting of both houses began at eleven-thirty A.M., and all parties expected prompt approval of the governor's "package" of laws designed to block court-ordered integration in the state's public schools.[95]

Two other vital changes to the Little Rock situation competed for space on the front pages of August 26, 1958. The Tuesday newspaper reported Chief Justice Earl Warren's announcement that the entire U.S. Supreme Court would meet in a rare off-season term to hear the Little Rock case, beginning that Friday, August 28. Justice Whittaker's response to Thurgood Marshall's request had thus expanded to the full court. Only five previous times in history had the Supreme Court heard cases before its planned October session.[96] The justices cut short their vacations, and some left early from the National Bar Association meeting in California to begin work on the case. School board attorney Richard C. Butler planned to argue the board's case before the high court, assisted by young John H. Haley. Thurgood Marshall planned to argue for the NAACP, assisted by Wiley Branton.

Blossom and the school board met and decided that a new date for opening schools was in order. Sharing headlines with the special session and the Supreme Court's announcement of a rare early session was therefore the news that all Little Rock schools would open on September 8, rather than on September 2.[97] Questions of whether Central High would open segregated or integrated repeated the previous year's battle between state and federal authority.

In the fall of 1958, instead of state or federal troops marking the argument, the Arkansas General Assembly was attempting to create new state laws to forestall any decision that the highest federal court in the country could issue. If a popular state governor with what amounted to a mandate from his voters could call into force new state laws, he might not stop integration, but he could certainly delay it. Students throughout the city rejoiced at six additional days of summer vacation, and Elizabeth and Glen Huckaby opened the silver they had given each other for their twenty-fifth wedding anniversary. The veteran teacher was as unsure as any other LSRD employee when she wrote: "It is beautiful. I'm glad we went ahead and got it—even if I may not have a salary check for long." Still employed at that point, she returned to school the following morning, where she completely retyped the preplanning-days schedules for teachers after learning that classes were to be extended in May 1959 to make up for the late opening.[98]

The Arkansas General Assembly was offered a six-bill package by Governor Faubus, all the bills intended to thwart racial integration. Surrounded by six state policemen and accompanied by his wife, Faubus spoke to the joint session in the House chamber. Appealing to the responsibilities of elective office, he stated, "We are here today, not through our own choice and desires but because it is our responsibility to face up to some problems that have been forced upon us, by unwise actions of others."[99] Later he criticized all levels of the federal courts, the local, district, and Supreme Court, and specific justices, over their recent decisions that had ruled against his wishes. Playing upon the public's greatest fears, and despite the fact that there had been little real violence at Central High the year before, Faubus said, "It matters not how bad the conditions that may exist; it matters not if a hundred people are slain in the streets or the corridors of school; it matters not how great the destruction of property; it matters not whether the parents know that their children may return home grievously wounded because of disorders or whether they may return at all. Integration is paramount to these considerations."[100]

During the first day of the session, Attorney General Bruce Bennett had representatives in the House propose his seven additional anti-integration bills. Three other bills appeared in the Senate. Among the sixteen bills, one measure gave the governor power to close any or all schools in a district. He alone would determine whether closing was necessary to preserve the peace and protect lives and property. The measure also gave him authority to close schools, if and when court-ordered integration was enforced, with troops or any other force at the federal level. It provided for a local-option election to be called within the school district within thirty days after closure. The ballot would require no title but would list simply two alternatives— "for" or "against" racial integration of all schools within the district. The final part of this measure concerning the local-option election required a majority of *eligible* voters to carry the election (Act 4). The detailed requirements of this bill would play out in the segregationists' favor in Little Rock in September, just as Faubus and his advisors intended.

Faubus's second bill concerned funding. State funds for closed schools were to be withheld on a per-pupil basis from the closed school and paid to whatever other public school or accredited nonprofit private school the pupil might attend (Act 5). This, in effect, would allow state money to be funneled to private education, similar to the idea of vouchers, proposed decades later. A third bill provided that no student should ever be denied the right to enroll and receive instruction in any course in any public school in the state by reason of his or her refusal to attend classes with a student of another race, while another bill provided for segregated class-rooms within an integrated school. The remaining measures created an appropriation of $100,000 for the governor's use in regulating the administration and financing of public schools and postponed Little Rock high schools' opening until September 15, 1958.[101]

Most of the bills proposed by the segregationist attorney general Bruce Bennett had to do with weakening the power and legal authority of the NAACP, but one would prove important within a few months. This recall law allowed for the removal of any school board member. A petition for such a recall required only 15 percent of a district's voters to force a recall election (Act 9). Also significant among the bills other politicians (besides Faubus and Bennett) proposed was one by Senator Artie Gregory of North Little Rock. It required all state employees, including public school and college faculty, to file an affidavit listing all organizations to which they had belonged for the previous five years—thus threatening the civil liberties of all teachers and state employees (Act 10).[102] Gregory had introduced a similar bill in March 1957 to root out subversives in the state's educational institutions. It mirrored many other massive resistance laws in the South that were tied to a fear of Communism. In 1957, Governor Faubus had vetoed the measure, saying, "No such measure could make people be patriots." But the General Assembly now passed the act, its members realizing that this bill could target NAACP members as well as Communists.[103]

The courts and the legislature met to do their work, and the Little Rock public school teachers did theirs. Teachers held meetings to prepare for the academic year ahead and to ready materials for their students. The delay of the school opening increased their planning days. Little did the high schools teachers realize just how many planning days they would have.

The state legislature passed all sixteen anti-integration bills, including the six Governor Faubus had proposed. In total support of Faubus's agenda, the legislators cleverly agreed to go home at noon on Friday, August 29, but they voted to extend the special session until January 10, 1959. In this way, the two chambers could hold the recently passed bills until the governor signed them: had they adjourned and sent the bills to him, he would have had to act on them within five days.[104] This way, Governor Faubus could simply call for the bills when and if he needed to sign them. Faubus was thus poised to take action as soon as the U.S. Supreme Court acted on the case of the LRSD board and the NAACP.

The emergency hearing of the high court began at noon on Thursday, August 28, 1958, the day before the Arkansas General Assembly orchestrated its noon recess. In Washington, representatives of the LRSD and the NAACP answered questions from the nine Supreme Court justices on the technical issue of the stay procedures. Just a little over three hours after beginning, the Court recessed at 3:33 P.M. Then at 5:10 P.M. it reconvened, with Chief Justice Earl Warren announcing that the Supreme Court would go on to consider the basic questions of Little Rock integration. The court recessed until September 11 and asked both sides to prepare oral arguments. The court also assumed that the opening of school would be postponed until September 15. This was the same date that the Arkansas General Assembly had voted on the day before.[105]

Soon after the noon "recess" of the Arkansas General Assembly, Elizabeth Huckaby held a scheduled meeting in her office with Walter Riddick, from the U.S. Attorney's office. Though he arrived one hour and fifteen minutes late and stayed until 4:45 P.M. on her Friday afternoon, she was "interested" in hearing that the Justice Department intended to be more rigorous "when and if" integration proceeded that fall.[106] Perhaps Huckaby would have welcomed an additional show of force by federal marshals, less obtrusive than federal troops. Attorney General William P. Rogers was preparing to be of greater assistance to the city of Little Rock and the school board, if necessary to preserve the peace, by increasing the number of federal marshals and deputy marshals. In a letter to the school board and in another to Mayor Dean Dauley, Rogers promised the help of the federal government without mentioning the use of troops, the tactic both the state and the federal government had taken the previous year.[107] In most later cases, the federal government turned to the use of federal marshals, rather than deploying the military to enforce court-ordered desegregation. Huckaby went home to news that the entire "Governor's Program" had passed both houses of the General Assembly.[108]

On Monday, September 1, Labor Day, the school board announced that the opening of all high schools in Little Rock would be delayed until September 15, as both the high court and the Arkansas legislature had determined. However, all other schools in the district planned to open on a segregated basis on Thursday, September 4. Elementary and junior high teachers had been in their buildings since August 27 and would soon have students. High school teachers, who had reported the same day, continued to report for work, but whether they would have students, and when, were still uncertain.

This uncertainty went far beyond the teachers. On Tuesday, September 2, while Huckaby was meeting with the tenth-grade English teachers, a concerned parent came by her office for advice about what to do with her girls' schooling for their senior year. Huckaby recorded, "I could not advise."[109] Naturally, the high school teachers were concerned and unsure of their future. Parents of high school students worried about their graduating seniors, or their returning juniors, or their fifteen-year-old sophomores who were anxious to begin their first year of high school. For 3,665 black and white high school students, their free public school education was in jeopardy. In their youthful exuberance, the students probably just enjoyed their additional days of summer vacation, but their parents were becoming increasingly anxious.

On Monday, September 8, Central High faculty attended a one-thirty P.M. meeting to hear Virgil Blossom before he went to Washington for the Supreme Court review of the Little Rock case, scheduled for Thursday of that week. Huckaby noted that Blossom was well received but that there were "some questions no one can answer."[110] By Friday noon, September 12, there were no more questions in the minds of the nine justices of the U.S. Supreme Court. They announced their unanimous decree that integration must proceed immediately. All four high schools should open on Monday, September 15, and Central High must continue to admit black students according to the original court-approved desegregation plan. By three P.M., the Little Rock School Board announced that all high schools would open on Monday, September 15, and that Central High would again be integrated. Within hours of the court's announcement, Governor Orval Faubus called for the bills that the Arkansas General Assembly had passed in late August, signed fifteen of them into law, and announced that all high schools in Little Rock were closed by his authority as governor and would not open on September 15. In accordance with the new Act 4, he set a referendum for October 7, 1958, allowing LRSD voters to approve or disapprove of his school closure. The federal courts had decreed, the governor had acted, and the matter appeared to be in the hands of the voters.[111]

Elizabeth Huckaby completed her administrative duties at school late that same Friday afternoon, then met her colleague Margaret Reiman at seven-thirty for Central High's first football game of the season, where she watched the Tigers defeat the West Monroe, Louisiana, Rebels at Quigley Stadium. By Sunday she was writing in her diary: "News of the day confused. No more moves likely till Monday, no high school classes then."[112] She and her colleagues, and the students and their families, were in limbo—thus beginning the aptly named Lost Year.

TWO

Nothing but Confusion

There was no 1–800 number to call to get advice.
—Sherri Daniel (Evans), Central High Student

LITTLE ROCK, SEPTEMBER 15–SEPTEMBER 29, 1958

SEPTEMBER 15. Planned day for opening of Little Rock public high schools. The schools are closed by order of Governor Faubus, who announces a referendum for October 7. The LRSD board interprets this to mean that all extracurricular activities are also ended.

SEPTEMBER 16. Faubus moves the referendum date back to Saturday, September 27.

SEPTEMBER 16. Mrs. David D. Terry organizes the Women's Emergency Committee to Open Our Schools.

SEPTEMBER 17. Football is restored by request of Governor Faubus.

SEPTEMBER 17. The Pulaski County Circuit Court grants a charter to the Little Rock Private School Corporation (LRPSC).

SEPTEMBER 22. High school classes begin on early-morning television.

SEPTEMBER 25. The Mothers' League of Central High is unable to gain sufficient signatures to recall four school board members.

SEPTEMBER 25. The school board petitions the federal district court for advice on leasing public school property. Judge John Miller claims no authority.

SEPTEMBER 26. The NAACP asks the Eighth Circuit Court to enjoin the LRSD board from leasing public school buildings.

SEPTEMBER 27. School-closing referendum. Little Rock voters reject integration in a suspect procedure.

SEPTEMBER 29. The LRSD board leases public high school buildings to the LRPSC.

SEPTEMBER 29. The LRPSC offers contracts to white LRSD high school teachers.

SEPTEMBER 29. U.S. circuit court judge Joseph Woodrough issues a restraining order forbidding the lease of public schools to the LRPSC.

In the fall of 1958, Mrs. Lee T. Pearcy's daughter Katherine was in Stuttgart, Germany, as a foreign exchange student. Her counterpart, seventeen-year-old Gerhard Maylaender from Germany, was residing with Mrs. Pearcy on Gaines Street in late September and expecting to attend Central High School with approximately 2,000 other students. When Maylaender was interviewed by the *Arkansas Gazette*, none of the high schools in the city was open to students, but teachers and administrators were reporting daily for work. Maylaender commented, "I'm not actually disappointed at the delay. In fact, it is kind of good for me to catch up with the language."[1] The LRSD board had changed the opening date for high schools from September 4 to September 8 and finally to September 15. Like so many other high school students and parents in Little Rock, Maylaender and his host family thought that the school openings had simply been delayed. Along with 3,665 black and white students from the four closed schools, the exchange student did not know if his school would open and did not know if it would be integrated or segregated. Governor Orval Faubus had officially closed all public high schools on September 12, but he spoke frequently of opening those schools on a private and segregated basis and had continued to encourage citizens to vote against integration in the upcoming referendum. He reassured them that private segregated education could occur using the public school buildings.[2]

Elizabeth Huckaby and all other teachers and administrators of the four high schools reported for work, as they had since August 27 or before. Under contract to the school district for the days they had already reported, they prepared for a delayed school year. But with Faubus's actions, many were beginning to realize that their students might not be coming. Huckaby recorded in her diary that a crowd of photographers and journalists were in front of Central High when she arrived for work on Monday, September 15.[3]

Central's faculty members were called to a late-morning meeting to discuss the peculiar situation of having no students. Huckaby, as vice principal for girls, compiled some of the teachers' ideas for "future work." She noted that there were "no students at school, of course," meaning that no classes were being held. However, she did record that the Hi Steppers, a girls' pep squad, was practicing inside the building. By 3:15 P.M., however, Principal Jesse Matthews had called another faculty meeting to announce that the school board had interpreted Faubus's Friday order on school closure to extend to all extracurricular activities, including football.[4] If this were the case, the Hi Steppers would no longer come to school for practice, and the previous Friday night's defeat of West Monroe, Louisiana, would end Central High's new football season after the team's thirty-fourth straight win. In Little Rock, high school football was second only to University of Arkansas Razorbacks football. Superintendent Blossom spoke out immediately, saying that the financial problems created by the cancellation of football games would have to be worked out with other districts, because Little Rock high schools had to guarantee visiting teams a certain amount of money for each of their home games.[5] Central High had guaranteed Paduchah, Kentucky, $900; other planned games ranged from $450 to $1,500.[6] That same day, Faubus charged that the school board was trying to arouse public sentiment against him by canceling the football program. The board president, Wayne Upton, telegraphed Faubus on September 16: "Our sole motive in yesterday's action stopping extracurricular activities was strict compliance with your proclamation closing the high schools, which was presumed to close all school activities. Your statement to the press today indicated that this was not your intention. Will you please advise us immediately as to which high school activities you intended that your proclamation cover?"[7] It is ironic that it took the governor's word to reinstitute football that season—his deeming the sport important enough to salvage, when academics were not. Blossom recounted in his memoir what was finally decided: "As a result [of Faubus's statements] the Board said it would carry out the football schedule and anything else the Governor would return to it. Only football was returned, and football was all we offered the youth of Little Rock that year."[8]

By Wednesday, September 17, the school board had agreed to the resumption of football so that players at the three high schools that fielded teams could return to practice and to playing games. This decision followed

Faubus's caustically worded telegram to Upton, insisting that it was only the school board that had stopped football.[9]

At Horace Mann High, Maude Woods, a math teacher with three years' experience in smaller Arkansas schools, and Jerome Muldrew, who taught social studies, were among the black teachers waiting for their students. Woods and Muldrew were among the young teachers whom LeRoy Christophe, the principal of Horace Mann, had hired. Christophe was a seasoned and respected administrator who had come to Horace Mann from Dunbar, the only high school for blacks in Little Rock until Horace Mann was opened in the spring of 1956, the Little Rock School Board having decided to open a new, modern black high school in the eastern part of the city and convert Dunbar to a junior high. Some blacks in Little Rock resented this decision, since Dunbar was the largest black accredited high school in Arkansas, located in a building constructed at about the same time as Central High and similar in design, if not in size. Dunbar, which had served as a high school and junior college for blacks since its opening in 1929, was at the center of a largely black neighborhood.[10]

Christophe had brought with him from Dunbar some "master teachers" and had added eleven new teachers—his "favorite picks," according to Muldrew, who says he referred to them as his "new thrusts."[11] Just as teachers at Hall, Central, and Little Rock Technical High waited, so too did the thirty-four faculty members at Horace Mann. Without students, teachers continued to prepare for classes, their hopes and expectations for open schools rising and falling as events unfolded in the legal and political arenas. Woods remembers preparing bulletin boards, creating teaching materials, checking textbooks, and cleaning her room. Christophe had no intention of allowing his teachers to waste or misuse time. Muldrew recalls that Christophe was "foresighted" enough to provide enrichment activities and in-service training by calling upon community members and Philander Smith College personnel. His organization kept teachers occupied in various types of classes and moving about the building with the bell, just as students would. They even prepared their own meals in the Home Economics Department, where they received lessons on nutrition. Muldrew jokingly notes that he remembers receiving more lectures than food.[12]

Their colleague Leon Adams, the band director, remembers worrying about where his students might go to school should Mann remain closed: "The black schools in Little Rock were the premier schools in the state, and our school was accredited by the North Central Association."[13] Adams points out that nonresident students traveled long distances to attend

Horace Mann and paid tuition to come to Little Rock. If Mann were closed, where could his students obtain a quality education? These same questions were troubling not only the Mann faculty but the ninety-two teachers at Central, the forty-three at Hall, and the eight at Little Rock Technical High.

The six men on the Little Rock School District Board of Education, the designated body that had been implementing the desegregation of the city's schools, were also concerned about the students. Along with board president Wayne Upton, board vice president William G. Cooper and board secretary Harold J. Engstrom Jr. had been heavily involved in this work throughout the previous year, with Superintendent Virgil Blossom. R. A. Lile aligned with these officers; together these four were the more moderate members of the board, when compared with Dale Alford, often labeled the most segregationist part of this 1958 team. The sixth board member, Henry Rath, had resigned from the board in frustration on September 12, when the Supreme Court ordered these six men and the superintendent to proceed with integration following the Blossom Plan. Rath was frustrated because he and the other board members were caught between federal court authority and state authority, each government entity dictating what actions the board should take.[14]

Richard C. Butler, part of the board's legal team, had recently argued before the high court that these men were public servants and capable, outstanding citizens. Two were medical doctors, one a certified accountant, one a civil engineer, one a lawyer, and one a banker. Butler pointed out that all served in unpaid positions and that all had done the best they could under "as trying circumstances as any public servant has ever faced."[15] Butler contrasted the Little Rock board with others in the South whose members were refusing to recognize the basic changes in the law mandated by the *Brown* decision. Butler argued that instead, "this board was studying and formulating ways and means of complying. They knew it was not an easy task, but they were willing to do their best."[16] Rath, for example, was the accountant for the Meyer's Bakery Company, which had suffered boycotts as a result of Rath's service on the school board.[17]

Division in the community over the issue of desegregation became more personalized over time, accompanied by ever-rising rhetoric. Along with boycotts of the *Arkansas Gazette,* segregationists discouraged the purchase of "black bread" from Meyer's Bakery and "black milk" from Coleman Dairy, both companies considered to be in favor of integration.[18] Rath's letter of resignation from the school board protested the Supreme Court's decision and declared Rath's belief that the LRSD board's request for a two-and-one-half-year delay of integration was "reasonable and just" and that the high court "had acted in complete disregard of the social customs of the South."[19]

Though Richard Butler had defended the board members' motives and frustrations, this same school board and Superintendent Blossom had in fact failed to demonstrate full support for court-ordered desegregation. The board had failed to follow the "Hoxie, Arkansas, model," which asked for a federal injunction to proceed with court-mandated integration. Further, this was the same board that had initiated the request for a two-and-one-half-year delay of the limited desegregation begun in 1957. Perhaps most significant, none of the board members or Blossom took a moral stand for desegregation—something for which they had criticized Governor Faubus in comments made earlier in the summer of 1958.[20] By failing to wage the battle to implement the *Brown* decision, these school board members continued to wedge themselves between directives from the highest court in the land and the intensifying rhetoric of segregationists championing the actions of their governor in closing the high schools.

The Supreme Court's September 12 decision (*Cooper v. Aaron*) not only prompted Governor Faubus to sign state legislation closing schools but brought responses from various other individuals and groups. The Mothers' League of Central High, a small but vocal segregationist organization formed in 1957 and sponsored by the Capital Citizens' Council, had been active in opposing the Blossom Plan and had opposed desegregation through lobbying efforts, sending representatives to school board meetings, encouraging a student walkout, and using telephone campaigns to gather participants for demonstrations outside Central High. Led first by Nadine Aaron and Margaret Jackson, this group announced in August 1957 that it would work as a "group of Christian mothers in a Christian-like way to oppose integration and violence."[21] By October 1957, it boasted 165 members. Issues of class influenced the membership of the Mothers' League. Historian Graeme Cope finds that the group "lived for the most part in or near the central area of the city," both its core support and its leadership coming from "the lower middle class and solid working employees."[22]

Despite the organization's name, only about one-fifth of its members were actually the mothers of Central High students. Throughout the crisis year, the Mothers' League and sometimes its members' children acted to thwart integration. One clique of girls and one boy, children of Mothers' League members, organized a campaign of ongoing harassment and intimidation inside Central High during the 1957–58 school year, aimed at the Little Rock Nine.[23] Early on, the Mothers' League had sought a temporary injunction against school integration in Pulaski County Chancery Court. Two members of the group later waged unsuccessful attempts to secure public office on the Little Rock City Board and allowed the use of their names as plaintiffs in several other lawsuits led by parties connected to the Capital Citizens' Council.[24]

On the Monday following the school closure, members of the Mothers' League initiated an attempt to use the new Arkansas recall law (Arkansas Act 9) to remove the remaining members of the school board, except Dale Alford, who was most closely aligned with their own thinking. By September 25, Margaret Jackson, the group's president, announced that the group would be unable to file the petitions on that Thursday, as planned. The new law required that 15 percent of voters sign a petition to call a recall vote; this would require 6,235 signatures.[25] Jackson later claimed that the Mothers' League had eventually collected, but never filed, 10,000 voters' signatures.[26]

The school board itself hoped to help the students with academics, as well as with the football it had restored. After the schools were closed, Act 4 required a referendum within thirty days to allow voters to either endorse or reject integration. Should the voters choose to accept racial integration, schools could open for all 3,665 black and white students who were presently locked out of their public school classrooms. As a stopgap measure before the vote, the LRSD board cooperated with the three local television stations, which provided broadcast time for several hours of courses on weekdays. Fifteen white teachers from the closed schools prepared lessons and went to the appointed television studios to learn the fundamentals of teaching on-camera. Little Rock's television stations were relatively new—all had opened between 1953 and 1955. The ABC, CBS, and NBC affiliates all provided seven A.M. live broadcasts of classes. Arkansas KATV gave time to teachers of English, applied mathematics, plane geometry, world history, and biology for sophomores. KTHV offered two hours of time for courses for juniors, and KARK broadcast more advanced classes, such as trigonometry and physics for seniors.[27] Virgil Blossom explained to the press that television teaching was merely a stopgap measure. He pointed out: "At Central High School we offer 87 different subjects. On television we're attempting only the four basic subjects—English, history, science, and mathematics."[28]

Nancy Popperfuss, an English teacher from Hall High, recalled the short run of television classes and her involvement in them. What stood out in her memory almost forty years later was how "terror-struck" she was after her department chair assigned her the very first lesson in eleventh-grade

American literature. She remembered worrying over her lesson on colonial literature the entire weekend before her Monday-morning performance, and she could even recall what she wore on camera. In one moment, Popperfuss, a young white teacher, became aware of one facet of separate-and-unequal education for blacks: "I think we saw how things worked. . . . Mrs. Henderson, my chair, took me aside and said, 'Now you can't give that assignment in that book to everybody.' We had different books than Horace Mann did. They [the black students] had the old books. So that showed that, see I never had known. Well, I never had asked about it."[29]

Another of the television-teacher personalities made quite an impression on the public. Emily Penton, a thirty-five-year veteran teacher of history and government, made her course in American history so interesting that she was retained for the rest of the year by public demand. Her program, entitled *Miss Emily,* ran from seven-thirty to eight A.M. daily, long after this quite limited experiment with television teaching ended.[30]

No black teachers were involved in the television presentations, though photos of black students positioned in front of their television sets appeared in *U.S. News and World Report* with the following caption: "Negro Students Barred from Central High School by Its Closing, Get the Same Courses and Same Teachers as Whites in the TV School."[31]

Access to education now reached beyond race to matters of economics. Ownership of or access to a television in a typical 1958 Little Rock home can only be estimated, but several statistics are available. The average Arkansas family earned $3,184 in 1958. Broken down by race, the average black median income was $1,636, while the same for whites was $3,678.[32] The same year, 84 percent of homes in the United States had television sets, but penetration in the South was somewhat lower, at approximately 76 percent.[33] At a time when a console television was advertised in Little Rock at a sale price of $229, some Little Rock students belonged to families that simply could not afford a television.[34] The day before the first broadcast, Superintendent Blossom said, "Nothing officially has been worked out to accommodate students whose families do not have TV sets."[35] This is but one example of the poorer students' reduced opportunities. If a student's family owned a television, this short run of teaching might have served him or her well, but this temporary solution to schooling ended on September 29, when a flurry of activity put television teaching in the same category as all other teaching—on hold.

As required by Act 4, the governor had first announced the referendum on school closure for October 7. But suddenly, on September 16—the second day that high schools were closed and just days after the Supreme Court decision—Orval Faubus moved the date of the referendum to Saturday, September 27. It was widely assumed that he changed the date of the election to a time before October 1, 1958, in order to keep unregistered voters from paying their new poll tax—a one-dollar charge required for voting. Since a 1957 poll tax was required, the number of voters was limited to those already registered. Many in Little Rock also questioned Faubus's choice of this particular Saturday for voting. The University of Arkansas Razorbacks were playing a home football game in Fayetteville, guaranteeing that a substantial number of Little Rock fans would be drawn away from their voting precincts that day. Faubus himself attended the game and made statements to the press after Arkansas lost to Tulsa, 27 to 14.[36]

Act 4 not only spelled out the exact wording for each ballot but also required a majority of *eligible* voters in the Little Rock School District, not just a majority of those voting, to change the status of closed schools. When Faubus announced the change in election dates, a *Gazette* editorial pointed out that the election was "rigged" and that any result was a "foregone conclusion" since this election, unlike any other ever held in Arkansas, would require that a majority of *qualified* voters must vote—and must vote to reopen the schools with integration in effect. The *Gazette* argued that the election would be "heavily weighted" against opening the schools and used Faubus's own recent landslide victory in the 1958 summer Democratic Primary as an example for comparison. Even Faubus had not carried a majority of *eligible* voters in that election, despite his vote being the highest ever recorded for a single candidate in a preferential primary.[37] The *Gazette's* quarrel echoed the concerns that many moderates in the community had over issues of eligibility and changing the date of the referendum.

The following day the *Gazette* "boxed" information and speculation regarding the upcoming referendum in the upper right section of the front page. First it listed the exact wording for the ballot that Act 4 dictated. The wording for opening the closed schools read, "For racial integration of all schools within the Little Rock School District." The other option read, "Against racial integration of all schools within the Little Rock School District." The ballot did not mention anything about the closure or opening of schools.[38] The *Arkansas Gazette* further explained that only 1957 poll-tax holders in the Little Rock School District were eligible to vote. Finally, the article tried to answer the question of "how many" by attempting to do the math—figuring out the exact number of votes needed to open the schools. The problem lay in counting the eligible number of voters in the

Little Rock School District, not in the city itself. Though Little Rock had 41,037 registered voters, some of those living in Wards 2, 4, and 5 lived in the Pulaski County School District. Additionally, some persons who lived outside the city itself were within the district, such as 509 qualified voters in Cammack Village. The newspaper also pointed out that a typical Little Rock school election drew fewer than 7,000 voters, while a record number of over 27,000 people in Little Rock had turned out for the summer primary, when Faubus won by only 430 votes within the city.[39] A heavy voter turnout would be necessary to meet Act 4's specific stipulation regarding the number of eligible voters.

If the upcoming election provoked turmoil, the decisions facing teachers, students, and parents were equally difficult because no one knew if the public high schools would open or if they would operate on a segregated or an integrated basis. Sherri Daniel (Evans) was planning her senior year at Central High. The school closure and the resulting uncertainty were "just a staggering blow to me," she recalled years later. "I felt like there was no help. There was no 1–800 number to call for advice. There was no one to give advice."[40]

Many parents waited until the September 27 referendum to make a decision about what to do for their students. But some did not wait. Anxious students or those with resourceful parents began quickly to make arrangements for alternative schooling before the upcoming referendum and even before television teaching began. Some students decided to leave Little Rock. On Friday, September 19, just four days after the school closure, Superintendent Blossom announced that 211 high school students had officially transferred, 130 from Hall High, 80 from Central High, and 1 from Little Rock Technical High. At that point no students had left Horace Mann High. Most of these transferring students enrolled in nearby public schools where they could remain at home but could carpool or arrange other transportation to schools in the county.[41]

New groups formed in reaction to the situation in Little Rock. The first week of the school closure, fifty-eight women met at the home of Adolphine Terry, the same seventy-six- year-old woman who had organized the dinner celebrating the Pulitzer Prizes for the *Arkansas Gazette*. This group of women was the first organization to take a public stand on getting the high schools reopened, and Terry felt that to be effective, the group had to be large and composed of a "core of white women with enough influence, clout, and drive" to recruit more members.[42]

Terry's group soon adopted four goals. The first two priorities were to get the four public high schools open and the students back in the classrooms.

Third, the group wanted to retain the schools' good teachers, and fourth, it wanted to maintain full accreditation by the North Central Association. (Accreditation would be lost if the schools closed.) Vivion Brewer, chosen chair of the new Women's Emergency Committee to Open Our Schools (WEC), joined Terry in making statements to encourage registered voters to go to the polls on September 27 and vote for racial integration, "as there is no other way to open our schools."[43] Terry did visit with Daisy Bates, inviting this black leader of the state NAACP and mentor of the Little Rock Nine to her home. After inquiring about the NAACP's plans regarding the school-closing law, Terry explained that to build acceptance for integration in Little Rock among white women and the white community, blacks could not be included in the WEC. In a later interview, Bates said she accepted this decision out of respect for Mrs. Terry.[44] In the 1950s, in Arkansas and throughout the South, women, in a still-paternalistic society, had to break one barrier at a time. As historian Lorraine Gates and others have pointed out, the "power from the pedestal" of southern womanhood gave white women sway only through acceptable venues and only quite gradually. And as historian Elizabeth Jacoway has noted in personal remarks regarding Little Rock during this period, "female questioning could somehow threaten the established order." In this atmosphere, it is understandable that the WEC would need first to fight for white women's influence before seeking to exert power as an interracial group.[45] Most historians have described the WEC as an elite group of white Little Rock women, but Sara Murphy, an early member, challenged the notion of elitism, saying that beyond the group's leaders, most members simply had "a heavy stake in keeping the public school system intact." She described the membership as "the committee heads and workers in the PTA and at church, who could not afford private education even if it were available."[46]

Another new group also competed for newspaper headlines in September of 1958. This group of six hoped to lease public high school buildings and to hire the public school teachers to operate the four facilities on a segregated and private basis. Five Little Rock businessmen and one woman had incorporated the Little Rock Private School Corporation (LRPSC) and secured a charter from the Pulaski County Circuit Court. Two of the incorporators were segregationist leaders: Malcolm Taylor, an osteopath who was a director of the Capital Citizens' Council (CCC), and W. H. Goodman, also a CCC member. J. C. Mitchell, a Faubus appointee to the state Merit System Council, was the group's third member. T. J. Raney, the Pulaski County Health Officer, and Ben Isgrig, a local seed dealer, were the remaining male board members of the LRPSC. Mrs. Gordon Oates, a civic leader and state representative nominee, was the only one of the six incorporators who would discuss the group's plans, explaining to the press that it could do little until after the referendum on closed schools. Oates did mention the recently passed law (Act 5) that stated that public school money could follow a student from a school threatened with integration to the private or public school that the student chose to attend, hinting at the possibility of public funding for the projected private school.[47]

Elizabeth Huckaby went back to Central High after lunch at home the day Oates made her statement. Hearing of this new group at school, she called them "a peculiar bunch." The following day she recorded: "New group to run schools as private looks even worse by morning light. Central High as we know it seems gone—no private school could be accredited. Our better pupils who can find other schooling are leaving. The city is going to let Faubus destroy an asset that it will take 25 years to rebuild, if people ever come to their senses."[48]

Faubus spoke on television the next evening, saying that the Little Rock School Board should rent its buildings to the new private school corporation. He criticized those who would "integrate our schools at any price" and explained his plan for private school operations, based on an 1875 state law that gave school boards permission to lease their buildings to private schools. He appealed for votes "for segregation" in the upcoming referendum, which he said would keep schools closed until they might be leased and opened as segregated, on a private basis.[49]

Since the school closings, the LRSD board itself had petitioned the federal district court for advice on leasing the public school property. Additionally, the NAACP had filed a petition to forbid the LRSD board from leasing any school property for the purpose of private, segregated education. Judge Miller heard the petitions in Fort Smith on September 25, two days before the referendum, and ruled that he had no power to make any decisions on the questions and that they should be heard by a three-judge higher court. Miller was the same judge who had bowed out of a "deal" he made with Blossom and Faubus in summer 1957.[50]

On September 26, the day before the scheduled referendum, NAACP lawyer Wiley A. Branton asked the Eighth Circuit Court of Appeals to enjoin the school board from leasing any of its property or from taking any action concerning the disposal of any school property without first obtaining the court's permission. He also asked the court to require the board to make provision to "secure the constitutional rights of the Negro children to attend Central High School and any other schools in Little Rock presently limited to whites" if such private schools were established.[51]

The community was divided over the issue of integration, as were the students who were waiting for schools to open. A few displaced students at Hall High took matters into their own hands, conducting a telephone poll of 501 junior and senior high students in the Hall attendance area in the western suburbs. They asked one question: "Do you want the schools opened immediately even if it means opening on an integrated basis?" The results of their informal poll found that 71 percent answered "yes," while 24 percent said "no" and 5 percent were uncertain. The day before these results were reported in the *Arkansas Gazette,* 65 Hall High students gathered at an informal meeting and voted for a resolution asking that schools be reopened. Only 2 of the 65 students attending voted against the resolution.[52]

In contrast to the thinking of the Hall High students, 4 displaced students from Central High sent out postcards to 1,236 Central juniors and seniors, asking their opinion on opening the schools. All recipients, students who had experienced the first year of integration in 1957–58, were asked the question: "Do you wish to have Central High School open, whether segregated or integrated?"[53] The postcard poll eventually revealed that 71 percent of responding students favored keeping Central closed rather than integrating it, but no record was made of how many cards were returned.[54] About 200 Central High students of a like mind—and free of school attendance—demonstrated their support for segregation and their governor by driving around the state capitol and the downtown business area in a five-block-long caravan of about forty cars, some with signs reading, "High School Students Against Integration." This group represented about 10 percent of the Central enrollment numbers. Some of these students demonstrated on the lawn of the governor's mansion, chanting, "Two, four, six, eight. We don't want to integrate." They intended to present the governor with a petition signed by 150 Central students that read, "We have seen the effects of one year of forced integration in Central High and not wishing to endure another term with armed soldiers or federal marshals, we are willing to make a few personal sacrifices right now rather than having classes interrupted throughout the year by racial turmoil." At the same time, the exodus of students from the high schools rose to a new total of 280, which now included three students from Horace Mann High. With only four days remaining before the voter referendum on school closure, this approximate one-tenth of registered students and their parents had already made the decision to leave Little Rock schools.[55]

North Little Rock High and its district administrators determined early on that no Little Rock student would be accepted into their system without a change of residence to their district.[56] However, they did make an exception for a group of thirty-five nonresident students from Central. These students lived in rural areas outside the Little Rock School District, and all but six of them were accepted at North Little Rock High in September, even before the referendum.[57] Twenty-six of these students lived in Scott, Arkansas, and their high school had closed at the end of the 1956–57 school year because of declining enrollment. These students had been offered the chance to be bused to nearby high schools such as the one in England, Arkansas, or Little Rock's Central High.

Among those former Scott students were Isao and Toshio Oishi, sons of a Japanese American couple—U.S. citizens who had been interned during World War II at Gila River Relocation Camp in Arizona. As the end of the war neared, interned families could be released from the camps if they could prove they had some type of employment and if they chose to go somewhere other than the West Coast. The Oishi family had moved to Wilson, in eastern Arkansas, in September 1945, when Toshio was four years old. Here they expected to develop truck farming on the Wilson plantation, a 63,000-acre estate that had previously concentrated primarily on cotton. Unable, however, to support their large family on their wages there, Hiromi and Tatsuye Oishi moved to Scott in 1952 to work on the vegetable farm of Mrs. Virginia Brown-Alexander. In Scott, Toshio and his siblings did backbreaking work alongside their parents for long hours on the truck farm, where, he later recalled, his father worked seven days a week. A total of five Japanese American families worked on Brown-Alexander land on Lower Steele Bend Road in Scott. These included the Nakamuras, the Yadas, the Yoshimuras, and the Oshimas, as well as the Oishis, who were seasonally joined by black, Mexican, and even Portuguese workers.[58]

Toshio and his siblings had attended segregated white schools in Wilson and later in Scott. Blacks, he recalled, had a school separate from whites in Wilson, whose movie theater had a sign denoting a separate bathrooms for blacks, who were required to watch movies sitting in the balcony. He and his siblings do not now remember any overt racism directed toward them in Scott, only the difficult farm work for less money than they required.

Arkansas had not always been this welcoming to Japanese Americans. During World War II, the federal government interned approximately 16,000 Japanese Americans at two camps in southeast Arkansas, at Jerome and Rohwer. Arkansas governor Homer Adkins passed laws forbidding

Japanese American students' attendance in Arkansas public schools and state colleges and even forbade Japanese Americans from owning land in the state.[59] In September 1957, the first year of desegregation at Central, Toshio, a junior, and his older brother, Kazuo, a senior, registered with fellow Scott classmates to attend Central High and were bused to school. Knowing that nine blacks were enrolling for the first time that year, Toshio remembered: "I was very concerned during registration and prior to attending Central High of being given a difficult time because my skin was very dark from working outdoors on the farm—this turned out to be an unwarranted fear."[60] Apparently, many Arkansans had narrowed their prejudices regarding race, and their children now accepted a few Japanese Americans into public schools, but they were not yet willing to accept blacks.

Toshio and a younger brother were bused to North Little Rock the year that Little Rock schools were closed, and after high school graduation, Toshio went on to earn a bachelor's degree in electrical engineering from the University of Arkansas. This is one story of displacement among more than three thousand others during the Lost Year. Toshio's education and life were in flux, as were the education and lives of so many. Some students would have a positive outcome despite troubling circumstances, as did Toshio, but others would not.

Just days after the public school closure, Trinity Episcopal Cathedral responded to parents in its congregation when its vestry voted to establish Trinity Interim Academy for the instruction of high school–age members of the church. Registration was to begin the following Monday, while teachers were being recruited.[61] This opportunity for private education was announced at the same time that the LRSD began television classes as a temporary measure. The Very Reverend Charles A. Higgins, dean of the cathedral, headed the board of the new school, announcing that students would pay nine dollars per semester per course. Higgins had moved to Arkansas from Waco, Texas, where he had started a parochial school, and he had convinced the Little Rock congregation to begin a school for grades one through three only one year before, in the fall of 1957.[62] The director of the school, Reverend Wade Wright Egbert, said that the school intended to operate until public schools in Little Rock reopened, whenever that might be. The Interim Academy had registered twenty-four students by September 23.[63]

One of these students' parents, Mrs. James Gates, recalled that Dean Higgins called parents together and suggested that the church could keep the students busy by renting typewriters and teaching typing or by engaging them in a "Great Books Series." As a parent of a high school senior, she—and others—preferred regular academic classes to prepare the students for transfer to accredited schools or back to local schools should they reopen. Within a short period, all senior-level students were being encouraged by the school leadership to attend some other accredited school, rather than risk taking courses that might not allow them into college. Gates's own daughter Ann, a senior, was admitted, along with a few other Little Rock students, to a nearby liberal arts college, Hendrix College in Conway, under a special early admission program.[64]

Trinity's first official day of classes was September 29. The teachers were all members of the Trinity parish, and all had previous teaching experience. Gates became the mathematics teacher, joining eight other faculty members in the parish hall of the church at Seventeenth and Louisiana streets. Students were offered a curriculum that included Latin, French, English, Spanish, mathematics, science, and history. Students completed a full school day, but faculty came only for their class times. Gates recalled that M. J. Kilbury, a surgeon, taught chemistry in the kitchen. By spring, Gates had become supervisor of instruction and could recount achievements from the school year, even as the school was wrestling with whether it would continue the following fall. It had managed a newspaper, a yearbook, and a play for the students, whose numbers had reached a high of twenty-five. Gates remembers doing the paperwork to gain certification for the school from the Arkansas Department of Education for the school's courses, but not for the school itself.[65]

In addition, the Anthony School, a private school that had previously offered only kindergarten and elementary classes, added high school classes for forty of its former students. Allen D. Anthony explained that classes were added for the upper grades at the request of parents and that the school had been pleased to start early and get the "cream of the crop" of teachers. Originally opened in 1944 as a kindergarten, the Anthony School had eventually added classes for lower grades.[66] Over time, both Mr. and Mrs. Anthony had learned about minimal brain dysfunction, and with the help of Sam Clement, a clinical psychologist, and John Peters, from the nearby University of Arkansas for Medical Sciences (UAMS), they geared the school's teaching toward addressing varied learning styles, using an assortment of special techniques to aid young learners. In 1958, when classes were added for high school students, the Anthonys drew some faculty from UAMS. High school classes met in the afternoon, after the lower grades had completed their time in the building.[67]

Chris Barrier, who attended the Anthony School for his junior year, recalled that the school opened some weeks after the public junior high and elementary schools. Classes began for high school students in the early afternoon and continued to about four o'clock P.M. Located in a converted house on Elm Street, the school was the same place where Barrier had attended kindergarten and where he had taken dance lessons in adolescence. No seniors attended Anthony—only sophomores and juniors—for the same reason that Trinity Interim Academy encouraged upper-level students to take classes that were guaranteed to be accredited for their graduation. Barrier's yearbook composite shows thirty-six students and two teachers; he recalled that Mrs. Wade Terral had taught English and Latin, but she was not pictured. Barrier recalled that Lily Major was his American history teacher as well as a teacher of Spanish.[68] Major, the wife of a Methodist minister, had recently returned from living in Latin America. One of ten children, she was the sister of T. J. Raney, one of the founders of the white segregationist private school that later took his name. She explained that the family was divided on the issue of desegregation and that her views were not those of her brother.[69]

Barrier recalled that students were not isolated from events in the community and that there was discussion regarding race and desegregation in these classes—especially in his American history class—"sometimes pretty heated." Barrier remembered that at some point, "Lily Major got tired of it and decided we would have a formal debate on racial equality." Barrier recalled that he was captain of the team for the affirmative and had Louise Crawford and Susan Kahn on his team. The opposition was headed by Allan Seibert, Tom Owen, and, he believes, Mary McKinley, the daughter of Ed McKinley, a segregationist who later became president of the LRSD board. The students researched material outside of school, which had no library, as they learned the rules of classical debate. Barrier remembered that the class held a vote to decide the winner of the debate, and the affirmative side won. He believes that the debate "did serve to reduce the verbal sparring in and out of class although it did not eliminate it."[70] Another student at the Anthony School was Dale Alford Jr., the son of the segregationist LRSD board member Dale Alford.

By late September, Faye Russ, a black sophomore displaced from Horace Mann High, had talked with her parents about a school choice. They contacted her aunt, a teacher, who worked in and lived near a county school: "I moved in with her to get the valid address so that I could enroll in her school, the Pulaski Country Training School located east of North Little

Rock." Russ did not remain in her aunt's home long, because she missed her family terribly. "I cannot do this, I need to be at home," she recalled saying. "I just figured out a way myself. I got a city bus schedule, I moved back home, I wanted to be at home." Russ caught a city bus at six A.M. and rode to the end of the bus line at Protho Junction, on the outskirts of North Little Rock. There she caught the Pulaski County school bus and reached her new school home. She recalled that, academically, her school year was disappointing: "I lost interest. In the ninth grade I had been on the honor roll, in the honor society, but that year is like—I don't know what it did to me. I didn't have the drive."[71]

The referendum vote on closed public schools came on Saturday, September 27. The ballot was worded, as the recent Act 4 required, with a choice between complete integration and complete segregation of all Little Rock Schools—a choice that Little Rock had not before been asked to make. The ballot made no mention of closed or open high schools.[72] On the Saturday of the referendum, Elizabeth Huckaby drove to Scott Street to take her father to vote. She tried to get a ballot for her mother. She wrote: "Tried County Clerk's office again. To be closed all day! No voting for invalids." She was also beginning to realize that enough people would be coming to vote to meet the requirement of eligible voters: "People seemed to be coming out of the gutters to vote. Rabble-rousing old sister on the corner getting signatures to School Board recall petition." Then she drove to her precinct to vote before going to the grocery store and back home.[73] Sunday morning's headline revealed that school integration had been rejected by a vote of 19,470 to 7,561, a vote that Huckaby labeled in her diary as "a rout—3 to 1 for segregation."[74] The number of voters far exceeded the average turnout for a school election by 20,000 votes, but Little Rock patrons—strongly influenced by the wording on the ballot and more importantly by the promise made by their governor and the new private school group—had voted just as the wily Faubus expected. As historian Numan Bartley argued in 1969, "The fact that Governor Faubus and the segregationists assured the voters that private segregated schools would promptly replace the public schools prevented this vote from being a true referendum on school closing."[75] Instead, the wording of the ballot made the issue one regarding race. Little Rock voters, some of whom had willingly accepted minimum compliance with token desegregation in 1957, were now being asked to accept wholesale integration—and they found it as unpalatable as Faubus expected in his trickery of syntax. An analysis of the vote count demonstrates that the predominantly black precincts supported the opening of fully integrated high schools. The upper-class white districts at this time did not, although the margins were much closer in those white precincts than in the overall city vote, of 3 to 1. Of the 7,561 "yes" votes, only 2,378 came from predominantly black precincts, leaving 5,183 predominantly white voters who did, in fact, support open and fully integrated schools. Despite the fact that the WEC campaign had stressed that a vote for integration was a vote for open schools, this was not enough.[76] In previous Little Rock votes stretching back to 1950, upper-class white and black precincts had voted together—making this particular vote a statistical "outlier."[77]

Public schools would now remain closed with what was interpreted as the consent of the voters. What was to be done with 3,665 students? What was to happen to the children, to education, to the community identity of Arkansas's capital city? For every displaced student, the closed schools also affected parents, siblings, and households. Huckaby wrote to her brother: "Of course it is the kids and their families I feel sorriest for. The financial and emotional disruption of local homes will never be assessed."[78]

The referendum closed the doors on public schools, but it brought no solution in itself. For weeks, Little Rock Private School Corporation leaders and Governor Faubus had stressed that should local voters use their franchise to support segregation, there would be no problem with the LRPSC's effort to open the former public school buildings on a private basis. Many in the community waited for news regarding these planned leases.

On the Monday after the Saturday referendum, Elizabeth Huckaby went to Central High, as did all the teachers of the four closed Little Rock high schools. Only those who were to teach on television were not yet there. Her diary records: "Everyone upset as we awaited leasing news. Radio carried it at noon."[79] The news was that the four public high schools had been leased to the LRPSC. She and all the other teachers were in for a hectic and dramatic afternoon. The librarian at Central, Lola Dunnavant, recorded her memories of that afternoon in her diary, just as Huckaby did. A general faculty meeting assembled after lunch in the library, where Jess Matthews passed out contracts for the LRPSC. The plan, Dunnavant recounted, was for the school district to rent its buildings to the private group. She noted that teachers "would resign from the public schools and sign contracts with the private school group."[80] The contract stated that should the private school fail for any reason, the teacher would be reinstated with the LRSD.[81]

The afternoon's events required each teacher to take a stand and thereby allow fellow teachers some awareness of his or her attitude toward private, segregated education for Little Rock. All the white teachers interviewed recalled that afternoon and the subsequent events of that evening and the next morning. They remembered being caught unawares, feeling mentally unprepared to make this decision. Howard Bell, a biology teacher at Central, wrote: "We were given what was left of the afternoon, less than two hours, to make our decision, and a multitude of questions arose and bombarded Mr. Matthews for much of the afternoon. . . . We wanted a chance to consult legal counsel and discuss it with our families at home. Yet the fact was that by mid-afternoon a report was received that Hall High teachers were 100% in signing the new contracts, and over half of the Central faculty had signed. In spite of Mr. Matthews's earnest pleadings to sign the contract, however, some of the teachers held out pending a consultation with lawyers."[82]

The participation of the LRSD in leasing the school buildings in cooperation with the Little Rock Private School Corporation had changed over time. In an article printed on Thursday, September 18, Virgil Blossom was quoted as saying, "The Board never had discussed leasing the schools to anyone." As to whether it would consent to leasing them, he said, "I'm sure they [the board] will cross that bridge when they get to it."[83] By the night of the referendum, when school segregation had received a 3-to-1 endorsement, the LRSD board began negotiations with the LRPSC. By Monday, September 29, when contracts were issued to Little Rock high school teachers, they not only contained the signatures of T. J. Raney and Ben Isgrig, of the new LRPSC, but included statements for the teachers' release from their previous contracts with the Little Rock School District. The second section of the contract was cosigned by Wayne Upton, the board president, and Harold Engstrom, the secretary—a clear indication that the new private school board and the existing public school board had cooperated to produce the document offered to Little Rock high school teachers. This was also an indication that the leasing of the buildings was assured. Huckaby's diary indicates that fifteen Central teachers refused to sign contracts with the private school, but she does not list their names: "15 of us held out but agreed to come back and conduct classes if needed. I told Mr. M[atthews], privately, that I would not sign at all. He expressed regret at losing me."[84]

Jo Ann Henry (Royster), like many white teachers, recalls that evening's events quite vividly. She had not signed her contract and was uneasy about her personal future as a math teacher because this was only her second year at Central. As the wife of a medical student, she was often alone in the evenings: "Now, that was some experience. When we left school that afternoon, we did not know what was going to happen. So that evening someone knocked on my door and I said who's there please and he said 'U.S. Marshall, ma'am with a restraining order.' I went over and got my neighbor on the other side of the house to go to the door with me because I just didn't open the door in the evening when I was by myself."[85]

This same day at three o'clock P.M., as teachers were offered contracts by the Little Rock Private School Corporation, the U.S. Supreme Court handed down its written decision in *Cooper v. Aaron,* which voided the private school scheme. The restraining orders, an outgrowth of that written ruling, caused the Eighth Circuit Court to respond almost immediately, acting upon the NAACP petition that had been filed in a lower court. The quickly created document prevented public school teachers and public school buildings from being used for private and segregated education.[86]

Howard Bell wrote about this eventful day and the federal marshals' delivery of the restraining orders to the governor, to members of both school boards (public and private), and to all teachers and administrators: "I went to bed early that evening with a sick headache brought on by the events of the day. Before daylight, a marshal was at the door to serve me with a notice to stay away from Central High School and, on his second attempt to get past my mother, succeeded in serving the notice. So I stayed home for a couple of days until the public status of Central High was clarified satisfactorily and faculty activities could be resumed."[87]

The legal restraints that federal authorities served to hundreds that Monday evening, September 29, and into the morning of September 30, had been issued at 4:10 P.M. by Judge Joseph W. Woodrough of the Eighth Circuit Court in St. Louis, just a few minutes after the teachers left their buildings. Huckaby later commented in a letter to her brother, "I'm sure that the private school bunch (and Mr. Faubus) were amazed at the speed of the federal court restraining order against the lease."[88] She expressed her belief that Faubus and the private school group wanted those schools opened quickly on a private basis so that federal intervention would require shutting down students in classrooms and teachers at work. This would have left another distasteful image of federal intervention in Little Rock schools and would have thus worked to the segregationists' advantage.[89]

Newspaper accounts regarding the Little Rock Private School Corporation frequently mentioned the lease of all four buildings for segregated education, but it is unclear whether the group ever intended to offer schooling for black students with black teachers in their existing building at Horace Mann High. Among the ten black teachers interviewed, none recalls being offered a contract by the LRPSC. Compared to the white teachers' vivid recollections of an emotional afternoon and forced decisions regarding their contracts, the black teachers' lack of such memories suggests that the LRPSC did not offer them such contracts. However, newspaper accounts attest to the fact that some of the 175 restraining orders were intended for all black and white teachers.[90] Whatever the intention of the LRPSC, the federal courts enjoined public school teachers from participation in the private school system and prevented the use of public school buildings for private use. As white teachers were served restraining orders on the evening of September 29, lawyers for the Classroom Teachers Association were calling to tell them not to report to school on Tuesday morning, September 30, lest they be considered in contempt of the restraining order.[91] Thus, no teachers, black or white, were in their buildings after September 29 until the Eighth Circuit Court of Appeals heard the latest manifestation of *Cooper v. Aaron,* planned for October 6. The orders also cancelled the television classes.[92]

In Howard Bell's account of events, he describes how that afternoon fully divided the faculty at Central High School. He notes what happened when they eventually returned to empty schools with no students: "Our contracts were returned to us without a comment, whether signed or unsigned. Every effort was made to forget the incident, since it had forced the teachers to take a stand. We knew now pretty well how the various teachers felt about integration, and we were not unanimous; we could not present a united front. In the interests of faculty harmony, therefore, the subject became taboo among us from then on."[93]

Huckaby's letter to her brother about the events of September 29 included more details regarding her decision and the decisions of the fourteen others who refused to sign contracts with the LRPSC: "I went home very low in spirits, of course. Glen agreed that if this meant the end of my career at Central that was the way it would have to be." She had opened this same letter by assuring her brother that she "was not incurring any unnecessary expenses" and that she and Glen would wait to make a decision about "dropping back to being a one-car family" until a later time. Her words reveal her anxiety—probably felt by all teachers—over the future of her professional as well as her public life. Earlier, lawyers had assured high school teachers that their contracts with the LRSD were binding and that they would be paid whether they taught students or not. But with the offer to resign from the public school and sign on with "anything sponsored by the Citizen's Council," as Huckaby describes the document to her brother, the issue became even more uncertain.[94]

Public school teachers in Little Rock high schools were "well-respected" members of the community, but they were certainly not paid well enough to be considered among Little Rock's elite. Their salaries were important to the maintenance of all of their households, and some provided the sole support for their families. Jo Ann Henry (Royster), a young math teacher and the wife of a medical student, was being paid $3,109 annually. Yet Jo Ann Henry and Elizabeth Huckaby, along with thirteen other white teachers at Central High, refused to sign on to work in what they considered a private, segregationist school. Their positions had forced them to clarify early on their personal views on race and desegregation, and now, after a year's trial by fire, they were risking their own paychecks and possibly their careers. Acting out of moral conviction, they took a stand that many others in the community would not take nor be asked to take. These fifteen courageous teachers should be acknowledged and lauded.[95]

CHAPTER THREE

Where Shall We Go?

When you close the schools and throw 3,600 kids out on the street,
that's an important story, too. Nobody covers our sacrifice.
—Phillip Moore, Central High Student

LITTLE ROCK, SEPTEMBER 30–NOVEMBER 12, 1958

SEPTEMBER 30. The LRPSC solicits funds for buildings and teachers for private education.

OCTOBER 6. A hearing of the Eighth Circuit Court continues the ban on school leasing and postpones opening until October 15.

OCTOBER 15. The Eighth Circuit Court takes written briefs regarding school leasing without giving a date for a decision.

OCTOBER 20. The LRPSC opens its doors to white seniors.

OCTOBER 27. The first day for Baptist High School (a new school directed by Ouachita College, together with Baptist Interim Academy, established weeks earlier).

OCTOBER 27. Dale Alford announces himself as a write-in candidate against Hays.

NOVEMBER 4. Thirty-eight Arkansas school districts solicit funds from Little Rock.

NOVEMBER 4. Alford defeats Hays for Congress in a write-in campaign.

NOVEMBER 10. The Eighth Circuit Court of Appeals rules.

NOVEMBER 12. Five of the six members of the LRSD board resign and buy
   out Blossom's contract.

On Tuesday, September 30, 1958, all public high schools in the city sat
closed to teachers, just as they had been to students since September 15.
Just the day before, late in the afternoon, the Eighth Circuit Court of
Appeals in St. Louis had issued restraining orders forbidding the Little Rock
School District and its board from leasing public school buildings to a private school group. The order also restrained public school teachers from
working for the Little Rock Private School Corporation. The LRPSC had
planned to conduct segregated private education in the city, using former
public school buildings and teachers, with classes planned to begin on
Tuesday, September 30. T. J. Raney, the president of the LRPSC board, along
with board members Malcolm Taylor and W. H. Goodman, appeared at
Central High at eight A.M. with their "no school" announcement and publicly solicited private buildings and private funds for segregated education
for high school students.[1] Raney read a statement that declared in part:
"Federal government officials, from the president on down, . . . must be
made to understand that the course they have chosen is leading our nation
to destruction. We have no alternative but to stand fast until there is an
awakening by the people of our nation."[2] It was another of the seemingly
unending battles between the federal courts and those citizens determined
to circumvent school desegregation in Little Rock. The September 29 ruling
by the Eighth Circuit Court and the restraining orders issued the afternoon
before had foiled the plans of the LRPSC and broken Faubus's promise of
private education in public school buildings. On this day, then, the courts
had won, but segregationists had not quit the battle.[3]

As Raney and the other two private school officials left the Central High
campus, the segregationist Dewey Coffman and two other men posted a
large four-by-six-foot misspelled sign: "This School Closed by Order of the
Federal Goverment." A guard working for the Little Rock School District
tried unsuccessfully to prevent them from posting the sign, and they then
moved on to the other three Little Rock high schools and erected identical
signs. When questioned, Coffman said, "I did it for the Private Corporation," admitting that he had not asked public school officials for permission
to erect the signs.[4] When photos of one of the signs appeared in the *Gazette*,
four boys wearing the fashion of the day for motorcycle-riding, blue-collar
society—leather jackets or upturned collars— posed with "thumbs down."
The caption asked, "Thumbs down to the government? the sign? or the
misspelled word?"[5]

Elizabeth Huckaby wrote her brother Bill that the signs would create yet another distasteful and inaccurate image of federal intervention in Little Rock schools, blaming the federal government for the closures, rather than state authority, the governor, and the voters. Had the courts not acted so quickly the day before, and had the LRPSC managed to open the former public buildings that morning, then any closures might indeed be blamed on the federal government.[6] Years later in his own book, *Down from the Hills*, Faubus recapped the same incidents, describing the federal court action as being "in unseemly haste." Like Huckaby, he believed that if the LRPSC had managed to open the leased buildings, it would have necessitated "sending U.S. marshals or even troops to arrest the teachers and force the children out of the school buildings."[7] No image could have played more effectively into the hands of the segregationists, but in reality this message was now a false one, because the schools had never really opened. Faubus referred to the signs defensively, noting that "someone" erected them and that the spelling mistake had actually brought "wider publicity than would have otherwise been obtained."[8] Jon Kennedy's cartoon regarding this sign in the *Arkansas Democrat* included a puzzled artist, with a caption saying "Whodunit?"[9]

Restrictions spelled out in the restraining order were to be in effect until a hearing set for October 6, 1958, in St. Louis. Public high school teachers remained at home, waiting for further word. Displaced students and parents searched for different schooling opportunities. Football, on the other hand, moved forward.

The Hall High Warriors planned to play Crossett, Arkansas, on Friday night at Quigley Stadium, despite the loss of six of their starting linemen since their opening win against Catholic High only weeks before.[10] Both Coach Ray Peters of Hall and Coach Gene Hall from Central High worried about holding their teams together for the remainder of the season with so many of their players leaving for alternate schooling. The *Arkansas Gazette* announced the rankings of Arkansas high school teams on October 1, and for the first time in years the Central High Tigers were not number one. Their glaring 42–0 loss to Istrouma High in Baton Rouge, Louisiana, the previous Friday had exposed weaknesses that sportswriter Jerry McConnell feared might not be remedied.[11]

Coach Hall had joined the Central High faculty in 1955 under Coach Wilson Matthews, who had taken the Central High Tigers to thirty-three straight wins. In 1958, the twenty-eight-year-old Hall was named head coach at his own alma mater: "Of course you can imagine how excited I was about being head coach, and then what do they do? They close us down."[12] Hall mentioned that a normal squad at his campus had over one hundred players, but that by the time of the Istrouma game, they were down to thirty-two boys. The Arkansas Athletic Association (AAA) had ruled that Little Rock high school football teams could compete but that the players could not enroll in any other public or private school throughout the season. As at other schools in the state, practice times were limited to after normal school hours, and all AAA rules applied to these teams despite the peculiar circumstances regarding their players' academic programs.[13] Bill Sigler, a starting lineman at Hall High, recalls playing the school's first game with the stands full, the cheerleaders in place, but with schools still closed. By the third game, he had joined five others from his team in transferring to Jacksonville High, where no one was allowed to play football because of Athletic Association rules. He and his classmates believed Hall High would not be able to muster many wins without them, but now he laughingly remembers that Hall won the Big Nine Championship that year—without their talent.[14] (Sigler was mistaken: El Dorado won in 1958–59, although Hall did win in 1959–60.)

Across town, Coach Fred Swinton held after-school practices for his team, the Horace Mann "Bearcats." On October 10, they were scheduled to face Temberton High School from Marshall, Texas, at Quigley Stadium, but they were off to their poorest start in years, having lost four of five games. Their decreasing number of players hurt them when they played Temberton, the number-three black team in Texas, but the Bearcats held on and managed a come-from-behind win, 12–7.[15] Although both black and white high school football continued, public education was at a standstill.

Superintendent Blossom and the LRSD board members continued their work, also waiting for word from the courts. By October 10, they had filled the vacancy on their board with a thirty-one-year-old insurance agent named Frank Lambright. Fellow board members had elected him to fill the unexpired term of Henry Rath.

LRPSC officials needed to act quickly. Before the referendum, they and Governor Faubus had assured the voters that Faubus's private school plan would work, but they had been stymied by the courts. LRPSC leaders now kicked into high gear, searching for new buildings, soliciting new teachers, and asking for donations. On October 3, T. J. Raney was quoted as saying, "We don't have any troubles except money," encouraging the *Gazette* reporter to publicize the LRPSC's address so that supporters could send in their donations. When the reporter quoted a public school spokesperson setting the cost of a high school program at $19,000 a week, Raney countered those figures: "We won't have all that expense because we won't have debt service, a hot lunch program and everything." Raney failed to mention that his group would also spend less money since they would not be providing any educational opportunities for Little Rock's black students.[16] He did ask that donors wishing to support segregated private education mail their contributions to an office next door to his, at 922 Marshall. He stressed that anyone with a facility that might possibly be used as classroom space should call this same office.[17]

That same day, sixteen-year-old Lin Phelps and her seventeen-year-old sister, Sue, accepted the offer of a temporary home with Mr. and Mrs. James Wharton of Memphis, Tennessee. Hearing of the need of displaced Little Rock students, the Whartons had announced their willingness to open their home to two young people—absolute strangers. After accepting the Phelps sisters, they turned down phone calls from others also hoping to accept the Whartons' generous offer.[18] The Phelps sisters were to have attended Hall High, but when it appeared that schools would not open, their father drove them first to Harrison, Arkansas. Hoping to live with their grandfather, Clifford Jordan, they were disappointed when the local school board decided against enrolling Little Rock students in its school. Later, a friend of the young girls' mother who worked for the Memphis newspaper called about the offer of housing at the Whartons' in Memphis. The Phelps sisters learned that Memphis public schools would not accept the girls, but they ultimately were able to enroll in the small Church of Christ School, Harding Academy, located not far from Jim and Terry Wharton's home. Both girls remained in Memphis for the fall semester, with Lin coming home to Little Rock on weekends for Hall High football games, where she cheered for the Warriors.

Both sisters returned to Little Rock at semester's end, and Sue was able to enroll at Little Rock University in January. But Lin, still a junior, faced a more difficult scenario. Lin's parents then made what Sue labeled the "scary" decision to allow friends in North Little Rock to adopt their younger daughter so that she could attend public schools in North Little Rock beginning in January 1959. Sue's final comments from the distance of fifty years summarize her feelings: "Being young and in the middle of the situation was more emotional than reasonable."[19]

On October 1, four more Hall High School seniors registered for classes at Sylvan Hills High, a Pulaski County school near North Little Rock, bringing the total of Little Rock students in that school to 21.[20] By October 3, however, the superintendent of Pulaski County schools, E. F. Dunn, had closed the doors to further transfers for Little Rock white students. More than 300 white students from the Little Rock district had enrolled in five county high schools before Superintendent Dunn turned away 250 more at Mabelvale High. In addition to overcrowding, he expressed concern that any more students would affect his high schools' Class-A rating. It appeared that sports determined his view of accepting more displaced students, since larger numbers would put his school in a higher competitive bracket.[21] One student who was able to enroll at Mabelvale before the cutoff was Gerhard Maylaender, the foreign exchange student from Germany. Mrs. Pearcy, with whom he lived, was a teacher at Meadowcliff Elementary in the southern part of Little Rock. She drove him to the Pulaski County high school, where he would complete one year of high school while her daughter, Katherine, continued her studies in Germany.[22]

Soon the Women's Emergency Committee publicly urged Governor Orval Faubus to take all steps needed to reopen the public high schools. Instead, he threw his weight behind the LRPSC, mailing thousands of letters on his official letterhead with the state's seal, soliciting donations for segregated education.[23] When reporters asked Clarence Laws, the field secretary of the NAACP, about private education for black students, he said he knew of no plans for them should private schools open. "We think this private school plan is an attempt to fool the people," he said, noting his belief that "the whole thing will collapse." Laws added that though Little Rock voters had overwhelmingly approved segregation just the Saturday before, "they would vote for integration if another election were held tomorrow."[24] The LRPSC had said little regarding educating black students, but from this point forward, it raised funds only for white private education.[25]

On Sunday, October 5, Elizabeth Huckaby wrote her brother Bill about the court decision expected the following day. Her copy of the restraining order stated clearly that the Eighth Circuit Court in St. Louis would hold a hearing then. She had expectations, as did many in Little Rock, that these three justices would be decisive in upholding the previous decisions of the Supreme Court. Projecting some possibilities in her letter, she spelled out several choices before the court and commented on each. She expected the court to make the restraining order permanent. This would continue to bar the lease of public schools to the LRPSC. She doubted that the court would take over the high schools and run them, something she felt would not lead to an eventual solution. The third choice she described was "really what [she] looked for"—that the school would remain closed all year. She told her brother that if this came about, she, as vice principal for girls at Central

High, would direct her attention to keeping up the "morale of faculty" and to "help[ing] teachers keep sharp." Her fear was that the ownership of the schools might remain in litigation and that teachers wouldn't be able to "gather at school each day."[26]

Monday, October 6, came and went, but the court only extended the school-lease ban and postponed a further hearing until October 15. Judges M. C. Mathes, Harvey M. Johnsen, and Joseph W. Woodrough called for briefs from interested parties and stated that no oral arguments would be allowed on October 15. At the morning's session on October 6, Richard Butler, legal counsel for the LRSD board, had given oral arguments with others in a short one-hour session. Just as he had argued the previous summer, Butler now suggested that the courts needed to declare unconstitutional the state laws that allowed school closure and the transfer of state funds to private education. The NAACP's Wiley Branton argued in favor of an injunction against the leasing of public school buildings to a private agency or, if not that, an order requiring that any private school be operated on an integrated basis. U.S. attorneys joined this short hearing with a twenty-five-page brief that emphasized that Little Rock had become the "testing ground" and that "if Central High is allowed to reopen on a segregated basis, the harmful effects both to children and to the country could in no way be undone by the courts."[27]

Little Rock's citizens were again waiting for the courts to act. Most groups followed the patterns of previous days. LRPSC forces continued their search for buildings, teachers, and donations. By October 8, they had hired W. C. Brashears, a retired principal, to serve as superintendent. His first public announcement reported that he had hired no teachers yet, but that there were "many" applicants from all over the country. He also said that "an enormous lot of space is available," but that the LRPSC had not settled on which facilities to use. He wanted to open for the senior class first and as soon as possible.[28] Four days later, Raney said the private school group was having "a little more difficulty than anticipated in obtaining teachers." Further, Brashears said, the curriculum of the private schools, when open, would be somewhat curtailed.[29]

It was a few days later that Elizabeth Huckaby received a phone call from fellow displaced teacher Nyna Keeton, who relayed the rumor that public high school teachers might be given twenty-day notice on contracts to force them into the private school system. Huckaby's diary captures beautifully her reaction to such a possibility: "charming thought for day's end."[30] Although this and other rumors were circulating, the following day an actual event troubled her. Glen, her husband and a retired junior high administrator, received a phone call from Brashears. He was searching for faculty for the LRPSC and called to offer Glen Huckaby a position with the private school. She wrote, "I hit the ceiling, no matter if we starved first, he mustn't consider it." She was relieved to find that he certainly didn't want to work for the same system that she had taken a stand against and with whom she had refused to sign a contract.[31]

With the absence of public education and the delays of Faubus's private school plans, Protestant churches attempted to fill in the gaps for their high school students. The Arkansas Missionary Baptist Association announced that it would open a high school "academy" on the campus of Conway Baptist College in Conway, about thirty-five miles northwest of Little Rock. Conway Academy would provide bus transportation from a church at Sixteenth and Arch in Little Rock, leaving at seven-thirty A.M. and returning at four-thirty P.M. A six-member faculty planned to teach basic college preparatory classes in English, French, mathematics, history, and science, as well as physical education. Dean Wassell Burgess announced that the tuition was to be fifty dollars per semester for classes, plus an additional thirty-two dollars per semester for transportation, with classes beginning in two weeks. Students would be able to buy their lunches for fifty cents per day in the cafeteria. Little Rock parents were beginning to realize that replacing a free public education for their children was going to be costly, and some simply could not afford it. At least this was becoming clear to white parents: the Missionary Baptist Association had no black members, and the Conway Academy would not be open to displaced black students.[32]

A second opportunity for white Baptists arose on October 13. The Second Baptist Interim Academy opened with forty students, all parishioners, at Eighth and Cumberland streets in Little Rock, in the educational building of the church. Dale Cowling welcomed the students with the following remarks: "This is school, not a police action. You will just have to grow up a little faster and meet your responsibilities."[33] Second Baptist's church minister of youth education, Marshall Walker, described the program that started that day. He had a faculty of twenty-one volunteers, all with college degrees. Teachers, he reported, would teach for only one hour a day, but students would be in classes from nine A.M. to three P.M. following chapel services at eight-thirty A.M.[34] The academy expanded later, with Ouachita Baptist College in Arkadelphia directing its academic program and an increasing number of students using additional facilities.

Thirty-five students from two additional churches gathered at Westover Hills Presbyterian church for classes scheduled to take place from eight-thirty A.M. to twelve-thirty P.M. Both St. Mark's Episcopal Church and St. Paul's Methodist Church sent children to Westover Hills. Here students enrolled in correspondence courses from the University of Arkansas, three teachers assisting them with their lessons in English, world history, and American history.[35]

Black high school students transferred to the only two public "Negro" schools in Pulaski County: J. C. Cook High School in Wrightsville and Pulaski County Training School near North Little Rock. Superintendent E .F. Dunn, the white administrator of all county schools, said: "A sincere effort will be made to accommodate 205 Negro students from Mann High" at J. C. Cook High School. Dunn planned to work with David Boswell, the school's superintendent, who had already admitted this number to his school. Dunn had cut off transfers of white students to his district nine days before but apparently was trying to accommodate the large number of blacks at Wrightsville somewhat later into the month. The two-year-old J. C. Cook High, with only seven classrooms for its own 395 students, hired four additional teachers and opened four more classrooms in the older frame building it had previously abandoned. Horace Mann had a total of 750 displaced black students looking for alternative education, but Cook High could accommodate only a third of them. No one in Little Rock was talking about private schools for blacks.[36]

Goforth Coleman was one of the black students who applied for admission to J. C. Cook as a sophomore that fall semester. One of six children and the second boy, he hoped to follow in the footsteps of his older brother, "the brainy one," who was attending Philander Smith College in Little Rock. Goforth explained that his family lived in the "projects" at Granite Mountain and that when they moved into public housing in southeast Little Rock in 1951, they were actually "moving up." He noted that they had previously lived nearby but had not had indoor plumbing. "It was a little rough," he added. Moving into public housing gave his family a refrigerator, a stove, a bathtub, central heat, and indoor plumbing. His father was a day laborer, and his mother did housekeeping and babysitting for white families. All six children hoed and picked cotton in the summers to make money, which they brought home and put on the kitchen table for his father to budget. He remembered that one summer after buying all the school clothes and supplies for each child, the family was able to buy a television with the money they had earned.[37]

Coleman knew that he needed to go to school, but he was already on the football team for Horace Mann. The school had fielded a championship team among black high schools in the Big Ten Conference, playing games as far away as Oklahoma City, against Douglas High, and eastern Texas. Like other displaced high school players in Little Rock, Coleman reported for practices and for games. Only after the season could he enroll at J. C. Cook High in Wrightsville. He hitchhiked and found rides to school with friends because his family had no car. Later in the year, when the Illings Bus Line made runs to Wrightsville and back, he recalled, he could not afford the sixty-cent one-way fare—well more than his lunch money per day.[38] Echoing the sentiments of Pulaski County Superintendent Dunn regarding overcrowding at Wrightsville, Coleman said that his classes had forty or more students: "We were still able to get . . . I won't say a quality education but I think we were able to continue the process."[39]

In Little Rock, many waited for the announcement of the Eighth Circuit Court's October 15 hearing. This turned out to be another disappointment for those who expected any change in the situation, as once again the session took less than an hour and no further ruling was made. The three judges extended the leasing ban again but gave no indication of when they would rule on the case. In the short session, the Justice Department attorneys joined NAACP lawyers in attacking the Little Rock School Board for claiming to be neutral in the case. This time a young and inexperienced lawyer named John Haley represented the school board, reiterating the belief that the board had to obey state laws "until they could be declared unconstitutional."[40] A month had passed since the official closure of the public high schools in Little Rock, and this afternoon session brought little change.

On Monday, October 20, 407 white students, grades 10–12, registered at the Baptist High School at Second Baptist Church, where teachers and students from the existing Baptist Interim Academy merged with the new organization headed by Ouachita Baptist College.[41] This college, an affiliate of the Southern Baptist Convention, was located in Arkadelphia, seventy-five miles southwest of Little Rock. Ouachita president Ralph A. Phelps and his board were expanding the existing Baptist Interim Academy, which would now be run by J. W. Cady, the dean of students at the college. Stressing that the school was not to be permanent, the board announced that its plan was to serve only because of the closure of public schools. This school would use the facilities of the Second Baptist Church, as the Interim Academy had done, and would add facilities at First Baptist Church and Gaines Street Baptist Church. Phelps stressed that Baptist High School would utilize no public funds even if they became available, "because such would violate Baptist principles of separation of church and state." He set tuition at twenty dollars per month, with the hope of later reducing the charges if possible. Cady opened an office in Little Rock to receive applications for teachers but planned to build around the core of teachers already volunteering at the existing facility.[42] Baptist High School, as the merged project was officially known, became the second-largest private school that operated during the Lost Year. Its academic classes met at the churches, while physical education classes were held at the YWCA and the Little Rock Boys Club. Baptist youth held priority for admission, but others also enrolled. Students chose from a broad curriculum of twenty-five credits.[43] While Ouachita Baptist College planned to regulate academic affairs, responsibility for the school's major problem—finances—rested with a board representing each of the major Southern Baptist congregations in Little Rock. Principal W. E. Middleton estimated that one-third of those enrolled in the newly merged school were not Baptist and that one-third of scholarship students came from churches other than those sponsoring the school.

The opening of the school called for the purchase of $3,500 worth of equipment, an expenditure that caused the school to be plagued by a $2,000 deficit for most of the year. When the board raised tuition to $25 per month, even scholarship students had to pay the additional $5. The board solicited funds from Sunday-school classes in sponsoring churches, the churches of students who attended the school, and the public. By March, Dale Cowling, of First Baptist Church, was optimistic: "We Baptists believe that if we tell our needs to the good Lord and the good people they will be supplied. We entered the school business to save our boys and girls from losing a year of academic training. We will accomplish our objective."[44]

In November, the board hired Lynn Nunnally (Blagg) to join the faculty at Baptist High. She was a spring 1958 graduate of Ouachita College and had belonged to the same Baptist congregation as Jim Cady, the new director of the school. One set of English classes had lost two teachers, and Cady had called Blagg and asked her if she wanted to begin her first year of teaching. Blagg taught one senior-level English class, three junior-level, and one sophomore-level. Being young and eager, she also served as the cheerleader sponsor and the yearbook sponsor. These extracurricular activities, along with basketball, track and field, a senior trip, and a Valentine banquet, were all intended to make the students' experience in the school as normal as possible. When asked if she believed that Baptist High differed in any way from the proposed Little Rock Private School Corporation's school (later to be named Raney High), Blagg said that Baptist was intended only to serve the students until public schools could open and that this school had no political agenda of any kind.[45]

Blagg described the facilities of Second Baptist's educational building as nice but indicated that classrooms with thirty desks made for crowded conditions. Teachers began to carry flashlights because the building had no windows, and if power was lost for any reason, they were completely in the dark. She referred to several bomb scares that Baptist High received. During bomb scares, teachers took the students across the street to the Little Rock Boys Club to wait while someone searched the building, but Blagg does not recall that authorities ever found anything dangerous in the school. Blagg remembers that neither she nor the students were excited about attending classes through early July but that the twenty-seven seniors pictured in the yearbook, *The Growl,* were pleased to graduate from Baptist High in the summer of 1959.[46]

The curriculum for the three grades was extensive, with offerings in Latin, English, Spanish, speech, mechanical drawing, trigonometry, plane geometry, American history, world history, home economics, applied mathematics, and biology. The board added physics, chemistry, and commercial subjects during the second semester in an attempt to meet the needs of all those enrolled. The yearbook pictures eight teachers and lists the names of six additional teachers. The school earned accreditation from the state of Arkansas in January 1959 but did not apply for state aid money under Act 5 because of its religious affiliation.[47]

Gayle Singleton (Gardner) attended Baptist High for her junior year. She had attended Hall High as a sophomore during its opening year and remembers being uncomfortable in that setting: "Central High had such a rich history and my brother had graduated from Central High. Everyone had always gone to Central, and Hall High was new and still feeling its way." When the schools didn't open early in September of 1958, Singleton remembers not being too disappointed. "My mother was much more concerned. She was a big reader and she encouraged me in school," Singleton said. She remembers that finances were an issue and that even purchasing the textbooks for public school could be a struggle for her family. Transportation to one of the county schools would have been difficult, so the family did not consider sending her to one. Her two younger brothers were elementary students, and only Gayle was not in school. She has vivid memories of the television classes offered by the LRSD in September, particularly recalling Emily Penton, the Central High teacher who continued to teach American history during early-morning sessions: "My great-grandmother, grandmother, and great-aunt lived across the street, and I remember that they watched Miss Penton every morning. If I can remember her name, you know she made an impact in the community."[48]

In the fall of 1958 she was attending Second Baptist Church with her great-aunt and had become an active member of the church's youth group. When the school opened there, Singleton's family could not afford the tuition, but "someone wrote a check. . . . I think the minister called some-one and they funded me," Singleton remembers. She recalls taking history, English, and geometry and walking to the YWCA for physical education. During the spring she walked as a group with classmates and an elderly teacher to Capital Business College, where she took typing and shorthand in an upstairs classroom: "I don't know how old my teacher was, but she seemed ancient at the time, and when we got upstairs she would have to get two chairs together and just lay out! I remember that she called all of us honey." In addition to her classes, her fondest memories of Baptist High included being a second-squad cheerleader and attending the Sweetheart Banquet at the Albert Pike Hotel.

Singleton is reflective regarding her own attitude and that of her family at the time, compared to the present. "My family believed that it was hon-orable to stand up for our rights, and my father believed that the federal government forcing desegregation with troops was wrong," said Singleton. "My future husband's views were different from my family's. He lived near Central High and had graduated in 1957, was waiting to leave for a Uni-versity of Arkansas track scholarship in the fall of 1957, and witnessed the protesting adults who surrounded Central High during the early days of the Crisis. He thought those adults were wrong, and he disapproved of their behaviors." Over time her own attitude also changed. Her older brother, Jack, became a Methodist minister, as did her younger sister, who was born later. "Through the years we have all grown, and my older brother helped open our eyes," she recalled. Looking back on the period, she believes that "it was larger than any one of us." When asked if she realized that black stu-dents at Horace Mann High were also locked out of school, she said, "I am embarrassed—I am embarrassed [to learn that]. I did not realize that."[49]

Singleton, who never finished school, remembers that there were others who did not complete high school. When public high schools did open in late summer of 1959, she did not want to return to Hall High. Instead she took classes at Little Rock University, which could count for high school credit for her senior year or for college credit if she continued. But instead of going further in college, she got married—to the man who helped change her attitude toward what happened in Little Rock during the Crisis and the Lost Year.[50]

On another front, Superintendent Brashears and the LRPSC board worked quickly to find a location and begin classes for seniors. On Friday, October 17, just nine days after he was hired, Brashears announced that the group had located classroom facilities at West Sixteenth and Lewis, had hired O. M. Owens as principal, and would register seniors the following Monday. At a press conference on the lawn of the fifty-year-old, two-story brick building fronted by large white columns, leaders of the group explained that the building had thirty-two usable rooms. Vance Thompson, a wealthy businessman from McCrory, Arkansas, had bought the building from the University of Arkansas just two days before and was leasing it to the LRPSC. Built in 1909, it had served as the Graduate Center for the University of Arkansas for ten years and had been a Methodist orphanage prior to that.[51] Brashears and others expected about five hundred white seniors to register, and about three hundred showed up at the LRPSC building the following Monday. Brashears announced that the school had filled the one building to capacity and that the LRPSC would use other facilities for juniors and sophomores after November 1. Reverend H. O. Bolin of Highland Methodist Church, located near the LRPSC facility at 4000 West Thirteenth, said that his church might consider leasing its new $140,000 educational building to the LRPSC. On the day of senior registration, several former Little Rock Technical High boys stood outside the large, imposing structure and said they had not registered because the school had no automotive or wood-work shop facilities. Organizers had said the school's college-prep curriculum would focus on basic courses; no specialty courses would be available for boys from Little Rock Technical High.[52]

All the teachers at the new school (which would take the name "Raney High" in December) held college degrees except the librarian, who had completed ninety hours toward a degree, and the driver-education teacher. Seven faculty members held advanced degrees. Some people in the community had the perception that many of the teachers at the private school had come out of retirement to teach, but in reality only seven were over sixty years of age and only two were over sixty-five. The average age for male teachers was thirty and for female teachers was forty-five.[53] The school's yearbook, entitled the *Rebel*, pictured forty-five faculty members. It offered classes in English, algebra, plane geometry, solid geometry, trigonometry, world history, American government, Arkansas history, biology, chemistry, physics, typewriting, bookkeeping, shorthand, applied mathematics, and driver's education.[54] The school also produced a newspaper, the *Rebel Rouser*, and fielded teams in both basketball and track. The seniors and juniors used the building at Sixteenth and Lewis, in addition to several portable buildings that had been brought to the property. The sophomores used the Education Building at Highland Methodist Church, which was nearby. [55]

Students paid no tuition at Raney High: the LRPSC had received private donations from all over the Unites States, totaling $300,480.43.[56] Faubus, who later wrote of the school's efforts toward accreditation and its lucrative fundraising, was frequently pictured in newspaper cartoonist Jon Kennedy's drawings as a supporter and champion of the private school system.[57] One expectation for the LRPSC and other private schools was that state funding of $176 per year per student would follow each transfer student who enrolled if the school received accreditation. This was based on the new Act 5, passed in the extraordinary session of 1958.[58]

Carol Lynn (Hallum) had attended Central High as a sophomore during the Crisis Year. She loved the school, her favorite activity going to the Campus Inn, a building on the school grounds with a juke box, where students could buy lunch and dance to their favorite music during the lunch break. She remembered the military's presence in the school in 1957–58 but did not consider it a disruption. She had little contact with the Little Rock Nine and witnessed no problems or harassment toward them. However, she did have a history class with Jefferson Thomas and recalled a "strange" situation. Normally, students were seated in alphabetical order, but Carol noticed that four football players were seated strategically in front of, behind, and beside Thomas: "They were obviously not in alphabetical order, and I don't know who set that up, if they did that on their own. I just know that the football players never bothered him."[59]

The next year, when schools were closed, Hallum attended Raney High. She doesn't remember when her family decided she would go there. They talked briefly about sending her to live with an aunt who was a teacher, but she lived in Mt. Vernon, Arkansas, a rural school that followed the crop year. Hallum commented, "There was no telling whether they were in school, out of school, or what." Hallum remembers that it was "really great" to be out of school into September while her younger sister was attending a junior high. She continued: "When they said there was going to be a private school, it would not cost you anything, my parents said 'you're going.' We didn't have the money for tuition at Baptist High." Hallum felt at home at Raney since many of her neighbors and friends from church whom she had grown up with also attended.

She looks back at her attitude toward desegregation as believing it was the right thing to do—the fair thing for black students—and contrasts her views with those of Sammie Dean Parker and David Sontag, two white segregationist students who had caused many disruptions at Central High the previous year and who both attended Raney. Hallum remembers that both were "prominent and active" in school activities at Raney, stressing that as a student she mostly cared about a social life of dancing on *Steve's Show* on television after classes, at the Optimist Club on weekends, or during the summer at Lake Nixon. Her views on race have not changed, and she is proud now that she raised her children to ignore race in making judgments about people.[60]

Regarding the academic rigor at Raney compared to Central High, Hallum remembers that she made the honor roll at Raney though she had never made it before. She says she was never outstanding in academics, but certainly average or above. Students, she recalls, had to go to school for approximately thirteen Saturdays in order to attend the correct number of days for accreditation. Hallum returned to Central High for her senior year in 1959–60 and says she was "delighted" to be able to return to the school she had loved so much as a sophomore.[61]

Phillip Moore, who had attended Central High as a junior, attended Raney High for his senior year, when the public schools closed. His comments reveal how important one's senior year can be. While juniors and sophomores in Little Rock might have lost a year of schooling, many were able to return to complete their education with old friends in familiar surroundings. But seniors had waited their entire academic lives for this year-long experience, this rite of passage to adulthood. From a distance of almost fifty years, Moore still harbors some anger about the Lost Year and is only now letting go of what happened to him and his fellow seniors. For years he was quite bitter: "Politicians and citizens of Little Rock closed our schools with no alternative available to us. . . . We students all felt like we had been used." He says that he and his friends at Central had "never worried about integration; it wasn't a problem for me and for most kids." Alluding to the Crisis Year and the limited number of troublemakers, he adds, "I believe if they had expelled about two dozen kids at Central they would have never needed the troops there."[62]

He doesn't believe that he shared the agenda of Governor Faubus or of the Capital Citizens' Council, but that media coverage portrayed Little Rock that way. The stories of the Little Rock desegregation crisis, he feels, "overtold" one part of the story and left out a significant part. "When you close the schools and throw 3,600 kids out on the street, that's an important story too. Nobody covers our sacrifice," he says.

Moore is grateful that Raney High opened and that he found a school to attend. He is glad there was no tuition because he believes the expense would have been a burden on his father, who was sixty-two years old at that time. He recognizes now that the school had no trained counselors who might have helped seniors prepare better for college or locate funding for tuition.

Moore was thoughtful and reflective in his 2005 interview, saying that over the years he had begun to "let go" of some of the bitterness he had felt earlier. He now believes that everything happens for a purpose and that his experience probably made him "stronger—it made us stronger for something down the road." His "letting go" is particularly clear when his 2005 remarks are compared to those he made six years earlier. Moore, heading a fortieth-reunion committee for Raney High in 1999, refused a suggested interview. He spoke for himself and the other members of the reunion committee: "I presented your proposal [for interview contacts] at our planning meeting last week. No one seemed interested in participating. I believe we all would just as soon put that to rest. The committee decided to keep our reunion low profile . . . so we wouldn't be interrupted during our gathering. You appreciate our misfortune to arrive at a time in history in which someone suffered needlessly and without recognition of that suffering."[63]

Moore's more recent responses indicate that he has since made some peace with events, but his comments characterize the feelings of many of the students affected by the Lost Year—a year that had many victims. There was enough suffering to share among the community's students and teachers, but no one was more victimized than the students who were denied a free public education. Some white students suffered as much as blacks when they found no school to attend. Even with substitute schooling, if it could be found, these young people were left looking for someone to blame for robbing them of their plans, their dreams, their rituals.

By October, thirty-three displaced Little Rock students were daily boarding a Trailways bus to the white high school in Hazen, Arkansas, approximately forty miles east of Little Rock. At the urging of white parents from Hazen and Senator J. J. Screeton, school officials had accepted these students into their local high school. Senator Screeton had encouraged a mass meeting of white parents, saying, "Every citizen of Arkansas should recognize that Little Rock's fight in this school situation is his fight too."[64] Superintendent A. H. McDonnel had received over seventy-five applications but assumed that some of those students would be enrolling in the newly opened private schools in Little Rock. Students commuting to Hazen had to catch the bus in downtown Little Rock at seven-fifteen A.M. and returned home at about five P.M., paying fifty cents each day for transportation, with any remaining costs to be picked up by the Hazen School District.[65]

Jerry Baldwin was a sophomore scheduled for Central High whose mother heard of the opportunity in Hazen and made arrangements for him to attend. Jerry remembers that it was forty-two miles one way from the bus station in Little Rock to the door of the school. He recalls that many of the students who rode with him for the eighty-four-mile daily trip were sophomores he had known in junior high. He doesn't believe that the year he spent at Hazen High adversely affected his plans for a strong education at Central High and later at Hendrix College, a private liberal arts college in Conway. However, he did recognize at the time that the same teacher taught all of Hazen's math, physical science, and chemistry offerings, so that his academics that year relied heavily on this one teacher. Baldwin recalls that the topic of segregation was an emotional one at the time, with 85 percent of the state endorsing separate black and white schools. He doesn't believe he or his parents were frustrated or angry about the closure of the Little Rock schools, instead maintaining that a principle was involved that was held by the majority of white people. While he uses words such as *inconvenience* and *adjustments* to describe his experience, he maintains he felt no resentment: "It was the thing you had to do to get an education."[66]

The courts permitted public high school teachers to return to their buildings on October 20, 1958. When the teachers returned, the LRSD assigned them a new duty—substituting in the elementary and junior high schools in the district. This was a cost-cutting measure, since these teachers were receiving salaries but had no students. Teachers from Horace Mann High covered all the black schools, and teachers from Central and Hall divided the white elementary and junior high schools according to geographic proximity. Hall, with a smaller faculty, was responsible for two of the five junior highs and four of the twelve elementary schools.[67] William C. Winchell, an auto mechanics teacher at Technical High, used the date to resign and take a position with a manufacturing company on the West Coast. Winchell later said he had accepted the position because of the "unsettled situation that prevails." By year's end, the LRSD would lose many other teachers as well.[68]

Several teachers became full-time substitutes. Jo Evelyn Torrence (Elston) was new to Little Rock, hired by LeRoy Christophe as a home economics teacher for Horace Mann for 1958–59. Early in the school year, she found herself assigned to Capitol Hill Elementary School for a first-grade class: "Some of the teachers were farmed out to other places . . . people who were idle were just given other responsibilities. Rather than hiring someone new, they took people who were at Mann who weren't teaching and just transferred them to whatever vacant positions that existed." Elston found other teachers in the elementary school very helpful, aiding her work as a first-time teacher in a subject area for which she was not trained: "It's probably the hardest work I've ever done in my life . . . trying to bring kids up to academic standards."[69]

Jo Ann Henry (Royster), a young math teacher who spent her first year after college teaching at Central High during the Crisis Year, recalls: "The school board decided to use us as substitutes all over the city because they were having to pay us. . . . I really didn't care for that too much." After weeks of substituting, she remembers, "a position became available in a third grade at Williams School. And I was asked if I would like to take the job. So I decided that would be better than driving to a different school in different parts of the city every day or every few days. So I took that position at Williams School as a third-grade teacher. . . . We thought we were guaranteed our salary through that year, but we didn't know what was going to happen after that year. That was a consideration since I was newly married and the sole support of the family while my husband was in medical school. . . . So I needed a pretty stable job."[70] At Central High, teachers chose to substitute at elementary schools on a voluntary basis. For those unwilling to do so, Principal Jess Matthews created a roster by subject matter and assigned work in the junior highs. Matthews usually made the early-morning phone calls assigning the teachers' duties or, when possible, gave them advance notice the previous evening.

Some considered substituting in the elementary grades an unwelcome assignment, one for which they felt unprepared as high school teachers. Patricia Williams and Mary Ann Lofton (Wright) remember that organizing the substituting duties was quite different at Hall High than at Central. Both were young English teachers at Hall, and they now remember that Claude Trickey, the assistant principal, solicited substitutes. When asked whether their substitution duties were voluntary or rotated, Williams recalled: "No, it was just kind of whoever he could catch. And, as I say, some of them wouldn't go to the grades. And one morning, I had just gone and gone and I was so tired of going and teaching little-bitty kids, which I didn't know the first thing about, and so a friend of my son's called him up and I said to him, 'Stay on the phone so Mr. Trickey can't get me.' So, when I got to school, Mr. Trickey was waiting on the porch and said, 'I want you to go to Jefferson School.' So I thundered off to Jefferson, mad as could be, and Tom, my son, was at Jefferson, and he looked out the window and he said to his teacher, 'Well, I see they got Mama.'"[71] Wright had few fond memories of substituting: "Discussing substituting is not pleasant. It was horrible. I was a teacher with one year's experience and was asked to go anywhere from ninth grade through first grade, and it was exceedingly frustrating. I had no idea what I was doing in elementary school, and in many cases, there were no lesson plans left. I can remember getting up in the morning and saying, 'Please Lord, don't let the phone ring.' . . . I can remember thinking that the only thing good about first grade was that they got out at two o'clock instead of three."[72]

At Horace Mann, LeRoy Christophe called upon many of the new faculty to substitute. Willie Brooks (Johnson), a recent graduate of Philander Smith College hired to teach science, said: "We were busy, and Dr. Christophe was very, very definite about what he wanted us to do. If the phone rang in the morning, he said, 'Mrs. Brooks, go to Granite Mountain and teach this; go to this school and serve as a secretary.' I would type off the milk reports, and that kind of happened in so many schools. . . . They expected us to be well-rounded folks and be able to do several jobs."[73]

Some teachers believe that as the year progressed, teachers in other schools took unfair advantage of the available substitutes. Arceal Terry, a typing and commercial-arts teacher from Horace Mann who had worked in Little Rock since 1946, did her share of substituting and working in the offices of other schools: "They were very nice to us when we went, but some people used to say they would stay out because they felt that absences would not be counted against them since we were on the payroll and we were substituting in their places."[74]

Several teachers kept track of the number of substitution assignments. Howard Bell, from Central, worked forty-two days as a substitute, while Patricia Williams, from Hall, worked forty. Elizabeth Huckaby's diary mentions substitution several times during the second semester. On March 17, 1959, Huckaby noted that twenty-three Central teachers were out substituting that day, besides ten others who were gone on a regular assignment for the rest of the year. By March 26, she wrote, a "good deal of bad feeling [was] growing about those not doing their fair share of teaching."[75] By late April, Huckaby was noting the cynicism that some must have been feeling, writing, "Mr. M. reported this is the first day with *no* calls for substitutes," and, the following day, "I went to school at the usual time. Since it wasn't payday some teachers in other schools needed substitutes."[76]

Mary Ann Lofton (Wright) describes the response she sensed from other teachers and from the public: "I do not remember a great deal of warmth. Of course, that varied from school to school, and how helpful the principal was varied. It's probably something I suppressed, that there was a feeling. I can remember people making fun—teachers, non-teachers, non–school people. 'Oh, you're getting paid for doing nothing.' And that was very, very unpleasant to put up with, even though they were being light about it. Because we were suffering a great deal. We were suffering for ourselves, we were suffering for the situation, and for the kids that we knew who might never come back to school, might never come back."[77]

Six weeks after the day that public elementary and junior high schools had opened, private education for whites in Little Rock was wobbling to a start, while private education for displaced blacks was nonexistent. Arkansas Baptist College in Little Rock and Shorter College in North Little Rock (two church-sponsored black colleges) were said to be considering establishing high school branches for the displaced black students by this time.[78]

Seven weeks into the semester, Jane Lewis (Huffman), a senior from Hall High, moved to Memphis to attend the Hutchinson School, a private day school that had a reputation for academic rigor. She boarded with a family whose children also attended Hutchinson and remembers studying very hard. Additionally, Hutchinson had a policy that if a student missed a day of school for any reason, every hour of that school day had to be made up. As a result, Jane stayed after school every day and attended Saturday school to make up the seven weeks she had missed.[79]

Beyond news of displaced students, political events continued to gain headlines. Dale Alford, the Little Rock ophthalmologist in his first term with the Little Rock School Board, had become the group's most outspoken segregationist. Suddenly, he announced on Monday, October 27, that he would be a write-in candidate for the Fifth Congressional District, a seat Brooks Hays had held for the previous sixteen years. Hays was more moderate than many Southern congressmen, although he had joined them in signing the "Southern Manifesto," a statement declaring that the U.S. Supreme Court had overstepped its authority with the *Brown v. Board* ruling by interfering with the South's social system. During the Crisis Year, when Governor Faubus called out the Arkansas National Guard at Central High, Hays had tried to broker a solution between the governor and President Dwight Eisenhower at a meeting in Newport, Rhode Island. The meeting was a failure, and Hays suffered for his part in it. In July, Hays won the Democratic primary for his congressional seat against segregationist Amis Guthridge, a lawyer for the Capital Citizens' Council. When Hays garnered 59 percent of the vote in this Democratic primary in a Democratic state, he felt assured of a November victory in the general election. Alford's subsequent filing as an Independent came as a surprise to many, but the fact that his announcement was made just eight days prior to the November 4 contest was even more stunning. For his campaign manager, Alford chose Claude Carpenter, an aide to Governor Faubus and the state chair of the Democratic Party's fundraising efforts. This connection clearly demonstrated how the governor felt about the Alford run and put a Democratic Party official in the position of working for an Independent against his own party's nominee, thereby discounting his party's candidate. Carpenter temporarily resigned his position with the party during the short campaign.[80]

To rouse the ire of segregationists, Alford's campaign circulated photographs of Hays with black religious leaders. Adding to the drama, one day before the election, Attorney General Bruce Bennett legalized the use of preprinted stickers with Alford's name and a box with an "x" already filled in. Some voters found these stickers on the tables of the election inspectors when they arrived at the polls. Hays lost his seat to Alford by a vote of 24,026 to 18,504. Alford said he would serve out his Little Rock term on the LRSD board, which would end with December elections.[81] Whether to seat Alford in Congress as a Democrat despite his running as an Independent became an issue, but Wilbur Mills (D-AR) helped get Alford accepted as a Democrat.[82] Congress did later investigate the election, but Alford remained in office until congressional redistricting in 1964 helped to unseat him.[83]

Election Day, November 4, 1958, was a triumph for segregationists, with Faubus's election to a third term over Republican George W. Johnson, who polled only 50,000 votes. James D. Johnson, former leader of the Capital Citizens' Council and Faubus's opponent in 1956, won a seat on the Arkansas Supreme Court, where he soon earned the nickname "Justice Jim." Additionally, voters agreed overwhelmingly to retain a 3 percent sales tax, something Faubus had endorsed.[84]

The morning before the election was the first day of classes for thirty-four displaced students commuting to Conway to attend classes at Central Baptist College. Reverend A. R. Reddin, the president of the college, welcomed students to Central Baptist Academy after a team from the state Department of Education visited the campus to check the facilities and the planned curriculum.[85] Myles Adams was one of the students who attended

Central Baptist Academy in Conway. As the year progressed, he estimated, about fifty students commuted from Little Rock on "the brand-new 1958 Chevrolet bus with a V-8 engine and dual exhausts with real loud pipes on it. The boys all got a kick out of that."[86] The college provided the bus and the driver, a college student who arrived every morning from Conway in his own car, drove the students to Conway, returned the bus to the church parking lot in the evening, and then once again drove his car back to Conway. Myles recalled that the driver was named Dan Fagala and that the high school students gathered at a Baptist church parking lot off Broadway near Seventeenth Street on the six days of the week that they had to attend classes. With the late start of the school year and several days missed for winter weather, they attended classes into June of that year.[87]

The American Baptist Association had opened Central Baptist College in Conway in 1952, in facilities that had once housed Central College for Women. Opening an academy for displaced high school students affected by desegregation in Little Rock served two purposes for the fledgling college. As historian Melvin Bender explains in his *History of Central Baptist College,* the new college's finances were a "saga of survival" in the 1950s. The college's president, A. R. Reddin, believed at the time that opening a high school academy would be a financial boon to the struggling new Central Baptist College. He later looked back with the belief that the college had survived the 1950s in part because of the income generated by the academy, at a time when the college student body included only eighty-one students.[88]

The second purpose of opening an academy was to serve students whose schools had been closed because of federally mandated desegregation. The Missionary Baptist Convention had taken a strong stand against racial integration, and several CCC leaders were ministers in Arkansas Missionary Baptist churches. Reverend Wesley Pruden, the pastor of Broadmoor Baptist Church, headed the CCC in 1958. In addition, Reverend M. L. Moser, the pastor of the Central Missionary Baptist Church in Little Rock, headed the segregationist group CROSS (Committee to Retain Our Segregated Schools), which would be active in May 1959. Many within the Convention also embraced the teachings of John W. Duggar of Laurel, Mississippi, who produced a Bible-based defense of segregation. "Through a careful exegesis of the Scripture and an equally thorough study of other classical sources," historian Bender writes, Duggar "encapsulated the viewpoint that so many in the denomination wanted to believe . . . the scripturalness of the segregation of the races."[89] By the time of the desegregation crisis at Central High in 1957, and the closure of Little Rock public high schools in 1958, Duggar's message had become the official credo of the Baptist Missionary Association of Arkansas.[90]

Myles Adams felt that his year at the Central Baptist Academy was "probably the best year of school I had my whole life. It was the most serious year, and I liked the attitude of the teachers. Quite frankly, I think I felt that I was lucky to get to go there." The classes were small and taught by college professors. Though Adams remembered "about fifty" students who commuted from Little Rock, the school's 1959 yearbook, entitled *The Towers*, pictures only twenty-nine in a group photo and ten seniors, fifteen juniors, and ten sophomores in official class photos. The yearbook also featured photos of churches that had sent students to the academy, with Temple Baptist in Little Rock sending eight students, including Adams.

Several of Adams's comments reveal both the exuberance of teenage boys and the racial attitudes of some of Little Rock's youth at this time. T he daily bus trips best capture the memorable adventure of commuting seventy-plus miles per day. Adams remembers that there were always people walking near the church where students gathered every morning, and one day, "somebody brought some potatoes and stuck some up the exhaust pipes [of the bus] and jammed them up there with a broomstick or something," he recalled. "When Dan started that thing up, it blew those things out and hit somebody in the back of the head down the street. . . . Guys were always doing stuff like that. We had three or four on there that were always looking for something to get into." Adams, reflective in his remarks on race, has experienced a change in his views over time: "I was pretty much a product of my generation at that time and said some, not all, of the ugly things that other people did. But I grew up down in East End in what is now a part of town people need to stay out of, a pretty rough part of town. . . . Most of the kids I played with, my age, were black kids. I had more trouble out of the white kids that were older and bigger than me, picking on me and beating on me all the time because I played with black kids. I was not taught by my family to hate them. I think the attitude that I have now is the fact that the same God that created them black made me white, is kind of what I grew up with as long as they didn't bother me they were okay. If they bothered me they were niggers. I grew up to be ashamed of that."[91]

Adams returned to Hall High for his senior year in 1959–60, where he was particularly aware of the social class system. "It was known that most of the people that lived up in the Heights area at that time had more, not to say that they were rich, but they had more than us folks did," he explained. Asked if he had ever attended a reunion of his Hall High class, he answered: "Never been to one. I just felt like I wasn't a part of most of that back then and most of the people liked to party and dance. It seemed to me that was what it was mostly about, and I just never cared about going. I didn't do it back then, and I don't care to do it now."[92]

By early November, thirty-eight different public school districts in the state had applied for funds for the students who had transferred to their schools from Little Rock high schools. Attorney General Bruce Bennett had recently ruled that payment of approximately $172 for each of the 166 transfer students was legal, based on Act 5.[93] Bennett also said transfer of money to accredited private schools would be legal, even though no private school had yet applied for funds. The largest single application came from Hazen, where 42 pupils had been accepted from Little Rock. The next two districts, Stuttgart and tiny Glendale in Lincoln County, had accepted 10 students each. Other public schools across the state by this point had accepted from 1 to 7 students, each meeting the accreditation requirement.[94]

The story of Glendale's enrollment comes from Robert White, a senior at Central High. He thinks he waited too long to find a school after attempting to enroll at North Little Rock High and Raney High. His best friend, Tommy Porter, and he simply got in the car and headed south, looking for any school that might take them. They tried Pine Bluff, Dollarway, Grady, Gould, and many other small towns in the area. Noting the issue of economics, he recalled that "the problem was that we were not from wealthy families and didn't have the money to pay room and board. We needed to find someone that would allow two boys from Little Rock that they had never laid eyes on to move in with them for an entire school year." Never thinking about how impossible this sounded, they knocked on doors in a small community about fifteen miles west of Star City (about ninety-five miles south of Little Rock) called Glendale. The first house they came to turned out to be that of the superintendent of the only school in the community, one with a total enrollment of approximately 150 students in first through twelfth grades. "They made the decision on the spot to allow us to share a bedroom for ten dollars a week," said White. The boys went back to Little Rock, told their parents, and shared the news with other displaced friends, who also chose to enroll at Glendale. This Little Rock group ultimately totaled ten, the four seniors doubling the size of the Glendale senior class.[95]

White recalls that his grades at Central had been less than perfect, but his experience at Glendale allowed him to improve his grades, to play on the basketball team, to be cast as the lead in the senior play, and to be voted king of the senior prom. He believes that he and the others learned life lessons at an early age and that the experience turned out to be a "blessing" for him.[96]

The week following the November general election, the Eighth Circuit Court of Appeals finally announced its official ruling regarding school leasing. After the restraining orders issued on September 29, and after several brief hearings on October 6 and 15, the court announced its final decision. Much less dramatic on its face than many had expected, the court's announcement forbade the leasing of public school facilities to private entities but returned the case to federal district court judge Miller and to the LRSD board, with instructions that it should oversee integration. The court did not specify when integration should take place or how it should be enforced. But it enjoined the board from "engaging in any other acts, whether independently or in participation with anyone else, which are capable of serving to impede, thwart, or frustrate the execution of the integration plan." Going beyond the notion of impeding acts, the court instructed the board to take "affirmative steps" as set out by the district judge.[97] The appellate court thus returned the responsibility for integration to the school board and to the very judge who had refused to rule on this same appeal weeks before.

The court's statements, and the congressional win of their colleague Dale Alford, frustrated five members of the LRSD board, and on November 12, two days after the court ruling and eight days after Alford's election, they resigned in a body, stating that they recognized the "utter hopelessness, helplessness, and frustration of our present position."[98] At this same meeting, and over the objections of Dale Alford, the five resigning board members bought out the contract of Superintendent Blossom, then in the fifth month of his second year of a three-year contract. The board president, Wayne Upton, said that they were allowing Little Rock to start with a "clean slate" by resigning and buying out Blossom's contract. A source close to the board said that in view of the previous Tuesday's election, the board members felt they were in the minority and that the majority should have the chance to name the kind of board they wanted.[99]

Some of the school board members were doubly involved in the controversy of closed schools. Not only were they serving as volunteers in a thankless, unpaid position in the community, but their own children were affected by the school closures. Polly and Grant Cooper, the children of the LRSD board's vice president, William Cooper, and Jimmy Engstrom, the son of board member Harold Engstrom, were among the almost four thousand students locked out of Little Rock high schools. By late September, these three adolescents, joined by Linda Shamblin, the daughter of Kenneth Shamblin, the pastor of Pulaski Heights Methodist Church, enrolled in Hot Springs High School. These four youths joined five other displaced Little Rock high school students, according to Principal Frank Sanders. Linda Shamblin's brother, Kenneth Shamblin Jr., recalls that several of the mothers took turns staying with the students in the Coopers' lake house near Hot Springs so that his sister and the other "school board" teenagers could live in that school district and come home only on weekends.[100]

Two days after his resignation, Wayne Upton made a statement in Knoxville, Tennessee, where he was attending a college reunion, boldly declaring that he and his colleagues had resigned because they were "tired of being Governor Orval Faubus' whipping boys." He said that the governor had identified him and four of his colleagues as an "integration school board" and that Faubus had used them "to win or help win three elections. We were tired of it." He explained that all the board members were "segregationists in feeling," but that they had been confronted with the problem of enforcing the law. "Our integration plan would have worked if it hadn't been for political interference," he said, making it clear that he meant interference by Faubus. He ended by giving advice to other southern school boards: "Get a plan, a concrete, definite, workable plan, to take into federal court when you are finally brought there."[101]

The frustrations of this long and tedious battle for LRSD board members were many. Now they were declining to play a further role in what had become a political game with stakes higher than anyone could have imagined. In the two days since his resignation, Upton had processed these frustrations and felt unsatisfied and even anxious over the still-unresolved problems. The one piece of wisdom he had gleaned from his long experience surfaced in his advice—that other school boards get a workable plan and stick by it. His own school board had not done so. It had started with a limited, token plan for integration, and in the face of stubborn resistance from the governor and the populace, it had retreated, asking for a delay in its own plan. Now its members were quitting the battle.

CHAPTER FOUR

Whom Shall We Blame?

Some people have said you can't do away
with public schools, but you can.
—Governor Orval Faubus, December 16, 1958

LITTLE ROCK, NOVEMBER 12, 1958—JANUARY 31, 1959

EARLY NOVEMBER 1958. The Arkansas Legislative Council attacks public school teachers.

NOVEMBER 12. The five resigning LRSD board members attempt to buy out Superintendent Blossom's contract for $19,741.41.

NOVEMBER 13. A lawsuit is filed by John King to prevent payment to Blossom.

DECEMBER 6. Thirteen candidates vie for six positions on the LRSD board. A three/three split emerges from each slate endorsed either by Faubus or by those touted as the "businessmen."

DECEMBER 18. Terrell Powell replaces Blossom as superintendent of the LRSD.

JANUARY 6, 1959. U.S. district court judge John Miller holds hearings in accordance with the Court of Appeals ruling and denies the LRSD board permission to open all high schools on a segregated basis while working on a new integration plan.

JANUARY 11. The Arkansas General Assembly opens in regular session.

JANUARY 17. Two preliminary hearings in federal court begin over
Arkansas Acts 4 and 5.

JANUARY 19. The Virginia State Supreme Court strikes down the Virginia
school-segregation laws, with schools to open integrated at semester.

JANUARY 26. The second semester begins with closed public high
schools.

The Arkansas Legislative Council (ALC) was established in the 1940s to provide guidance to the Arkansas General Assembly between sessions. Made up
of twenty-one senators and representatives, it was led by some of the most
powerful and senior members of the legislature. Its connection to the teachers of the Lost Year began in the spring of 1958, when it directed members
of the Arkansas State Police to conduct individual interviews with every
teacher at Central High. Elizabeth Huckaby wrote of the "voluntary" interviews in her memoir, explaining that teachers could have been subpoenaed
had they not willingly testified and that she felt "intimidation" at what the
police called simple "fact-finding."[1] Few of the interview transcripts remain,
but those conducted with the principal, Jess Matthews, and the vice
Principals, J. O. Powell and Elizabeth Huckaby, are available because the
three hired a transcriber for their own protection. Sergeant L. E. Gwyn and
Chelsey C. Clayton conducted the interview with Huckaby and explained
that the information was needed to help others around the state prepare for
integration. They insisted that the results would go only to the Legislative
Council, which wanted to understand the facts and opinions of those
closely involved in the process of integrating Central High. Clayton and
Gwinn said that the ALC also planned to hold hearings to aid other school
districts in preparing for racial integration.[2] Interview questions centered
on events within the school, the presence of troops in the building, and
teacher opinion regarding school desegregation.[3]

Four other Central High teacher interviews, held in the Faubus Collection at the University of Arkansas, tell a different story than those of the
school administrators. These teachers went on the record complaining of
special treatment for the black students and disruption of the educational
process with the presence of troops, expressing the consensus that "most"
teachers and students wanted the black students "out."[4]

The ALC took a more public and vocal stance regarding many of the
state's teachers in November 1958. The Arkansas Education Association
(AEA) held its annual meeting in Little Rock on November 6–7. This large,

statewide white teachers' organization made a policy statement during its conference supporting public schools and adopted a plan for statewide monitoring of the upcoming 1959 General Assembly, for the purpose of preserving public education. Not using the word *integration* or mentioning the Little Rock situation itself, the organization stated, "We are deeply concerned over the continuing school crisis—for fear that long-sought and hard-won gains for public education may be lost." It continued, "We shall find answers to the complex problems emerging from the present crisis— answers which do not undermine the one institution upon which all we have and all we hope for rests, the public school system."[5] The AEA's pledge to fight for public schools was made in reaction to reports that some legislators believed abolishing the schools would be preferable to integration.[6]

The ALC was outraged by the AEA's policy statement. The legislators declared themselves supporters of the schools but ordered the Legislative Committee on Subversion in Education to investigate the AEA report. Additionally, the ALC passed a resolution threatening to withhold the third penny of the state's recently passed sales tax, which was expected to produce about fourteen million dollars a year for public schools. When the ALC members heard the AEA's comments that "no issue" should change the importance of public education, Representative Marion Crank of Little River County interjected, "They're blind as hell then."[7] The ALC ordered a poll of all AEA members to check their agreement with the policy statements made by the group's leaders. Representative Paul Van Dalsem of Perry County, the ALC's vice chair, appointed a committee to arrange the poll, headed by Senator Roy A. Riales of Mena. This group of legislators complained that no other group had more friends in the General Assembly than the school lobby and that the legislators had risked "political suicide" by raising the sales tax from 2 to 3 percent for the benefit of education. Representative John P. Bethel of Prairie County said: "We stuck our necks out to pass the sales tax. Now it's time we laid it on the line. It's time for the teachers to get on or get off and I mean from the Commissioner of Education on down."[8] Clearly, the state's white teacher organization and the ALC did not feel the same way regarding the importance of public schools. On November 8, an *Arkansas Gazette* editorial commented that it was only logical that an organization of public school teachers, whose livelihood depended upon the operation of the public schools, should not ignore the fact that Little Rock's public high schools had been closed by the state: "The very violence of the legislators' reaction to the AEA's mild resolution is an indication of how desperate the impasse really is—and how far we are from a practical answer to the grave problem."[9]

Though the legislators' threats were loud and menacing, within a few weeks the idea of a teachers' poll had fizzled. In *Arkansas Gazette* articles published later in November, several members of the ALC reported that teacher sentiment in their own districts was so solidly against the AEA stand that it was not necessary to spend money on the poll.[10] However, five members of the ALC were quoted as saying that "they would close the schools rather than integrate them."[11] Sentiment against the public school teachers, especially those in Little Rock's public high schools, was also mounting because they were drawing a paycheck even though they were often assigned to empty classrooms.

As students continued to relocate and seek education in venues both within the state and beyond, the recent mass resignation from the Little Rock School Board played out in the community. On November 12, 1958, the same evening that five of the six board members resigned from their positions in protest, they also, as noted earlier, authorized buying out the remainder of Virgil Blossom's three-year contract. Blossom's services were to end officially on November 30, 1958. But immediately, John King filed a suit to prevent this payment, and chancery judge Murray Reed issued a restraining order to the treasurer of the school district, forbidding him from paying the money to Blossom. The treasurer believed that he was prohibited from giving Blossom even his November paycheck, but Blossom telephoned King's lawyer, James Sloan, who agreed to call the judge and ask that Blossom be paid for that month, but not for the rest of his contract.[12] Virgil Blossom took his check, planning to seek work in another location.

The regularly scheduled election of school board members was to be held on December 6, and the board members' resignations had come just in time for new candidates to file for their positions in the upcoming election. The sixth member of the board, Dale Alford, recently elected to Congress, planned to serve out his term until the December date. With less than a month until new members could be elected, Pulaski County judge Arch Campbell chose not to appoint any interim members. His authority to fill the vacancies stemmed from a 1935 law, but some questioned it, since 1941 legislation had created a county board of education vested with appointment powers.[13] Who held authority did not become an issue, and no one filled the short vacancies.

The filing deadline was at midnight, November 15, giving any interested party a very small window of time to announce for office. Immediately after the resignations and the firing of Blossom, only one candidate had signed on for the race—Jimmy Karam, a downtown clothier and segregationist friend of Governor Faubus. Blossom's description of what transpired in locating new candidates for the school board demonstrates the paralysis in the business community. Approximately thirty-five "of the city's business and civic leaders," Blossom said, met first to urge the resigning board members to reconsider their decisions. Failing this, the group sought six representatives from the six downtown banking institutions, one to seek each of the available positions on the empty board. This would fill each of the slots with a different bank representative, so that segregationists could not boycott all of the city's financial institutions and so that each business shared in the responsibility of leadership. Blossom describes the bankers' refusals, explaining their dilemma. "Our banks would not be protected at all," they claimed, because each depended heavily on the subsidiary deposits of banks in eastern Arkansas, where segregationist sentiment was the strongest.[14]

Sara Murphy's account repeats this story, adding information about the involvement of the Women's Emergency Committee. Ted Lamb, an advertising agent, was willing to run for election and to endorse opening the closed schools. Billy Rector, described by Murphy as a "blustery businessman full of self-importance and with large real estate and insurance holdings," also agreed to run.[15] With only two days left between the resignations and the filing deadline, Grainger Williams of the Chamber of Commerce brought a list of possible candidates to WEC founder Adolphine Terry, asking her to call for willing male candidates from the list. Terry agreed, as long as she could add the name of one woman, and she was subsequently able to coax Margaret Stephens, a WEC member and the former Central High PTA president, to run. By Saturday, Terry had enough names for five slots, and she sent WEC members scurrying about for the required signatures on petitions, needed by six P.M. that evening for the candidates' filings. Making up the slate of candidates backed by the "business-civic group" were Ted Lamb, Billy Rector, Everett Tucker, Russell Matson, and Margaret Stephens (Mrs. Charles W.). A photograph of Lamb, Stephens, and Rector appeared as they filed with W. H. Laubach, the secretary of the Pulaski County Election Commission.[16] Russell Matson was out of town in Fayetteville for a Razorback football game, and thus, although he had agreed to run, he was not there to sign the petition for his race. Terry forged his name on the petition, "but when Matson returned he went down to the courthouse to correct the forgery."[17] Vivion Brewer, the president of the WEC, saw Rector as the self-appointed spokesperson for the businessmen's slate, finding him "decisively abrupt, almost belligerent."[18] His interactions with Brewer demonstrate the awkward position the men on this slate held in the community. They were running against vocal segregationists, but they felt they could not allow the needed support of the WEC to be made public. As Brewer said, "He wanted total efforts of our organization on behalf of 'his' slate but he made it clear that no one should know of our alliance."[19] The WEC was controversial for its double labels—"integrationists" and "women," neither of which was an acceptable descriptor in Arkansas leadership in the 1950s. Authors Elizabeth Jacoway, Sara Murphy, and Lorraine Gates have explained the dilemma facing this group, as well as the issue of its acceptance into the mainstream.[20]

Rector insisted that Ed McKinley's name be added to the businessmen's slate, a demand that the WEC met but later regretted. McKinley, running for the slot then held by Dale Alford, was the only candidate who had no opposition, while all the other candidates had at least one opponent. McKinley was soon endorsed by segregationists, and by December 3, the large ads running in the *Arkansas Gazette* listed only Lamb, Rector, Tucker, Matson, and Stephens as a slate.[21] By this time, the WEC was exhibiting its improved organizational skills, with Irene Samuel naming captains in each city ward and precinct workers distributing flyers by mail or personal delivery. The WEC used poll-tax records for telephoning and for arranging carpools to the polls. Earlier in September, the WEC had quickly prepared for the referendum called by Faubus; after this defeat in opening the schools, it had steadily improved its campaign tactics during the intervening elections.[22]

A total of thirteen candidates managed to file for the six school board positions, with the surprising withdrawal of Jimmy Karam. By November 30, the Capital Citizens' Council endorsed Ed McKinley Jr., Mrs. Pauline Woodson, Ben D. Rowland Sr., Margaret Morrison. C. C. Railey, and traffic judge R. W. Laster. The current president of the CCC, Reverend Wesley Pruden, said that his executive board had unanimously endorsed these six candidates and that none was a member of the CCC. By endorsing these six candidates, the CCC was snubbing George P. Branscum, a dentist and a former member of the Citizens' Council board who had also filed for election. Branscum had resigned from the CCC in protest the previous June, when the group expelled three others from membership. These three and Branscum, along with fifteen others who had resigned from the CCC, organized the State's Rights Council. This second segregationist group promoted its own slate of candidates, with some overlap with the segregationists endorsed by the CCC, ultimately splitting the segregationist votes in the community.[23]

The CCC mailed letters urging its members' support for its group of six and stressed that the school board election was "the most important school election in our history." Noting confidence in its chosen candidates, the letter stated that all thirteen "claimed to be segregationists" and continued: "Some of them are honestly prepared to carry out the will of the great majority of Little Rock voters in maintaining segregation. Others we think are trying to get into office by fooling the people."[24]

The atmosphere in the community convinced the "business slate," or at least its self-appointed leader, Rector, that in order to win they had to soft-pedal their association with the Chamber of Commerce and the WEC. One ad stated that these candidates were "qualified by their backgrounds of business experience, integrity, and community service," but went on to say that they pledged to do whatever they could "to maintain our public schools on a segregated basis."[25]

During the short campaign, the divided white community exchanged charges and countercharges. Advertising by the CCC declared that Daisy Bates, the state president of the NAACP, had attended PTA meetings at Central High School when one of the business slate's candidates, Margaret Stephens, had been PTA president.[26] On the eve of the election, Faubus took a stand, charging that the five-member business slate was "the integration slate."[27] Rector countered these charges, producing a canceled check showing that he had donated $100 to the CCC.[28] Rector and Faubus had disagreed previously, starting in February, when Rector blamed the loss of a $10,000,000 shopping center on the integration crisis and the governor's actions. Faubus responded by calling Rector an integrationist and saying that he didn't think Rector "tells the truth."[29]

Everett Tucker Jr. ran his own advertisement as the executive director of the Industrial Development Company, stating clearly, "I honestly and sincerely feel that segregated schooling is the ONLY way in which the maximum educational advantage can be provided for children of both races."[30] That the more moderate candidates felt compelled to claim segregationist sympathies says a great deal about the sentiment in the community. Little Rock's white community was divided ideologically. Historian David Chappell wrote in 1995 that whites "differed so much in the degree of importance they assigned to segregation that they ended up fighting each other as much as they fought the NAACP." Chappell sees the white community as including extreme segregationists, moderate segregationists, and the "small but crucial number of whites" who were willing to openly identify themselves with desegregation.[31] At this point in the year of closed schools, Everett Tucker Jr. was straddling the line, hoping to gain the most votes.

As voters decided on their candidates, several events marked the lives of displaced students, teachers, and their families. On November 17, Nelson High School, near Scott, Arkansas, opened for the fall. This rural black school in Pulaski County annually opened late, after the cotton harvest. Months after most public high schools were in session, here was another chance for displaced black students from Horace Mann High to find schooling. The other nearby black county high schools, such as Wrightsville and Pulaski County Training School, had reached capacity and cut off any more transfers in September. Among the normal enrollment of approximately four hundred black students at Nelson, Little Rock transfer records show that forty-four had officially transferred, despite the fact that Nelson was not an accredited school.[32] These transfers to Nelson reflect black families' desperation to find education for their high school children, even if this meant they had to attend an unaccredited school.

In November 1958, Daisy Bates, the president of the state convention of the NAACP, accounted for all of the nine black students who had integrated Central High in 1957. Carlotta Walls, Melba Patillo, Thelma Mothershed, Elizabeth Eckford, and Jefferson Thomas had registered for correspondence courses and were working with several volunteer tutors at the Dunbar Community Center. In order to continue his schooling, Terrance Roberts had moved to Los Angeles to live with relatives, while Gloria Ray had moved to Kansas City to live with her brother. Minnijean Bown, who had been expelled from Central High in spring 1958, continued her high school studies at New Lincoln High School in New York, where she had been invited after her expulsion. Ernest Green, who had graduated from Central in May 1958, attended Michigan State University.[33]

Some in the national black community advocated a financial campaign organized by the NAACP to pay for extension courses for all displaced black students. The *New York World Telegram and Sun* endorsed such a campaign in November 1958. One contributor sent in a check for ninety-six dollars but presaged the sentiments of many in the NAACP in his accompanying letter, predicting the possible negative consequences of this kind of financial support: "It is unfortunate that such a campaign is necessary for *any* student in Arkansas, for if outside help is given, the day may only be prolonged when we shall see the integration of schools there."[34] By December, Henry Moon, the NAACP's director of public relations, had released a response to all Scripps-Howard newspapers, deploring the tragic consequences of Governor Faubus's decision to close Little Rock's public high schools. Quoting Executive Secretary Roy Wilkins, the document went on to "set forth the NAACP position" on displaced black students:

Some have wondered whether colored citizens should not set up a school of their own. This we cannot do. We cannot ourselves finance Jim Crow schools for our children. We cannot choose deliberately to set up the kind of system which has been ruled illegal and unconstitutional. The segregationists have set up their temporary schools to defy the law. If we join them and set up our schools, we will be defying the law, also. Besides, we would be doing just what they want us to do. In addition, we would be selling out the youngsters who endured persecution at Central high last year. We would be betraying all other Negro children throughout the nation who hope to go forward to full opportunity, not backward to segregation and second-class citizenship.[35]

There were enormous and very human consequences to the lack of private black education in Little Rock. Not only were black students shut out of public high schools, but they were asked to sacrifice even more for their civil liberties, since no nearby private school for black students was encouraged. One half of all black students did not go to school that year. Bowman Burns, John Dokes, and Myrthene Rowe (Wroten) are instructive examples of this population.

Bowman Burns was to be a junior at Horace Mann during the Lost Year, but he stayed at home in Little Rock and worked. "My mom and dad were pretty firm about leaving home after high school and being out on your own. Back then a high school education really meant something," he recalled. Burns was the only son among five sisters and the second-oldest in birth order. "When you are that age you really don't look at or question what could happen. As a kid that age you don't really think, you really don't. You don't know what's going on," he said. He waited for a while to see if schools would open and then went out to find a job. "I didn't have to be reminded either, my mother was very long-winded about that," he recalled with a laugh. Burns worked for a while at Frankie's Cafeteria, where his mother worked, and later at another cafeteria. Looking back, he wishes he had gone to school somewhere so that he could have graduated with his own class. Instead, he returned to Horace Mann in 1959–60 as a junior and graduated with the younger students. He never went to college and was drafted in 1963. He described his high school experience as "just downhill, it wasn't fun at all. I felt depressed, empty."[36]

John Dokes is another Horace Mann student who missed his junior year. Dokes was the oldest of three sons, but his brothers, enrolled in junior high and elementary school, were able to attend classes that year. Complicating the Dokes brothers' young lives was the loss of their mother during 1959. An aunt moved into the home to support the family, but Dokes remembers the difficulty of being isolated from friends that year. The work he could find was cutting yards and doing janitorial work with a cousin who shared his own paycheck with John, so that he could become one of the "bread-winners" in the new family arrangement. John's future wife was a class-mate. She was able to enroll in nearby Wrightsville High, but she had to pay to ride with a friend to the crowded county high school. Dokes remembers that it took "money to go to outlying areas to school," which he simply did not have. Today he believes the Lost Year changed his life and blocked him from some of his dreams. He looks back on the experience with some bit-terness, saying: "Some kids didn't miss a beat, the white kids had nearby private schools to attend. But blacks suffered the most." He returned to Horace Mann when it opened, but he had lost the skills he had accrued in running track, something that at the time he had thought might bring him a college scholarship. Because he was a year behind in his studies, he watched his classmates move on, while he adjusted to being with the younger class. "I was happy to be back in school, but I was disappointed not to be with my friends," he recalls. Dokes believes that he has achieved suc-cess in his life. He and his wife left Arkansas, and he attended two years of college, sold insurance for seventeen years, and retired as a professional in Alameda County Social Services in California. He always believed that edu-cation was the ticket out of poverty and that he was able to instill this idea in his younger brothers—focusing them on their dreams. One brother is retired from the military, and one is in corporate America, in Silicon Valley. Dokes feels that the Lost Year inspired him to "reach for the stars—to over-come that year," but adds, "I didn't get to complete the dream I had of being a lawyer, but I have achieved success in my life. Many of my class-mates have gone on to great achievements"—in spite of this year, he believes. He ended by saying, "It doesn't make what happened to us, it doesn't make it right."[37]

Myrthene Rowe (Wroten), a year ahead of Dokes and Burns, expected to complete her senior year in 1958–59. Like them, she did not attend school that year. She remembers listening to the radio with her mother and wait-ing for news of a school opening. Eventually, she and her mother went to St. Bartholomew School, hoping that the nuns would allow Myrthene to enroll. By that time, the Catholic high school was filled and could not take additional students. Myrthene stayed home but eventually enrolled in some correspondence courses from the University of Arkansas. She worked on her lessons at home and remembers making very good grades. She returned to Horace Mann in 1959–60, joining younger classmates, as did John Dokes and Bowman Burns.[38]

Myrthene attended a Baptist church, where her friend Merriam Lupper (Lindsay) and Little Rock Nine student Jefferson Thomas were also members. Merriam was luckier than Myrthene because she was able to enroll at St. Bartholomew High School, at Fifteenth and Marshall. She lived fewer than three blocks away, which pleased her mother, who did not want Merriam to go miles away to attend school, like some of her friends who attended Carver High in Lonoke and the Pulaski County Training school. Merriam remembers that most of the families in her neighborhood were Baptist but that her neighbors across the street were Catholic, so her mother asked them if they thought she might be able to enroll at St. Bartholomew. "The neighbors were recognized and respected by the teachers and the Father at the school," she recalls. Merriam said that when she was accepted, there were many rules she had to follow. She had to attend Mass every Tuesday at eight A.M. and participate in the service. She was told to pray after every recess, and at the end of the day she had to offer the prayer, "Hail Mary full of grace . . ." She recalls that it didn't take her long to learn the prayers: "I was young and I was eager to attend the school and graduate on time, although I wanted to graduate at Horace Mann High with all my friends. At that time, I did not know how long the schools would be closed." She describes the school as small, with an enrollment of between 250 and 300 students. There was no cafeteria for hot meals and no auditorium on campus, so meetings were held on the school playground. She was grateful for the excellent teachers, all of whom were nuns. Since most of the students had attended the Catholic school since the early grades, she felt that "they seemed to resent our transferring there because of the closing of our school." According to Little Rock School District transfer records, 19 of Horace Mann's 750 students were admitted to St. Bartholomew High during the Lost Year, a statistic that demonstrates the few opportunities for displaced black students. The absence of private education and the limited slots in the only black parochial school clearly affected transfer opportunities.[39]

On November 26, Thanksgiving morning, Central High and Hall High played their final game of the football season at ten-thirty A.M. on a cold and gray day.[40] This was the first year of what was to become a long football rivalry, as Central beat Hall 7 to 0. Gene Hall, the head coach at Central, recalls that the game ended a peculiar season for the Tigers. Traditionally, a group photo of the team was taken, but that year, because many of his players had scattered for alternative schooling, the school photographer, Ben Lincoln, used the individual photos of players made in August to create a composite of the year's team. Hall still has that photo in his collection of memorabilia of Central teams.[41]

At the suggestion of students, the LRPSC had by December named its school "Raney High," in honor of Thomas J. Raney, the president of the board. The board declared the school mascot and sports teams the Rebels, despite the students' first suggestion of the Trojans. Since Little Rock Junior College already had the Trojans as its mascot, the Raney board and students ultimately chose a symbol associated with the Confederacy—and, as they pointed out, with a Mississippi team that often gave their beloved University of Arkansas Razorbacks a tough time. Raney High was issuing report cards for the first six weeks at about the same time as the name change was announced; Baptist High planned to issue its report cards for the first term the following week.[42]

The day before the Saturday vote for new LRSD board members, teachers at Central were upset about the school election. The gossip circulating was that Jimmy Karam, the friend of Governor Faubus who had withdrawn his name from the school board race, might be appointed as the next superintendent. After voting on Saturday morning, the Huckabys attended an event that evening honoring former LRSD superintendent Virgil Blossom and his wife. Hosted by Little Rock's principals at Forest Heights Junior High, the dinner served as a farewell to the Blossoms, who soon afterward moved to San Antonio, Texas.[43] Huckaby's Sunday-morning diary entry reports the results of the school board election: "Newspapers report School Board evenly split 3 and 3. Not much can be accomplished that way, but at least there are some sensible ones on the board."[44] Election results reported Robert Laster, Ed McKinley Jr., and Ben D. Rowland Sr. winners. All three were attorneys, and all had supported the governor. The three other members elected were Ted Lamb, Everett Tucker Jr., and Russell H. Matson Jr., all labeled by Faubus as integrationists. Though the board was evenly split, some believed that the election of the three moderates was the first significant rebuff of segregationists at the polls.[45] Lamb, a true integrationist who won a three-year term, defeating Woodson and Branscum, attacked the governor: "Our victory is the beginning of the end for Orval Faubus, a 20th century Machiavelli."[46] Calling the election "Little Rock's Strangest School Board Election," the *Arkansas Gazette* reported that three of the losers planned protests. Mrs. Charles W. Stephens, who had lost to Laster by eighty-one votes, and C. C. Railey considered challenging the vote, and Billy

Rector lashed out at Governor Faubus for attacking him during the campaign. Rector claimed that Faubus's attack had "very definitely" affected his chances, because Faubus had labeled Rector and others integrationists.[47] Unlike in the September referendum, voter turnout for the school board election was light. With approximately 42,485 voters in the district, only 14,300 votes were cast. This was a higher number than cast in a typical school board election, which usually attracted around 7,000 voters, but much lower than the over 26,000 votes cast in the referendum on school closure. Adding controversy was the fact that the last five boxes of votes to come in went heavily to the Citizens' Council slate. Laster won his race with the forty-fifth and final box, while Rowland got his victory with the last two boxes counted.[48]

As the requested recount began, Robert Laster's humorous comments summed up the winners' feelings: "If the check shows that Mrs. Stephens won I'll send her the box of aspirin I bought when I thought I had been elected."[49] The recount took two days with seven four-man teams working, but it failed to change the outcome of the election.[50] The winners' daunting challenge was summed up by an editorial in the *Gazette:* "They will take over a school system with four high schools closed by order of the governor, without a superintendent and with mounting financial problems. Beyond this the Board will shortly be before the federal court which originally ordered integration in the high schools, and inevitably will renew and strengthen that order in the course of coming hearings."[51] The reference to more court action was prompted by a December 9 announcement that federal judge John Miller had set another school hearing for January 6, 1959, as mandated by the order of the Federal Appeals Court for immediate integration. Judge Miller was being instructed by higher courts: he could not again shirk his duty or their rulings.[52]

The six new voices and personalities elected to run the Little Rock school system found the situation among displaced high school students alarming. According to the board's own December records, 604 of the 3,665 students were doing no academic work, while 1,299 were attending private schools full-time; 527 were engaged in part-time work through correspondence courses; 1,168 were enrolled in other public schools in Arkansas; and approximately 100 were enrolled in public schools outside the state.[53] Handed the challenges of displaced students and closed schools, the new board members were probably asking themselves why they had ever chosen to run. Russell Matson, reflecting on what might become a deadlocked board, said: "Right now we're between two dilemmas—the federal court on one side and the state laws on the other. Just which course we'll take, I don't know."[54]

The election raised emotions in the community but solved little. The acrimony between segregationists and active moderates was rising. A week after the election, the *Gazette* announced it had learned that Ed McKinley Jr., a winner for the segregationists, was actually a member of the Little Rock Private School Corporation board, though he had denied this fact when running for public office. McKinley, an attorney, the former state banking commissioner, and a former city attorney, had joined the LRPSC board just weeks before his election to the public school system.[55] He would be forced to resign from the private school board, but there was little question where his loyalties lay.

As a cold front entered the state, and temperatures dropped to as low as five degrees below zero in the northern areas, many rural schools closed temporarily because of weather.[56] In a speech to the annual conference of the Agricultural Extension Service, Governor Faubus raised the issue of school closures of another kind: "Some people have said you can't do away with public schools, but you can. . . . .The public school system is not so important that it has to be maintained at the expense of freedom." Faubus's remarks, added at the end of his speech on agricultural programs, contrasted with the remarks he had made a few weeks earlier, when he declared there was a place for public schools.[57] The events of the Lost Year were moving Faubus further into the segregationist camp and further away from free public schools for all.

At the same time, Attorney General Bruce Bennett was targeting many blacks by attacking the NAACP through laws passed in the summer of 1958. In 1957, Bennett had convinced Faubus to sign off on Arkansas's Sovereignty Commission. Such state commissions, modeled on national groups that perpetuated the Red Scare, led investigations and propaganda campaigns in efforts to expose Communists in the civil rights movement. An interlocking network of local, state, and federal institutions tied southern states to groups such as the House Committee on Un-American Activities and the Permanent Subcommittee on Investigations and to the actions of J. Edgar Hoover, the director of the Federal Bureau of Investigation.[58] Often in the South, these commissions were closely tied to "massive resistance" to racial integration. Unlike in other southern states such as Mississippi, Arkansas's Sovereignty Commission did little. However, Attorney General Bruce Bennett was able to use the Education Committee of the Arkansas Legislative Council to bring publicity to what he called a Communist conspiracy in the civil rights movement. The politically active ALC had focused on teachers as early as November, when they attacked the AEA, but now it was going well beyond the ranks of teachers. The opening hearings of the Special Education Committee of the ALC began on December 16, and for three days Bennett promoted the rising southern belief that the forces of Communism and integration "had signed a devil's pact to destroy the region's way of life."[59] The first day was devoted to criticizing L. C. Bates, the owner of the *Arkansas State Press,* and his wife, Daisy Bates, the president of the state conference of the NAACP and a mentor to the Little Rock Nine. Bennett used a photo of two known Communists, featured eating breakfast with the Bateses and former vice president Henry Wallace. Bennett's intent was to prove that Communists were behind racial unrest in Arkansas. Bennett was placing himself to the right of Faubus, with hopes for future office, probably as governor. By proposing several bills in the extraordinary session of the previous summer that targeted the NAACP, he was now using the same technique used by other southern attorneys general to link Cold War fears of Communism to integration. The NAACP called the hearings a "smear." After three days of testimony by persons such as J. B. Matthews, once an investigator for the House Un-American Activities Committee and later fired from the McCarthy Committee in the U.S. Senate, the hearings drew to a close.[60]

Christmas was coming for all of Little Rock's families, and those with displaced students were awaiting the vacation days of their missing children, who would soon be home for the holidays. The Women's Emergency Committee to Open Our Schools mailed Christmas cards to out-of-state friends, including a "Little Rock Letter" identifying the group's purpose. The letter began: "We know it will be a long time before the state of Arkansas can live down the shame and disgrace with which it is now viewed by the entire world. We thought you might like to learn that there is one group here dedicated to the principle of good public education with liberty and justice for all."[61] Despite the fact that all Little Rock high schools were closed, Hall High's cheerleaders were attempting to bring a degree of normalcy to any former students who would be in town on Saturday, December 20, sponsoring an afternoon Christmas "tea dance" for students at the Hall High gymnasium. A live six-piece combo called The Rebels provided the music, and admission was fifty cents.[62]

The newly elected six-member LRSD board took office on December 16 and appointed the principal of Hall High, Terrell E. Powell, as the new superintendent of the Little Rock school system. The same week, the Capital

Citizens' Council elected a new president, Malcolm Taylor, to replace Reverend Wesley Pruden. Taylor, a charter member of the LRPSC, was joined by three other new officers and three new board members.[63] Orval Faubus, speaking in Monroe, Louisiana, to a rally attended by about seven hundred persons, where he was raising funds for the LRPSC, claimed that Democratic friends had dangled before him the possibility of their support for the vice presidency of the United States, while urging him to back school segregation at the outset of Little Rock's racial crisis. In his speech, he criticized President Eisenhower, the U.S. Supreme Court, and the "ultra-left-wing press," including the *Arkansas Gazette.* After a standing ovation, he commented on Bruce Bennett's state investigation of racial unrest and agreed that Communist subversive influences were at work.[64]

Arkansans celebrated the holidays in unusually cold weather. The news for moderates the week of Christmas brought disappointment along with the intermittent snow. On December 22, the Arkansas Supreme Court upheld the "Bennett Ordinances." These laws to determine which groups or organizations should be paying a municipal privilege tax had been adopted by both Little Rock and North Little Rock. A side effect of the laws was to expose the membership rolls of organizations. The NAACP did not wish to comply with the demand for its membership and contributor lists and a fifty-dollar-per-year state tax on corporations. The Arkansas Supreme Court ruled by a 5–2 margin against the NAACP, saying it must open all its records to the public. Fearing exposure to intimidation for its members and contributors, the NAACP promised to appeal to the U.S. Supreme Court.[65]

These same "Bennett Ordinances" would be used against the WEC when one segregationist member of the Little Rock City Board of Directors, L. L. Langford, invoked the ordinances' rules and harassed WEC members with letters delivered by two plainclothes policemen to the door of the group's secretary, Dottie Morris. Each of the three times this occurred in early 1959, the WEC responded with a letter listing officers, some budget figures, and finally some policy statements—but with no list of its membership, despite the rising "belligerent and threatening tone" found in Langford's letters.[66] During this period, the WEC never released the names of all of its more than one thousand members, fearing intimidation by segregationists toward the women and, even more, toward their husbands.[67]

Word of the WEC's tireless work had spread among supporters of integration outside Little Rock and outside the state. *The Loretta Young Show,* broadcast from New York City, had expressed an interest in dramatizing the history of the WEC on the show scheduled for February 1959. When news of this program leaked out, Malcolm Taylor, the new CCC president and a new member of the Raney High board, sent threatening letters to the network, to the sponsors, and to Loretta Young herself. The letter began with a report of the show's intent to dramatize the work of Vivion Brewer and the WEC, stating that the group had been organized after voters in Little Rock had voted "to close schools rather than race-mix them." Taylor challenged the show's intentions: "Is this motely [sic] crowd of clandestined [sic] frustrated women to be portrayed as modern day counterparts of American women heroines? Is it your job to show the parents in Georgia, Louisiana, South Carolina, Mississippi, and Alabama that we in Little Rock who believe in our time honored and successful (for both races) customs and traditions are bigots and hate-mongers?" Taylor ended his letter with both a demand and personal insults for Young: "We demand that the plans to portray the Little Rock WEC be canceled. We are sending copies of this letter to the Association of Citizens Councils of America, newspapers all over the South and to other publications with nationwide circulation. We are certain that they will help us spread the word across the country and cause you and your sponsor to learn a well-deserved lesson on public relations. I suspect that you have flounced into many living rooms, with your wide-eyed innocence and swirling skirts, for the last time."[68] The CCC efforts worked, and the television show was never filmed.

Three days after Christmas, the announcement came that Governor Faubus had been voted the Gallup Poll's tenth most popular man in America. However, the number-one place went to President Eisenhower, something that probably pleased moderates more than Faubus's place pleased segregationists.[69] At the same time, the Women's Emergency Committee asked the Little Rock city manager board to establish an interdenominational, interracial "City Commission on Civic Unity," according to a plan drawn up by WEC member Velma Powell, the wife of Central High's vice principal, J. O. Powell. The intended purpose of the proposed commission was to advise city government on ways to build better community relations. Little Rock's mayor, Werner Knoop, told Vivion Brewer by phone that there was no need for her to discuss the WEC proposal with him because he did not plan to support it. WEC workers mailed copies of the proposal to all members of the city board with the encouragement of the lone woman among the city directors, Mrs. Edgar Dixon. However well intentioned, the WEC proposal ultimately failed.[70]

A court hearing scheduled for January 6 bolstered the hopes of those who counted on Judge Miller to demand that the public schools open. He had been instructed by the higher courts not to impede the schools moving toward integration. In the 1950s, public schools often ended their first semester in mid-January, having started their school year after Labor Day, and some thought that the judge might act in time for Little Rock high schools to hold at least one semester of classes.

Arkansas was not completely alone in its wait for the opening of closed public schools. Some Virginia public schools were also closed in 1958–59 to prevent desegregation. Those Virginians affected, like those in Little Rock, hoped that the second semester might bring a solution. Just as some in Arkansas had cried state's rights, white supremacy, and massive resistance to the Supreme Court's ruling on school desegregation, so too had many in Virginia. Just as the Arkansas legislature had voted power to its governor to close schools to prevent racial integration in August 1958, other southern states had passed similar legislation. By the end of 1958, every southern state except Tennessee had enacted school-closing laws. As early as 1956, the Virginia General Assembly had passed twenty-three segregation laws that ranged from school closing to anti-NAACP measures.[71]

In addition to Little Rock, only the state of Virginia actually closed schools that year. On the same day that Faubus announced the closure of all four Little Rock high schools, Virginia governor Lindsay Almond removed Warren County High School from Virginia's public school system and ordered it closed. One week later, he closed two schools in Charlottesville. Later in September, he closed six white schools in Norfolk. Unlike in Arkansas, Almond closed only those schools actually threatened with desegregation. While Little Rock denied public education to almost 3,700 students, Virginia school districts denied public education to 12,725.[72]

Unlike Arkansas's laws, Virginia's massive resistance laws cut off all state education funds to a school district the moment a single black child registered in a white school. In Norfolk, 151 blacks applied for white schools. At first the school board rejected all applications, but after federal judge Walter E. Hoffman ordered the board to reconsider in view of the *Brown I* and *II* decisions, it admitted 17 black children into six all-white Norfolk schools. By mid-September, Norfolk's segregated elementary schools and one white junior high opened, while six junior and senior high schools had not. Unlike in Little Rock, black schools remained open.[73]

Almond closed a total of nine schools in Virginia: six in Norfolk, two in Charlottesville, and one in Warren County. Virginia denied a free public education to three times more students than Arkansas had and disrupted the careers of 543 teachers. Mary Johnson, a Norfolk teacher of thirty-six years, describes her own situation and that of fellow faculty members: "The teachers put their whole lives into public schools. They see what they have spent all their lives building up—falling apart. I can't really describe to you the feelings of insecurity."[74]

Unlike in Little Rock, Virginia courts did not restrain the teachers from instructing students in private schools or in settings other than public school buildings. Of Virginia's 543 displaced teachers, 405 tutored in improvised classrooms located in churches and homes. They did this either for no pay or merely for expenses. None of Virginia's public school teachers agreed to teach at the Tidewater Education Foundation, a private school system established by the Defenders of States Rights and Individual Sovereignty, which had originally proposed a full-scale private school plan to handle more than 5,000 students. This organization, Virginia's version of the White Citizens' Council, hoped to hire public school teachers. Advice from lawyers convinced public school teachers not to work for the private group for fear of breaking their contracts and losing their salaries.[75]

Virginia's state education organization collectively rejected Almond's school closure at its statewide meeting, in a move similar to Arkansas's AEA's. The vote was merely a survey of teachers' views, which by a four-to-one margin fell in favor of opening schools even if this meant racial integration. One teacher explained: "There was a real unity among us all—but don't misunderstand. We weren't voting for integration; we were voting for public education."[76] This same sentiment—"not integration, but public education"—continued to be voiced by moderates in Little Rock as a more palatable approach to gaining support for opening the schools. As the new year came, parents, students, and Virginia and Little Rock communities waited for schools to open, while segregationists recognized that school closures had put both states on the front lines of massive resistance.

As promised, federal judge John E. Miller followed the mandate from the Eighth Circuit at his January 6 hearing. Both he and the LRSD board had been instructed to prevent Little Rock public schools from being used as private segregated schools and to take affirmative steps toward carrying out the court-approved plan of integration. The Eighth Circuit's ruling had come back in November, and now Miller and the new members of the LRSD board needed to act. Miller had promised to rule after he received the mandate he received in December. He set the January date knowing that the higher courts expected a showdown in the long battle over Little Rock desegregation. Through this decision, especially following the *Brown II* ruling, the higher courts were handing local school boards and federal district judges the job of overseeing school desegregation. The problem in the South was that many justices did not want this job and felt that they had no power of enforcement, while many school boards and their patrons lacked the courage or even the convictions needed to go forward with full implementation. At the January 6 hearing, new counsel represented the newly elected LRSD board. Attorney Herschel Friday of the Mehaffy, Smith and Williams law firm opposed the lawyers of the NAACP, who now represented forty-two black student plaintiffs. Attorneys for the Little Rock Classroom Teachers and the U.S. Department of Justice also attended the hearing.[77] One of Judge Miller's first actions was to incorporate the new school board members and new superintendent into the case and then to change its name from *Aaron v. Cooper* to *Aaron v. McKinley,* because Ed McKinley had been elected the new board president. Demonstrating some new tactics, Herschel Friday tried to get the new LRSD board members removed from the case since they had not been part of the original legislation. Miller refused. Then Friday tried to get the Justice Department, which had entered the year before as a friend of the court, dismissed from the case. Failing that, he asked for and received more time for the new board members to study the case.[78]

On January 10, Miller instructed the new board members and superintendent to "move forward within their official powers" to carry out integration in Little Rock public schools and asked for a specific report of their plan within thirty days.[79] Miller did not order them to open the closed schools but delegated to them the task of moving forward—or even of interpreting "moving forward." Only his second statement appeared to coincide with the higher courts' directive: if public schools were opened, he said, "there seems to be no alternative" but to make them integrated. Miller did, as always, "reserve jurisdiction herein to enter such further orders as may be necessary and appropriate."[80] Following the hearing, he mailed his twenty-page opinion to the Little Rock clerk's office.

The following day, Monday, January 12, the Arkansas General Assembly convened for its regular biennial session. The Sixty-second Assembly met for general organizational activity and then waited for the governor to outline his plans in a speech scheduled for the next day. On January 17, the LRSD board went back to court—with a plan to open Little Rock high schools for the second semester by January 26. However, its proposal would have opened the four high schools on a *segregated* basis, with the court's permission; the board promised to have a new plan for integration by August 15 "that would satisfy both the federal courts and the residents of the school district." Board president Ed McKinley said he had discussed the matter with Faubus and that he believed that the governor would give the board permission to open the schools in this fashion if the court approved.[81] Miller set a February 3 hearing date for this motion. As might be expected, both the NAACP and the Justice Department objected to the new proposal.

Unlike Little Rock, Virginia reopened its schools after one semester. On January 19, 1959, the Virginia Supreme Court of Appeals ruled that closing schools and withholding state funds were violations of the state constitution (*Harrison v. Day*, 1959). On the same day, a three–judge federal district court decision held that both measures also conflicted with the U.S. Constitution (*James v. Almond*, 1959).[82] Unlike Arkansas's leaders, Virginia's governor, Lindsay Almond, vowed to start over—something Governor Faubus didn't need to do. The Arkansas Supreme Court had not been asked to rule on the legality of Arkansas's school-closing law or on the law withholding funds. For this reason, it appeared that Arkansas's governor could simply add more and more state laws with the new legislature's blessing.

Actions on January 12 changed all that. A new filing by the Legal Defense Fund of the NAACP appeared to offer a chance of opening Little Rock's high schools—at least at some future time. The same day that the General Assembly opened its new session, the black plaintiffs asked the district court to add to the existing Little Rock case a request to nullify Arkansas Acts 4 and 5. Finally, someone in Arkansas was officially requesting that these two state laws, one allowing school closure and one allowing state money to follow displaced students to accredited schools, be declared unconstitutional. As Virginia had just settled its own cases with similar court appeals, now Arkansas and the plaintiffs were forcing the specific issue of state authority against federal authority through the courts. Thurgood Marshall and Wiley Branton decided to file this new case, rather than appealing the previous decision by Judge Miller, because it was obvious to Marshall that Miller would not hand down a favorable decision.[83] It would take a three-judge federal panel to consider the new case, but it was not scheduled to convene until spring. Always acting to delay and complicate, Attorney General Bruce Bennett began challenging the two acts (4 and 5) in state court and asking that the federal court not act until the state court had completed its work. Bennett recognized that the Arkansas Supreme Court would not be easily swayed to support integration; asking that the state courts act first would be a useful delaying tactic.[84]

Beyond the courts and the Arkansas legislature, students' lives were in flux. Joyce and Jane Franklin were sisters who were to attend Hall High in

1958–59. Joyce had been a junior at Hall during its opening year of 1957–58 and was looking forward to her senior year; her younger sister, Jane, was to be a sophomore. Like the Franklin sisters, not all students remained with one choice for the entire academic year. The choices the Franklins made in the fall of 1958 set them on one path, but events subsequently altered their course; by the beginning of the new semester, they were responding to their circumstances in a new way. In September 1958, the Franklin sisters had waited with other students and parents for courts', politicians', and voters' decisions. Joyce recalls: "I just didn't understand what was going on. I waited day after day, being sure the next day the schools would open. I watched TV every single night, and I talked with friends who were in the same situation." Weeks passed, and many parents "panicked," looking for alternative schools, but Joyce, Jane, and their mother waited. "Students disappeared overnight," Joyce recounts, as they rushed to enroll in nearby county schools such as Mabelvale, Jacksonville, and Sylvan Hills, and in the Catholic schools in Little Rock. Added to the anxiety and uncertainty of making these life-changing decisions for her daughters, Mrs. Franklin was still coping with the recent loss of her husband, who had died the previous spring. About five weeks after Labor Day, then, Mrs. Franklin packed up both girls and went to Montgomery, Alabama, where she had family. She enrolled them at Sidney Lanier High School, where they met with a counselor who tried to find appropriate classes for each girl: "Our mother went to buy our school books, but by the time she returned for us that afternoon, we had talked to one another and decided we were not going back to that school." Jane remembers that six-week exams were scheduled for the following day, and she had been told that she would be required to take exams in Latin, in algebra, and on a book she had never read: "I knew at that moment that I couldn't do it. . . . Joyce and I knew it was a recipe for failure because we had never had some of those courses." After a few days, the threesome packed up and returned to Little Rock; after some time, Joyce enrolled in correspondence courses from the University of Arkansas that were being offered at Westover Hill Presbyterian Church. "I remember taking only English or literature and history and earned two credits by semester, so that I could enter college early," she recalls.

As a sophomore, Jane could not take correspondence courses, so she was enrolled downtown at Draughon's School of Business for typing and shorthand. Joyce's classes ended at noon, and no meal was provided for students at Westover Hills. Jane, being fifteen, could not yet drive, so Joyce picked her up after her morning business classes. Both of the Franklin sisters were glad to be back in Little Rock and stayed in touch with any friends who remained there. They looked forward to the Hall High Warrior football games remaining in the season and attended them with hopes of seeing their scattered acquaintances. By semester's end, both girls had to make new choices when it became apparent that efforts to reopen the public high schools would not be successful.

In describing her parents' views on the situation in Little Rock, Joyce remarks that her father was liberal in his views and speculates that he would have been active in encouraging integration. The Franklin family were among only 1,400 Jews in Little Rock in the 1950s, in a city population of 110,000.[85] Historian Carolyn LeMaster and author Irving Spitzberg characterize Little Rock's Jews as being strongly active in Little Rock's desegregation controversy, generally holding moderate to liberal opinions.[86] Joyce believes that "maybe because of that, he would have done the right thing. Being Jewish and growing up in Little Rock we really didn't feel a lot of prejudice and maybe it was out there. . . . I have had other people say—'Oh Joyce, you're so naive,' but maybe we were just protected; but I always felt comfortable living in Little Rock." At semester, Joyce headed to Lindenwood College in St. Charles, Missouri, while Jane enrolled at Harding Academy, a residential high school sponsored by the Church of Christ's Harding College in Searcy, Arkansas.

If the Franklin sisters knew little of prejudice toward Jews in Little Rock, Jane was to learn more than she wanted at Harding. Classes there were held on Tuesday through Saturday because many of the male college students served churches, preaching on Sundays around the state. This meant that though Jane returned to Little Rock every weekend, she missed the services at her own synagogue. She found the classes at Harding academically challenging, since most were taught by college professors. Jane adjusted to the requirement that she take classes in the New Testament, but she recalls, "I felt prejudice for the very first time." There was little interaction between the high school students and the college-level ones, but she has vivid memories of the day she and a friend walked along the sidewalk, within earshot of several college students behind her. When they said, "I don't see any pitchfork, or any horns, or a tail," she had no idea they were talking about her. Only her friend verified that they were. "Many of them were from small rural areas of Arkansas and had never seen a Jewish person before, and they had very fundamental ideas regarding the biblical Jews," she remembers.

Jane found a personal hero that semester at Harding Academy in another brush with a different doctrinal interpretation. One of the other Hall High students who attended Harding was Jim Guy Tucker, a future Arkansas governor (the forty-third, 1993–96). They were both sophomores and often sat together at the required morning chapel or evening vespers. One morning, Jane fell asleep during the chapel service when the headmaster was preaching and awoke to Tucker standing up beside her and saying to the speaker, "You shouldn't say those things . . . you shouldn't say that the Jews killed Christ." To this day, Jane regards the actions of her very young defender as both laudable and daring.[87]

Like some other Lost Year students, each of the Franklin sisters had three different schooling experiences that year. Many of the senior students enrolled in correspondence courses moved on to college by semester, and there is no way of accounting for students who left one high school venue for another. The official transfer records were well documented and analyzed in 1963 by J. Harvey Walthall, the principal at Forrest Heights Junior High during this period, who detailed where students were sent by each of the closed high schools.[88] The LRSD transfer records, however, indicate only where the transcript for each of the 3,665 students was first sent, or if it was sent.

By tracing these documents, Walthall chronicles the enormous displacement of students and reveals dramatic differences for students by race and even by class. Most dramatic of all was the disparity among blacks and whites for locating any type of education. All but 7 percent of the 2,915 displaced white students found alternative schooling, while 50 percent of the 750 blacks found none. Private education for whites in Little Rock drew 44 percent of white students, while 35 percent of whites managed to enroll in public schools either near Little Rock or scattered about the state, students moving in with relatives or friends. A greater percentage of black students than white enrolled in public schools either nearby or with relatives or friends across the state. Although 37 percent of blacks went to public schools within the state, no black students attended a private school in Little Rock because no such opportunity existed. Ninety-one black students, or 12 percent, were able to attend public or private school out of state, while 275 white students, or 9.4 percent, were able to do the same. Only 6 black students entered college before graduation, amounting to only .8 percent, while 116 white students, or 4 percent, entered college before graduation.[89]

These various statistics demonstrate without question that blacks suffered disproportionately in their loss of education. This chapter in the history of the Lost Year is unfortunately one of complete inequity for the 50 percent of black students who were unable to attend school at all. Some joined the military, some married early and started families, and some simply worked in the community and waited for public schools to open. Some black students never finished school.

How does one measure hardship? The young white men who joined the military were just as lonely and frightened as the black ones. The black parents were just as disappointed as the white parents for the lost aspirations they held for their sons and daughters. Many black students and some white ones suffered from having their personal dreams and expectations interrupted. Some white parents opened private schools for their students, but the national NAACP discouraged this in the black community because private schooling would go against the efforts of the Little Rock Nine—not to mention play directly into the hands of the segregationists. The actual number of students who did no academic work that year was 208 white students and 376 black students. There is no greater evidence that 1958–59 was "lost" than this denial of a free public education to these 584 young people.[90]

Owen McMillan was to have been a tenth grader at Horace Mann in 1958, even though he was only fourteen, having been academically promoted in grade school. Like his classmates, he waited for schools to open, but Owen never finished high school. Though he returned to Horace Mann when schools opened, he finally dropped out. He joined the military but was not allowed to finish his enlistment. He jumped from job to job and place to place. At the time of his interview, some forty-four years after his high school was closed, he was working as a telemarketer and living with his mother. Looking back, he recalls: "I remember running the streets, taking odd jobs when men came into the Ninth Street pool halls looking for laborers. . . . I became cynical, lost any respect for authority I had, and blamed adults for not doing the right thing for young people. You take on certain characteristics when you do not have structure in your life. . . . You couldn't tell me anything. I had no respect for authority. . . . The only school I ever graduated from was the school of hard knocks."[91] Those black students who could not crowd into the nearby public schools or live with relatives in or out of state were simply denied an education. One can measure this loss with statistics and count it in numbers, but nothing clarifies it as well as the voices of the students themselves.

CHAPTER FIVE

Enter the Politicians

*I learned something could happen in my life that would
just make me take a totally right turn without
expecting it and start on a whole new path.*
—Linda Collins (Newsome), Hall High student

LITTLE ROCK, JANUARY 13–MARCH 12, 1959

JANUARY 13. Orval Faubus swears to uphold the federal and state constitutions during his third oath of office as governor.

JANUARY 13. Faubus presents his third-term program to the regular session of the Arkansas General Assembly during his inaugural address. This includes a local-option proposal for funding schools.

JANUARY 14. Grainger Williams, the new president of the Little Rock Chamber of Commerce, mentions the "unmentionable"—the cost of education or the lack of education.

JANUARY 15. The Arkansas Revenue Department says that the expenses of sending Little Rock high school students away from home is not deductible from state income tax.

JANUARY 17. Bruce Bennett and his Special Education Committee submit their report from the three-day hearings in December to the public and to the Arkansas House of Representatives.

JANUARY 18. Raney High holds an open house.

JANUARY 26. The Chamber of Commerce endorses opening schools on a segregated basis.

JANUARY 26. Faubus disputes an American Association of University Women report on the loss of business because of the desegregation crisis.

JANUARY 28. Two of Faubus's three school bills pass the House.

JANUARY 29. Representative John P. Bethell introduces a bill demanding that the *Arkansas Gazette* drop the use of its masthead because it appears to be a corruption of the state seal.

FEBRUARY 3. Federal judge Miller denies the LRSD board's motion to open all four high schools on a segregated basis.

FEBRUARY 10. The *Arkansas Gazette* leaks a plan to purge many high school teachers and administrators. Faubus mentions those teachers he would target.

MARCH 2. House Bill 546 (the Tyler board-packing bill that would allow Faubus to appoint three new members to the LRSD board) passes.

MARCH 3. Senator Ellis Fagan uses powerful oratory and appeals to table the Tyler bill in the Senate. The Senate votes to table it.

MARCH 4. Senator Max Howell introduces an alternative bill for the election of three new members to the LRSD board (SB421).

MARCH 5. A connection is made between the threatened purge of high school teachers and administrators and the Tyler board-packing bill.

MARCH 11. The House passes SB421 (the Howell bill) but fails to vote an emergency clause.

MARCH 12. On the last day of the regular session of the legislature, Senator Sam Levine from Pine Bluff filibusters the Howell bill to its death.

The new year of 1959 began as students in most schools across the state returned to class and to the end of their first semester. Displaced Little Rock high school students, scattered among private or parochial schools in the city and other schools across the state or nation, did the same. Of course, many had no school to attend and had already joined the military, enrolled in correspondence courses, or entered college early; some simply were not enrolled. By January 7, Superintendent Powell and the Little Rock School District released official numbers for the first time in months. The report said that 2,873 displaced students had found some type of education, leaving out at least 500 who were not enrolled anywhere. The figure used for total displaced students was an estimate based upon average daily attendance the previous year. No one could be sure of the exact number of enrolled students, because Little Rock's public high schools had never opened this school year.[1]

A second important question for the displaced students—or, more importantly, for their new schools—concerned the funding of their education. Nearly two hundred public schools in Arkansas had applied for and were receiving state money in the amount of $24.50 a month per displaced student enrolled. The money that would have gone to Little Rock for high school students was now going elsewhere, according to Arkansas Act 5. Only accredited schools could receive funds, and the matter of accreditation for the private and parochial academies that had opened quickly in the fall in Little Rock was about to become an issue.[2]

Almost two weeks into the new year, Governor Orval Faubus took his oath of office before the Arkansas General Assembly for the third time, the second man in the state's history to serve a third term. Accompanied by his wife and only child, Farrell, he walked down the aisle toward the podium as the band played "Dixie" in the gallery. As television cameras operated with large banks of lights, the temperature in the crowded House chamber rose during the governor's one-hour address.[3] His speech included three proposed laws regarding segregation, as well as laws regarding the minimum wage, a new state agency for agriculture, an increase in unemployment benefits, an extension of the penalty deadline of the reassessment law, and the adoption of a new insurance code.[4] His three suggested bills to resist federal court decisions on racial integration included one to initiate a constitutional amendment under which local districts could close their schools and pay their students equal shares of state and local money. The second was a stopgap state law putting the proposed amendment into effect until the people could vote on it. The third would permit public school teachers to retain their public school retirement if they switched to private schools.[5]

An editorial in the *Arkansas Gazette* called the governor's ideas a "tragic last resort." It pointed out that Faubus's plan would remove Arkansas's constitutional requirement for mandatory public schools as had already happened in Georgia in 1957 under Governor Herman Talmadge—a circuitous route to what Talmadge himself had labeled a "tragic last resort" even as he proposed it. The plan would allow state money to flow directly to each student, who in turn could pay tuition to the private school of his or her choice. The *Gazette* pointed out that such a solution, even if it could stand the test of the law, would run short of money. Considering that the existing per-capita expenditure of state and local funds in Arkansas was among the lowest in the nation, the *Gazette* predicted that the amount would barely cover the cost of instruction. This would leave nothing for the capital outlay for construction and maintenance of buildings or for equipment and laboratories. And then *Gazette* editor Harry Ashmore raised the crucial dilemma: "The well-to-do can likely make up the difference between this state stipend and the far larger tuition fees normally charged by first-rate private schools, but the rank and file of our citizens certainly can't." He then suggested what Arkansas might be moving toward: downgraded public schools that would be opened on an integrated basis as some lesser parallel system alongside private and segregated schools. This editorial presaged the overarching question that citizens would ask again and again in the spring of 1959 and even in recent years in Little Rock. Would Little Rock have free, equal, and public schools for students of all races and economic classes?[6]

Because Little Rock parents were paying taxes for public schools that were closed, and some were paying additional fees for tuition and expenses for their children to attend other public or private schools, the Women's Emergency Committee formally asked the state's revenue department if such expenses might be deducted from state income tax.[7] Governor Faubus had suggested in November that donations to Little Rock's private schools might be deducted from the donor's Arkansas tax bill.[8] Ironically, he had made this remark to a crowd of over ten thousand in Crestview, Florida, while on a swing across southern states, not to an Arkansas audience. He later refused to elaborate on his statements in response to press questions and never mentioned the idea again. In January, the Arkansas Revenue Department answered the WEC with a resounding "no." Parents of displaced students were entitled to no tax break.[9]

On the evening of January 14, Grainger Williams, the new president of the Little Rock Chamber of Commerce, gave his inaugural address before a large crowd at Little Rock's Robinson Auditorium. Some look back at these remarks as a turning point in the white community's attitude, a mark of newfound resistance to the policies of segregationists.[10] Williams's remarks astonished his listeners because Williams chose to mention the school situation —a previously unmentionable topic among business moderates. His remarks spoke to the climate of real social repression many felt: "The time has come for us to evaluate the cost of education and the cost of the lack of it. I have neither the purpose nor the desire to discuss the political and social aspects of the integration problem. . . . I would urge that no matter what our personal feelings might be—each of us encourage the reestablishment of all areas of communication. . . . To achieve this climate of communication would be one of the greatest contributions we could make, and to that end I am dedicated."[11]

Author Sara Murphy explains that Williams's rise to the Chamber presidency came after the tenures of the head of Southwestern Bell Telephone Company and the head of the Arkansas Power and Light Company. Because of their business positions, neither would openly oppose Governor Faubus, but Williams, an insurance executive, now publicly mentioned the state of the public schools. As courageous as Williams's remarks appear in the climate of that moment, the Chamber's action twelve days later reveals how far that body was willing to go. The new LRSD board asked the Federal District Court to allow the city's four closed high schools to reopen immediately on a segregated basis.[12] The Chamber of Commerce then not only endorsed opening the schools as segregated but pledged the Chamber's efforts to assist the school board.[13] These actions demonstrate what the business community was indeed willing to do at this point, long after the WEC had advertised extensively to endorse opening schools. Historian Elizabeth Jacoway calls this particular Chamber of Commerce action "regrettable" because it sent the wrong message to the community and to the courts.[14]

If Judge John Miller accepted the new proposal by this new LRSD board to open the schools on a segregated basis, he would do away with the gradual-integration plan Little Rock had adopted in 1955 and he had endorsed in 1956. The new LRSD board, in effect, was trying to abandon the Blossom Plan, which it called "stalemated." The board members insisted that it was "impossible under the circumstances" for them as defendants "to carry into effect" the existing plan.[15] The board, which had hired a new set of attorneys to represent it, was acting in its new term as a group that wanted schools open but segregated. The six-man school board, as it began to work together, was following a more conservative approach than the previous board. Its hiring of Herschel Friday and the Smith law firm, and its actions in early January 1959, demonstrate its attempt at backtracking, at abandoning even the most limited and token integration plan. Some saw the change in legal representation as a conflict of interest. Both Pat Mehaffy and William J. Smith were close advisors to Governor Faubus, and Herschel Friday was the attorney the firm assigned to the school board. Author Irving Spitzberg remarks that this demonstrated "the enormous power the Mehaffy,

Smith, and Williams firm wielded in Arkansas."[16] Spitzberg also quotes two businessmen, one of whom claimed that Herschel Friday was hired to "neutralize the Mehaffy firm's role in the Little Rock situation." The second said that the board knew that the Mehaffy firm "could get things done."[17] Author Roy Reed saw William Smith and his law firm as "the third side in a power triangle that included Stephens, Inc. and the governor's office."[18] Faubus had learned in his earlier terms as governor to work effectively with powerful economic interests that could provide him crucial financial backing. Among the most prominent of these interests were Wilton "Witt" Stephens and his brother Jack.[19]

In reality, the new school board members who had hired the new law firm were all segregationists. Each had publicly claimed this status in the December election, and by January they appeared to be acting in a unified manner and speaking in one voice. When Judge Miller refused the board's request to open the schools immediately on a segregated basis, however, their unified public status dissipated, and a real split ensued. The deadlock held and became an issue during the Arkansas General Assembly's regular session, with board-packing bills intended to break what became a three/three split on the new LRSD board.

Probably the most interesting of the new LRSD board's public strategies was its use of figures related to displaced black students. Stating that "only a few Negroes had found alternative schooling when compared to whites," the board asked that reopening schools be segregated, with Horace Mann High reserved for black students.[20] The school board's argument was ironic, using the very students most displaced by the state law to prevent integration as an excuse to return the city's schools to totally segregated education.

Judge Miller, already under pressure from the Eighth Circuit Court to "take affirmative steps" with the previously approved desegregation plan, disappointed those hoping for a speedy reopening of the schools. He doubted that he could hold a hearing on the board's request within the next few weeks. Additionally, the NAACP called the board's request unacceptable, and Daisy Bates said that her organization could not accept the board's "start again" plan.[21] By January 24, Wiley Branton, the NAACP attorney, asked the federal court at Little Rock to reject the LRSD board's request that it be allowed to write a new plan to be presented in August. Representing black students in the original Little Rock integration suit, Branton contended that the district court was "bound by the decree of the United States Supreme Court as the law of the case and could not give relief then sought by the defendants."[22] He continued that the LRSD was trying "to move backward rather than forward."[23] The Justice Department, remaining a "friend of the court," also objected to the school board's proposed changes, saying that its proposal was offered "in bad faith to avoid compliance" with previous court orders. U.S. attorney general William P. Rogers signed this motion, demonstrating that the federal government was continuing to be a presence in Arkansas's battles with the federal courts. Judge Miller called a hearing for February 3, well after most schools' second semesters had begun—frustrating the hopes of any who thought Little Rock high schools might be open for the second term.[24]

Arkansas attorney general Bruce Bennett submitted a report to the Arkansas House of Representatives from the Special Education Committee of the Legislative Council. The House voted to include his detailed report in its *Journal*. This report laid the community's racial unrest at the door of the Communist Party and criticized the work of the NAACP, the Arkansas Council on Human Relations, and the Southern Regional Council—all groups with interracial memberships. The report was based on the three days of public hearings Bennett had directed in December, during which none of the accused persons appeared and none of the witnesses who did testify was directly involved in the school situation.[25] Ever the political hopeful, Bennett, along with his committee, continued a program of harassment toward the cited groups.

On Sunday afternoon, January 16, T. J. Raney, the president of the Little Rock Private School Corporation, welcomed hundreds of well-wishers to the high school named in his honor. Visitors inspected the main building at Sixteenth and Lewis, as teachers and students stationed about the campus showed off their school's facilities. Governor Orval Faubus, besieged with autograph seekers, dropped by and signed the guest book, the words "institution of a free people" near his name.[26]

When headlines revealed that the state laws Virginia had used to close nine white public high schools had fallen in federal and state courts, Governor Faubus used the occasion to defend his newest "local-option" idea for school funding, announced to the General Assembly the week before. Claiming that he didn't believe "that the Virginia segregation setback in the courts would have much effect on Arkansas," he declared his proposal an almost "foolproof" solution to federal integration moves. By essentially taking desegregation issues away from the state, the new rules would put them in the hands of local school boards, which would let voters decide whether to have desegregated public schools or no public schools at all.[27] Unlike in Little Rock, the nine white schools in Virginia that had been shuttered since September opened for classes by late January or early February. Little Rock public high schools remained closed.

As the Arkansas General Assembly continued its regular sixty-day session, Governor Faubus publicly commented on several issues at his regularly televised press conferences. The Little Rock branch of the American Association of University Women (AAUW) had recently conducted a poll of eighty-five businesspersons, asking if Little Rock businesses had been hurt by the school-integration crisis. Results showed that forty-five said their businesses had suffered, while thirty-five said they had seen no effect; six, including two moving companies, said their businesses had improved. Speculating that the results were meant to embarrass him, Faubus challenged the findings. He disputed the survey results because retail store sales over the previous few months had increased, according to Faubus. Asked about the possibility of opening the public high schools, Faubus discounted the chance of this happening any time soon. Probably his most surprising remarks centered on a proposed bill by representative T. E. Tyler of Pulaski County to create a state militia—the Arkansas Mounted Rangers—under the governor's control and not subject to the federal government, as was the Arkansas National Guard. Faubus said he would not view the bill with disfavor.[28]

As the end of the month approached and Faubus's three proposals moved through both houses of the legislature, some state solons continued to propose punitive bills. Representative John P. Bethell of Prairie County, a segregationist member of the Legislative Council, denounced the *Arkansas Gazette* for its editorial stand and proposed a bill to force the newspaper to drop the use of its front-page emblem. He claimed that the *Gazette* had forfeited its right to display what he called a "corruption" of the Great Seal of Arkansas. The newspaper had displayed this logo on its masthead since 1908. Though it was not a copy of the state seal, its eagle was similar in design. The bill called for a fine—from five hundred to five thousand dollars—for any business that used a replica or corruption of the state seal. Ironically, Bethell did not mention the *Arkansas Democrat,* a newspaper that many segregationists supported. Instead he commented, "I am sick to my stomach that I don't have a state paper I can be proud of." Although many segregationists had long before canceled their subscriptions to the *Arkansas Gazette,* most supported the *Arkansas Democrat.* Apparently, Bethell was upset with both newspapers, as well as with the Associated Press, for printing a copy of a speech that Hugh Patterson, the publisher of the *Gazette,* had made to an audience in Boston, criticizing Governor Faubus.[29]

As February opened, some legislators focused more and more on issues of desegregation. Legislators introduced about fifty measures dealing in some way with integration in the regular session of the Sixty-second General Assembly, including the three Governor Faubus had discussed publicly in January and a fourth measure that would allow students who did not wish to attend a desegregated school to take their state appropriations with them to another school.

Representative T. E. Tyler introduced House Bill 546 at the behest of Governor Faubus and Ed McKinley Jr., the president of the LRSD board. Acknowledged popularly as the "board-packing bill," Tyler's proposal called for three new members to be added to the LRSD board by appointment of Governor Faubus. The three/three split in the six-member board elected in early December had solidified, and the board could take little action.[30] By March 2, the board-packing bill had passed the House with a seventy-one to twenty-three vote, with bitter opposition from the Pulaski County delegation, except Tyler. Representative Gayle Windsor of Pulaski County responded with a blistering attack, calling the bill "a monstrous piece of legislation." Also on hand to voice objections were "about 16 to 20 women representing the PTA and the WEC," who were photographed stopping Representative Tyler and surrounding him on the steps to the House chamber a few minutes before the session opened. Some of the women said the bill was dictatorial, and many accused Tyler of letting the governor dictate to him. Finally, under their questioning, Tyler shouted, "Lady will you please shut up?" He defended his actions by saying that the bill might break the deadlock that existed on the LRSD board. The women later sat in the balcony, warned by the speaker against any demonstration.

The same afternoon, the bill came up in the Senate, where it was derailed when Senator Ellis Fagan "roared his disapproval," calling the bill "a disgrace. This bill seeks to take away from the people the right to elect our School Board. It is the lowest thing that has ever happened to me," he said, "having to stand here and defend the quarter million people who elect the School Board in the city." To add more insult to the governor, Fagan shouted, "I am ashamed of it." He noted that never in his twenty-six years in the legislature had he put forward a bill on a personal basis, and then he added his most dramatic challenge to his fellow senators. Saying that the bill would take away the right of the people to choose, and his own right to represent the voters of Little Rock, he threatened to resign his seat if his fellow senators voted approval, because "we would no longer represent our people." The senators then refused to consider the bill and tabled the measure with a roaring voice vote.[31]

Senator Ellis Fagan was the president pro tempore of the Arkansas Senate, as well as the owner of the Fagan Electric Company. Arkansas Power and

Light Company (AP&L) was his principal customer. Fagan had a close political association with AP&L that stretched at least as far back as the governorship of Sid McMath. McMath had supported the rural electrical cooperatives over the giant utility monopoly, and when McMath sought a third term in 1952, it was Senator Fagan who launched a critical radio attack on every phase of his administration. Fagan had also introduced into the Arkansas General Assembly a Highway Audit Commission, a five-member group that conducted public hearings regarding McMath's highway commission and a possible link to his campaign contributions. In his memoir, McMath argued that the electric utility had in effect defeated him in his run for a third term in the statehouse.[32]

These previous political battles, and the accompanying political alignments, were driving some of the events in the legislature in 1958 and even in the headlines of the city's two newspapers. It was again Fagan who challenged Faubus's "school board–packing" bill and dramatically put his own job on the line in getting the bill tabled. But there would be retribution.

Ellis Fagan and his wife, Alta, had one daughter, Judy, who was scheduled to be a senior in 1958–59 at Hall High. Like her classmates, she had to find alternative schooling. Judy attended Sylvan Hills High for her senior year, carpooling with friends to the school in northern Pulaski County. Beyond losing her senior year with her lifelong classmates, Judy became a target of some of her father's political enemies. In late February, in the midst of the legislative session, Orval Faubus called a news conference to announce that the Arkansas Sate Police had "uncovered a state-wide teenage vice ring involving both whites and Negroes."[33] Although Herman Lindsay, the Arkansas state police director, was at his side, the governor did all of the talking.

Elizabeth Huckaby's diary sums up the shocking news in succinct phrases: "Marijuana ring—integrated! White and black kids. Donna Wells (a fellow teacher) told me two names—earth shaking if revealed."[34] The *Arkansas Democrat,* the evening paper, got the story first, as it was Faubus's custom to make announcements in the afternoon so that the *Gazette* would have to carry the story later, the following morning. The headlines were as shocking as the details. Two adult black men were in custody and would be charged with possession of narcotics. A group of underage youths, of both races, had been questioned. Although Faubus refused to identify the teenage marijuana users because all were juveniles, he did state that some were from "very prominent families."[35]

The state police arrested the two black men at their apartments in Little Rock. The governor said that each apartment had "a special party room," where smoking parties were held. He said that "the rooms had red curtains on the window, red and blue lights and artificial flowers."[36] When a reporter asked the governor whether the youths committed acts beyond smoking marijuana, Faubus turned to Lindsay, who said, "yes, the teenaged [white] girls have admitted having other relations with the Negroes," elaborating no further.[37] Though Faubus did not give the names of any of the teenage girls, he did mention that two were sixteen-year-old white girls from Raney High, striking fear into the heart of every parent of every young white female in the state and appealing to the basest fears of race-mixing. Unable to resist, Faubus continued, "You'll pardon me for adding, these [the marijuana parties] are some of the fruits of integration."[38]

News reports describe the roundup of ten people, who had been questioned for hours on the previous day, some held overnight in custody. Faubus explained that the marijuana had come from Dallas, where federal narcotics agents had aided in tracking the source of the supply to Arkansas. He explained that a "Hot Springs Negro night club" was one source for the drugs.[39] Though none of the names of the juveniles was listed in the newspaper, radio reports hinted that children of the leaders of the Arkansas House and Senate were involved.[40]

Judy Fagan, the daughter of Senator Ellis Fagan, was taken into custody and questioned. To this day, she believes that segregationists were punishing her for her father's politics. Although she admits that she loved jazz music and had been to a black nightclub in Hot Springs to hear it performed, her greatest sin was underage drinking. She was not involved in this incident. She says that she didn't even know what marijuana was.[41] She recalls being questioned at state police headquarters; being kept over thirty hours without seeing her family; and appearing before Jack Holt, whom she remembers as "some kind of judge." The *Arkansas Democrat,* however, stated that "three Negroes being questioned . . . were taken to the prosecuting attorney's office to talk with Prosecutor Jack Holt."[42] Fagan remembers that Holt did question her but exonerated her of all charges. Within days, newspaper accounts credited Faubus: "The charges of selling narcotics would not be pressed and the white teenagers described as 'users' were released after questioning, because he did not want to reveal their identity and did not want them to have to appear in court as accusers." It was too late, since the damage of the gossip had been done.[43]

Fagan recalls that the publicity made life difficult for her. When she went back to school at Sylvan Hills High, the other students pulled their desks away from her in the classroom. Some of the students who had carpooled with her were no longer allowed to ride with her to school. Her reputation as a drug user—and "more"—followed her even after graduation, when she attended college at Texas Women's University and a girl in the cafeteria refused to serve her, saying, "You're the girl from Little Rock who sleeps with niggers." Today Fagan works with a mental-health agency, providing drug and alcohol services within the court system in north Arkansas.[44]

If the segregationists were painting the children of some politicians with a broad brush of shame, another story was breaking in the headlines targeting the other side. Next to the news of the board-packing bill in the legislature and the front-page stories on the youth drug ring was a story that tied a segregationist school board member, traffic judge Robert W. "Bob" Laster, to a bribe paid to an *Arkansas Democrat* reporter, Bob Troutt. Two Little Rock pinball machine operators claimed that they had paid two thousand dollars to Troutt to keep him from printing articles harmful to their business and that Bob Laster had arranged for the payment.[45] Laster, a segregationist member of the LRSD board, said the same day that the situation was "too damned ridiculous to even comment on." He challenged the two pinball operators, Cecil Hill and Harold Dunaway, to prove the validity of the audiotapes they had taken to the city manager's office to support their claims.[46]

By March 3, Governor Faubus was charging that the alleged pinball bribe payoff "was part of a plan by integrationists to gain control of the Little Rock School Board and force open the four high schools under 'controlled integration.'"[47] Faubus charged that the integrationists wanted to get Laster off the board, which would create a vacancy. This would give the integrationists three votes, with only two for the segregationists.[48] Faubus charged that "the mastermind" behind the plot to remove Laster was Harry Ashmore, the executive editor of the *Arkansas Gazette.* Then he accused the Arkansas Bar Association and the Little Rock Chamber of Commerce of moving to "crush Laster." The plan, he said, was either to disbar Laster for allegedly being involved in the payoff scheme or to remove Laster from the LRSD board through an election contest filed by his opponent in the December election. Most telling of all of Faubus's comments was his answer to a reporter's question: if Laster were forced off because of the pinball charges, would Faubus support Laster? Faubus answered that he would not. He added, "Perhaps Laster deserves what he gets because of his inept actions."[49]

LRSD board member Bob Laster had been elected in December 1958 by a narrow margin, only eighty-nine votes, over Margaret Stephens, the candidate Adolphine Terry had suggested. Stephens had immediately brought suit against Laster over the vote count. The liberal attorney Edwin Dunaway, a close associate and friend of former governor Sid McMath and *Arkansas Gazette* editor Harry Ashmore, represented Stephens. When the pinball operators, Cecil Hill and Harold Dunaway, went before the grand jury, Edwin Dunaway represented them as well. Each side in the battle for Little Rock was using unfavorable publicity against the other.

The same day that Faubus spoke out about Laster, the Pulaski County delegation in the House of Representatives introduced bills to abolish Laster's job. There were actually two bills, one to do away with the Second Division, Little Rock Municipal Court, and the other to re-create the court and allow the governor to appoint a judge—but no one who had served over the previous five years. The members of the delegation who made the proposals said that they understood that Governor Faubus had approved the two bills and would sign them.[50] If this day passed with the public being unsure of who was on which side and where politicians' loyalties lay, the following day made the situation even more problematical: the Pulaski County delegation withdrew its bills to abolish Laster's job, stating that they feared that their bills "might make a martyr of Laster in the view of the public."[51]

Historically, Arkansas politics have been something close to incestuous. If not that, at least political alignments ebb and flow frequently, and loyalties vary by situation. During the Lost Year, each side appeared to be using unwanted and unwarranted publicity to hurt its opponents. As further demonstration of this tangled web of intrigue, with charges and counter-charges, several other facts are of interest. First, Bob Laster had served as the lawyer for the black musicians who were implicated in the teenage drug ring. Second, Laster and Fagan were political enemies who had run for the same Senate seat several times, with Fagan the victor. And probably most peculiar of all, Bob Laster's mother clerked for Ellis Fagan.[52] At this point in March 1959, Laster was still in office both on the school board and as traffic judge.

The *Arkansas Gazette* noted the tabling of Faubus's board-packing bill as the "first legislative setback for Faubus on a piece of segregationist legislation since September of 1957." The newspaper ran a parallel article on page 1 entitled "Minimum Plan Approved by 819–245 Vote."[53] The Little Rock Chamber of Commerce now endorsed the reopening of the Little Rock high schools even with a "controlled minimum" of racial integration, based on a citywide vote of members. Finally, the tide was turning, and even the Chamber of Commerce had found its voice by early March. It called upon the Arkansas Supreme Court to rule on the constitutionality of Arkansas Acts 4 and 5; as president Grainger Williams said, "We're trying to get something done so we can have public schools this fall."[54] The announcement of the Chamber vote and Williams's statement came less than two months after the Chamber had voted to support the school board in opening the schools on a segregated basis, but after a ballot had been mailed to members, with 1,064 returns out of 2,014. Opposition to Faubus's bill in the legislature and the Chamber announcement substantiated the fact that Little Rock's support for the governor and for extreme segregationists was finally waning. As proof, the *Gazette* ran a photo of Senator Ellis Fagan, along with over two hundred telegrams he had received in support of his actions against the board-packing bill.[55]

With the Tyler bill tabled and with the twenty-four senators necessary to vote for bringing it back before the Senate, Governor Faubus and his supporters exerted pressure to make the board-packing bill viable. The Mothers' League of Central High sent representatives to the Senate chamber before its daily session. They cornered Senator Artie Gregory from North Little Rock and vocally encouraged him to bring the bill up for a vote. Senator Jerry Screeton of Hazen, the only senator heard to vote against tabling the bill earlier in the week, was taking a personal poll, trying to get a count of possible votes. Rumor had it that he could only count on sixteen votes—not enough to resurrect the bill.[56] The next day Senator Max Howell of Little Rock proposed an alternative bill. This bill would also add three new members to the school board, but by popular election rather than by the governor's appointment. Howell's bill would allow the Pulaski County Election Commission to call a special election to choose additional members within thirty days. Governor Faubus had not agreed to this, and the press reported that he called thirty-three of the thirty-five senators to his office, pressuring them to bring his board-packing bill back to the chamber.[57]

A few other Pulaski County representatives were finding ways to support the Little Rock school board and defy the governor's proposed plan to choose additional members. Representative Gayle Windsor of Pulaski County stated publicly that he was locking up his desk in the House chamber and spending the time remaining in the session working in the Senate chamber to defeat HB546. "After two days of worry and a prayer with his pastor," Windsor said, he wanted "to show how serious he thought the bill was and to give moral support to the Pulaski senators."[58]

By this time, talk was circulating about the real motive for the Tyler bill. The *Gazette* revealed that one reason for breaking the deadlock on the LRSD board was to purge high school teachers—an issue that had first been mentioned in February. Rumors of a purge began to emerge in print, suggesting an agreement involving the three extreme segregationist members of the LRSD board and community segregationists. The *Gazette* revealed a "scheme" to recover a half-million dollars in withheld state funds by "firing as many as a hundred teachers and administrators at the behest of local segregationists."[59] On the day it revealed the planned purge, the press mentioned four administrators who were to be fired: LeRoy Christophe, the principal of Horace Mann High, and the three top administrators of Central High.[60] The same day, Governor Faubus claimed to know of no such plot but added that he had no objections to the firing of three district employees. He named Jess Matthews, the Central High principal, Elizabeth Huckaby, the vice principal for girls, and J. O. Powell, the vice principal for boys, adding, "They did everything they could to discriminate against white students" during the crisis year.[61] Huckaby kept a running commentary in her diary about the legislature's actions and the feelings among her colleagues. She wrote that "people at school are more cheerful because of the tabling of the school board packing measure and Senator Fagan's stand against it." She added that Jess Matthews had made her laugh at the daily faculty meeting when he asked teachers not to criticize school board members because the teachers wouldn't like it if school board members criticized them. She added, "as if three [school board members] hadn't pushed for him to be fired along with J.O. and me!"[62]

Blossom's replacement, Superintendent Terrell Powell, had announced in February that money was a problem for the LRSD. The district was $139,844.59 short of having enough money to pay its bills that month. Powell blamed the shortage on the state's policy of withholding money from the LRSD to pay other districts where Little Rock high school students had transferred. Powell said that he would pay the bills for that month out of the activity, cafeteria, and bond funds. He hoped to replenish those funds with the next allotment of tax money, but he also noted that he expected ongoing deficits for the remainder of the school year.[63] Segregationists were concerned at the expense of paying 177 teachers and administrators who were in empty schools with no students. The LRSD had already employed cost-cutting measures regarding these teachers, using them, as noted earlier, as substitutes in elementary and junior high schools and replacing vacancies at those levels with high school teachers. Segregationists also considered that if the district fired all teachers from the closed institutions, the federal government's reopening of the public schools would be for naught—or at least further thwarted. As the Tyler bill, tabled in the Senate, was on the minds of the public and the legislators, many discussed its connection to the teacher purge. This brought the executive committee of the Little Rock Parent Teachers Association (PTA) Council to take a stand against the Tyler bill, the group's first official action in the school crisis. The PTA Council represented thirteen thousand members in twenty-six PTAs in Little Rock. However, Mrs. Leon Hoffman, the group's president, was careful to point out two things. First, she said: "We have not commented on integration and are not doing so here. We are just commenting on the ethics of this particular bill."[64] Further, she stated, the comments came from the twelve-member executive committee only—not necessarily from the larger membership.[65]

The General Assembly's regular session was to last sixty days, the planned adjournment of the Sixty-second General Assembly on March 12. Time was short for the governor and his followers to resurrect the Tyler bill from the Senate, but this only increased the pressure Faubus's office exerted on senators. The alternative bill proposed by Max Howell called for increasing LRSD board members to nine, not by appointment of the governor but by special election of the voters. If either of the bills passed, it would need an emergency clause to be put into effect immediately. Normally, legislation passed in a regular session does not immediately go into effect. In 1959, legislation passed in the regular session of the General Assembly would not go into effect until June 12, but an emergency clause could make it effective immediately.[66]

According to existing Arkansas law, a teacher's contract was automatically renewed within ten days after the end of the school term. Only a notice from the school board to the teacher, or vice versa, altered this. The date for automatic renewal for Little Rock teachers in 1959 was June 10. The drama playing out in the General Assembly on the emergency clause, board-packing bills, and the rule on teacher contracts created high emotions in the legislature. On the next to the last day of the session, the House passed the Max Howell version of the board-packing bill (SB421) by a vote of 63 to 24. However, within minutes, it had refused the emergency clause by a vote of 55 to 21. Representative J. H. Cottrell of Pulaski County was instrumental in arguing against the emergency clause, saying: "We don't want our teachers fired like this and scattered to the four winds. We don't deserve that and they don't either."[67] He explained that without the emergency clause, Little Rock teachers would be safe by June 10. The drama intensified as Representative T. E. Tyler, author of the other bill that Faubus had wanted, shouted, "We need the emergency clause." "Vote, vote," called Representatives Talbot Field of Hempstead County and Paul Van Dalsem of Perry County. "We need more yes votes to get the emergency clause passed."[68] On the final day of the legislative session, the Senate took up the bill passed the previous day in the House without the emergency clause. This bill was SB421 (the Max Howell version), which would allow the voters to add three members to the LRSD board. Senator Sam Levine of Pine Bluff filibustered this second bill to its death.[69]

Elizabeth Huckaby wrote in her diary on March 6, when the Howell bill was being discussed, that "no one feels good about it." When Senator Levine filibustered the bills, she recorded that the "purge is halted, at least temporarily." During the days surrounding the legislative session, Huckaby recorded much of the activity within the closed school. A writer named Gowran, from the *Chicago Tribune,* came to visit her at Central High. He had been to Raney High earlier and visited with Sammie Dean Parker, the young white troublemaker who had taunted the Little Rock Nine inside Central. Parker had told the reporter of Huckaby's attempts to "brainwash her" during that period. Huckaby recorded that the reporter was unable to learn of any academic "failures" at Raney High; she was further distressed to record that he predicted a "two system" scenario for Little Rock, one a private tuition-based school system and the other a "downgraded public one." Adding to the teacher's anxiety regarding a purge, Gowran said that he had eaten dinner with school board president Ed McKinley, who had said he did not plan to rehire any high school teachers if he controlled the board. Despite the victory in the Arkansas Senate defeating the board-packing bill, Huckaby recorded that two teachers were emptying their classrooms and carrying things to their cars—"They have finally given up"—while a third teacher said she had turned down a job in Hobbs, New Mexico, because "she couldn't face leaving." Huckaby herself wrote letters to some members of the Arkansas General Assembly, thanking them for their efforts for teachers. At the same time, she was sending requests for letters of reference to people who might be able to help her find some future type of federal employment, should she need it.[70]

Resistance to segregationist legislation in the General Assembly had finally emerged—another small victory for those who opposed Faubus and his legislative followers. By not adding members to the LRSD board, whether by the governor or by the voters, the General Assembly had refused to give the governor all he wanted: the deadlocked three/three split on the LRSD board remained. But such a victory must be viewed in the context of thirty-two measures related to desegregation that were passed within the sixty-day session and sent on to the governor for his signature, including the four Faubus had personally proposed.[71]

Though Little Rock politics were moving at a rapid pace, many youths were far from home as the legislative session ended and Easter approached the very next Sunday. Cathie Remmel (Matthews) and her friend Betty Copeland (Meyer), both scheduled to be seniors at Hall High, had been attending classes at Hendrix College, a liberal arts school about thirty-five miles northwest of Little Rock. They had spent their fall semester in Little Rock taking correspondence courses, tutoring the football team, and working after school hours with a Hall High teacher to prepare for college entrance exams. At semester, they and several other friends had entered Hendrix for the spring semester, but both wanted to go out of state the following year, to schools they had planned on attending before the school closure intervened. They often went home for weekends in Cathie's white Nash Rambler and remember that they were late on the Saturday morning they were to take the SAT—a test they needed to go out of state to college.[72] Later in the semester, after her application to Agnes Scott College in Atlanta was denied, Betty was shocked to learn this was because she had no high school diploma. None of the Hall High seniors of 1958–59 expected to receive such a diploma, so in late spring some of their parents took matters into their own hands, intending to give their children something that Little Rock was denying them. Cathie's and Betty's parents, along with many others, planned a prom at the Marion Hotel and made mock diplomas for those in attendance.[73]

Much farther from home, Dick Gardner, a seventeen-year-old junior at Central High, had joined the U.S. Navy with his parents' permission. His basic training began in October 1958 in San Diego, California, and he recalls that he did get to come home and see his folks for Christmas that year before being sent to Norfolk, Virginia, assigned to the USS *Tidewater,* where he was a metalsmith. By the time the Arkansas legislative session was ending, Gardner was repairing U.S. destroyers that pulled into his port, or he was out on cruises to Canada, Cuba, and the Mediterranean. His mail from home reminded him that his parents kept a large world map on the wall with pins to mark his travels. Gardner finished high school with equivalency courses through the navy: "I was eager to learn everything they would give me, any training I could get."[74]

Paul H. (Pete) Hoover, the son of a Little Rock surgeon who was scheduled to be a junior at Hall High, had stayed in Little Rock during the fall semester and even played football for Coach Ray Peters as a Hall High Warrior. By January, his parents had investigated a residential prep school called McCauley located in Chattanooga, Tennessee. He enrolled there after Christmas with several other Little Rock boys, including his roommate, Otis Hood. He found the school quite academically challenging: "I have come to the realization that was the finest and best decision that my parents made for me. It turned my life around. . . . At McCauley you had to work for everything that you got."[75] Paul remembers that he did get to fly home for a week at Easter that spring. This was about that time that he and his parents decided he would stay on at McCauley to finish his high school degree. He stayed in Tennessee for summer school, completed his senior year at McCauley, and stayed through a second-session summer school, graduating twenty-second out of a class of 112 in August 1960. His schooling at McCauley also influenced his college choice: he remained in Tennessee, attending Vanderbilt University, along with twenty-two McCauley classmates.[76]

Linda Collins (Newsome) made a similar decision about schooling, leaving Little Rock to live with an aunt and uncle in Kansas City. Linda was also a Hall High junior, and her parents wanted her to be in an environment as much like home as possible and be able to attend school. Her mother's sister and husband had no children of their own, but they were close to all their nieces and nephews. They agreed to take Linda into their home so that she could enroll at Shawnee Mission East High School. She was surprised to learn that a classmate from Little Rock, Jim Redheffer, was also enrolled there, though neither had known the other was coming. Linda came home for the Christmas holidays, and her parents visited her often that year. At Easter, her mother came to see Linda and stayed for about ten days. Linda's aunt and uncle had a cabin on Table Rock Lake, and in the spring, the family sometimes gathered there on weekends. Linda believes that it was on such a trip to the cabin that she and her parents decided that she would remain in Kansas City the following year and graduate among her new friends. The schooling situation in Little Rock was uncertain, and they all agreed that finishing high school in Kansas City was the best solution for Linda. She did come home and work for her father during the summer, but she was eager to return to new acquaintances and new experiences in the broader world. She later chose an out-of-state college for two years before finishing her degree at the University of Arkansas. She believes that leaving home at that young age taught her what she could do and led her to a long career with IBM outside the state, all over the country, and with diverse people. Examining the lives of other women her age, she considers having gone away important to her later choices: "I think it changed my life. . . . I think it affected all of our lives, but I don't think it changed everybody's life like it did mine and I did not realize that for many years. . . . I learned something could happen in my life that would just make me take a totally right turn without expecting it and start on a whole new path. . . . I think that comes from making opportunities from bad hands that are dealt to you."[77]

Issues of race and class played into the "right turns" and "opportunities" available to displaced students. Often whites, especially those of means, enjoyed more and better chances. While Paul Hoover was in Tennessee and Linda Collins was in Kansas, Bowman Burns was washing dishes at Frankie's Cafeteria in downtown Little Rock. Also a junior scheduled to attend Horace Mann High, Bowman worked that entire school year, earning money and saving to return to the public schools when they opened: "I worked eight hours, sometimes nine, ten hours a day. I saved my money because my daddy raised me up and told me when I was a kid that out of every dollar you make, save just a dime out of it. So I had that going for me. . . . When school opened, I was able to save my parents money."

P. H. Gilkey, Burns's classmate, did not stay in Little Rock all year. In February, he and several friends went downtown to the marine enlistment office, but it was closed for lunch, so they went into the navy office, next door. After his visit, Gilkey decided he would enlist because the navy promised to help him earn his high school degree, and he had been out of school since September. Any money Gilkey could earn would add to the family income for his mother and younger siblings. His two older brothers were married and out of the home, so he had worked from a young age at the Marion Hotel as a waiter and a busboy. He had worked after school from three to eleven six nights a week, paid $37.50 for each two-week period. He regularly logged forty-eight hours a week, while still maintaining high grades in junior high and tenth grade. He knew he wanted a college degree, and he knew he was capable, known as "the star of the east end" because he was always seen with library books and school books in his arms. The navy would pay him, and he could send some of this money home to his mom; the navy would also get him an education. Among the friends who went with him to the navy office, only Gilkey signed on. It was February 24, 1959, and he flew out of Little Rock on February 25. He had never spent the night away from home, and now he was off to San Diego for basic training. That spring, when the Arkansas legislature ended its session and people in Little Rock celebrated Easter, he was in basic training. Weeks later, he was able to come back to Little Rock and his family before being shipped out for duty. He took an express bus from San Diego to Little Rock, and the trip took three days. When they reached Texarkana, Texas, they changed drivers and buses, but Gilkey was asleep, and no one noticed him. He found himself on an empty bus inside a bus barn. He terrified the guard, who did not believe his story at first, perhaps because he was not wearing his military uniform. Eventually, he got to Little Rock by bus, visiting before spending twenty years and eleven days in the U.S. Navy.[78]

All 3,665 displaced students in Little Rock made life-changing choices when their schools closed—but not all students were offered the same choices.

CHAPTER SIX

Why Not Blame the Teachers?

I was young and new but I was honored to be
in the company of Mrs.Elizabeth Huckaby.
—*Jo Ann Henry (Royster), purged Central High math teacher*

LITTLE ROCK, APRIL 1—MAY 25, 1958

APRIL 1. Arkansas begins enforcement of Arkansas Acts 10 and 115.

APRIL 30. A University of Arkansas dean attacks Act 10.

APRIL 30. Superintendent Powell indicates that 176 certified personnel might not return to the LRSD for the 1959–60 school year.

MAY 5. The LRSD board meets and splits over contracts. Three moderates walk out, and the remaining segregationist board members fire forty-four teachers and administrators.

MAY 5. The WEC is the first group to publicly support the fired teachers.

MAY 6. Little Rock Classroom Teachers calls the firing an illegal action.

MAY 7. Moderates organize STOP to recall the three members of the LRSD board who purged the teachers.

MAY 16. Segregationists organize CROSS to recall the more moderate LRSD board members.

MAY 25. The recall election removes the three extreme segregationist members of the LRSD board.

April was a disheartening month for Little Rock high school teachers, centering on two issues. First, two new state laws targeted public employees, and second, these teachers' professional lives and careers in nationally accredited high schools were uncertain. The Arkansas General Assembly, in its extraordinary session of summer 1958, had passed Act 10, which required that state employees sign affidavits listing all organizational memberships and any organizations to which they made regular contributions. The law affected not only public school teachers but faculty in all state colleges. Arkansas did not begin to enforce this new requirement until April 1959, after the regular legislative session, when the Arkansas General Assembly added yet another attack on civil liberties through Act 115. This second law, which prevented the state employment of any member of the NAACP, was part of Attorney General Bruce Bennett's harassment of that organization.[1] Elizabeth Huckaby's diary mentions that she filed the list required by Act 10 at school on April 9, the same day it describes Faubus's public comments as the "governor thundering as usual." Huckaby had mentioned two days before that black teachers and others were being required to list their organizations and follow other "segregation laws aimed at the NAACP," which she labeled "ridiculous."[2]

Bernice McSwaim, a black teacher at Gibbs Elementary, signed her affidavit on April 13 and listed ten different organizations to which she belonged, including the National Education Association and the Mt. Zion Baptist Sunday School. Under the category for organizations to which she paid dues or to which she regularly contributed, she listed ten organizations, with some overlap from the first list. She added her quiet personal protest in her own handwriting: "The above information is complete and correct relying solely on memory." The document was sworn and notarized by a Mamie Jackson, notary public.[3] Maude Woods, a black teacher from Horace Mann, remembers that black teachers often did not list the NAACP as an organization to which they belonged, but she recalls making contributions to the NAACP that year. "You didn't write a check," she says, but she remembers being asked to boycott certain stores. "You stopped buying and that's how you made your contribution." She gave her money in cash, so there was no record.[4]

Howard Bell, the biology teacher at Central High, spoke of this requirement years later: "I thought that was too much prying into a person's background. That invaded [our] privacy, and it was a background for a new Nazism which had just almost devastated the world in World War 2. Every time I see its head rising on the horizon, I have something to say about privacy and individual freedom to express oneself, or to join organizations."[5]

If public school teachers were annoyed with the requirements of Act 10, some college professors were irate, outraged at being targeted by such legislation. The dean of the College of Arts and Sciences at the University of Arkansas, G. D. Nichols, best expressed the emotion felt by many Arkansas educators: "Perhaps the greatest objection to *Act 10* is the contribution it is making to an atmosphere of fear and insecurity and the consequent threat to academic freedom." He predicted the exodus of faculty from the state.[6] Historian Jeff Woods describes both Act 10 and Act 115 as an expression of the southern connection of segregation to Communism. Studying the "red and black menace" and its ties to southern nationalism, Woods focuses on the civil rights movement through the lens of Cold War fears, citing the American Association of University Professors (AAUP) and the NAACP as the most vocal opponents of these two Arkansas laws.[7] The constitutionality of both of these acts took months—or even longer—to resolve, two Little Rock high school teachers bringing the first lawsuits against both.

Working with the NAACP, B. T. Shelton, a longtime teacher at Dunbar and later Horace Mann, filed suit against Acts 10 and 115 in April 1959, just as teachers were responding to their requirements. Shelton refused to sign Act 10, as did Vice Principal J. O. Powell of Central High, who denounced it as "totalitarian." Powell did list all of his memberships, saying that he had no intention of resigning his position and objecting to the use of the required information as a condition for reemployment for the following year. He said: "The time has arrived in Arkansas as it did under Hitler and Stalin when it is not enough for one to refrain from opposing the policies of the powers that be. It now seems that one is to be required to actively support those policies." Powell joined in the suit with Shelton, which was originally filed in late April by J. R. Booker for the NAACP. After losses in the lower courts, Booker added another plaintiff, T. W. Coggs of the Arkansas Negro Teachers' Association, and appealed the case to a federal district court. Finally, in June 1959, a three-judge federal court upheld Act 10 but overturned Act 115, stating that it violated the Fourteenth Amendment to the U.S. Constitution and set a precedent for lawsuits against similar laws across the South.[8] Arkansas attorney general Bruce Bennett commented that Act 115 had served its purpose so far as he was concerned, because it was designed to harass the NAACP and had accomplished that purpose: "I've cost them a lot of money and membership. I will continue to fight the NAACP in whatever court I can get them into."[9]

In order to end the power of Act 10, the University of Arkansas branch of the AAUP, represented by Little Rock lawyer Edwin Dunaway, brought about a new challenge. Separating it from the issue of race and concentrating on its power to intimidate, Dunaway argued that the law infringed on the academic freedom of teachers. It took until December 1960 for the U.S. Supreme Court to reach a 5-4 decision to overturn the Arkansas affidavit law. Despite the victories in court, however, the personal stories of University of Arkansas professors fired under Act 10 were less encouraging. The university fired four professors for their failure to sign the act, and the national AAUP censured the school when it refused to reinstate them. Censure by such a national rights organization hurt the university's reputation among faculty across the country. Still, each side claimed a victory. Governor Faubus and the segregationists agreed with the university's actions, claiming that "the wrong kind of teachers" had been kept from working in Arkansas. On the other hand, southern moderates eventually won two victories in federal court that gave greater protection to teachers.[10]

Beyond the courts, morale among Little Rock's high school teachers was spiraling downward in April. Their job uncertainty for the following year was one worry. Concerns over the accreditation of new Little Rock private schools, the subsequent loss of tax dollars from the public school district, and worry for their displaced students added to their problems. Beyond these issues, nothing upset teachers as much as the news in April that Little Rock Central High, Hall High, and Horace Mann High had all lost their accreditation from the North Central Association of Secondary Schools and Colleges (NCA). This news surprised the teachers and the administrators when they read of the NCA's annual meeting in Chicago, where the loss of accreditation was announced.[11] Lola Dunnavant, the Central High librarian, mentioned this event in her diary: "Last week, the State Department of Education requested our withdrawal from the North Central Association. This was inevitable—we would either withdraw or be put out for we have not had a single day of school."[12] Huckaby's diary mentions how upset Central High principal Jess Matthews was over the loss of accreditation and over the circumstances. On April 22, Huckaby recorded, "Mr. M. disturbed about the story that the high schools had *asked* to withdraw from the NCA.[13] The following day, she continued: "A very disturbed morning. Near tears over story on withdrawal under peculiar circumstances of LR high schools from NCA. Faubus wants to kill us for the sake of Raney and get us into Southern Association, I think."[14]

In reality, the request to withdraw NCA accreditation from the three high schools had come from the state NCA Committee, which argued that when the schools reopened, they would have a better chance of regaining accreditation[15] The committee had not bothered to inform the public school administrators of its actions in advance. Huckaby continued the following day: "At school, atmosphere not good. No explanation of North Central withdrawal explains not informing [our] superintendent of planned move. Mr. McCuiston succumbed to pressure from the governor, no doubt."[16] Ed McCuiston was the assistant Arkansas education commissioner for instruction and the chair of the Arkansas NCA.[17]

One of the things in which teachers at Central, Hall, and Mann took the greatest pride was their schools' academic programs. Now teachers in all three schools had seen the honor of accreditation stripped from them, and they were disheartened.[18] At Hall High, English teacher Nancy Popperfuss recalls, "That was the thing that scared everyone. Once we lost North Central—there goes your college entrances, you see."[19] The new private schools in Little Rock had been accredited by the Arkansas State Department of Education, not the North Central Association. The NCA was a national group accrediting 3,500 high schools and 401 colleges and universities in a nineteen-state area that included Arkansas.[20] The new state law Act 5 allowed state money to follow students only to an accredited high school, and the state decided that its own accreditation of the newly opened private schools or their coursework would suffice to meet the letter of the law. This accreditation allowed $24.50 per student per month to go to the new school chosen by displaced students.[21]

Worry about their own careers affected both black and white teachers. Lola Dunavant, a veteran librarian from Central High, wrote in her diary as early as February: "Nearly everyone seems to have lost spirit—they just go from day to day. I do hope that I will not have to leave Little Rock next year, but one never knows. If the schools do not open, I will have to get another job. . . . But to go away alone and leave my home and friends— that's hard."[22] Notes in Huckaby's diary provide evidence that several teachers were looking into new teaching options for the following year. On March 2, she recorded, "Helen Conrad was back from guidance meeting in Austin. She made some contacts in Texas." On March 9, Huckaby noted, "Loreen Lee turned down Hobbs, New Mexico job, just couldn't face leaving." On March 24, she wrote, "Al Lape came in. He has decided to risk staying."

At Horace Mann, Leon Adams, the band director, recalls, "we weren't so sure what was going to happen that next year. Some of us began looking for jobs. As a matter of fact, I left the district at that time to attend graduate school at the University of Illinois."[23] The public learned of the impending exodus of teachers from the closed public schools at the end of April, when

Superintendent Terrell Powell reported that 176 teachers planned not to return the following year.[24] Based on the official personnel records of the Little Rock School District, the specific numbers of teachers employed at Central, Hall, and Mann high schools in 1958–59 whose names do not appear in 1959–60 records were thirty-two out of ninety-two at Central, twelve out of forty-three at Hall, and five out of thirty-five at Horace Mann. All these teachers' professional lives were profoundly affected by the Lost Year.[25]

A lower percentage of black high school teachers left the district than white teachers. Maude Woods, a math teacher from Horace Mann who remained in the Little Rock School District until her retirement in the 1990s, said that morale at Horace Mann "wasn't too low. We had each other and there was a lot of support. Everybody just looked forward to the next year." She summarized the morale at Mann by describing the philosophy of an older, well-respected English teacher named Vivian Hegwood: "She talked very softly and distinct. 'We don't have a lot to worry about. We will outlast any school board and we'll outlast any governor. . . . They can't get rid of all of us.'"[26]

■ ■ ■

May 5, 1959, was a day of high emotion in Little Rock, especially for high school teachers. The monthly meeting of the LRSD board promised to deal with the issue of renewing of teachers' contracts; this annual renewal had been on the agenda for the April meeting, but it was delayed because two members were out of town. In addition to this publicly given reason, Superintendent Terrell Powell had purposely pushed the contract meeting back another month because of his unease with a possible teacher purge. He had physically "sabotaged the school district's printing press" to delay the printing of contracts and buy more time for the teachers.[27] As the meeting opened at nine A.M. in the administrative offices of the school district, representatives of several teacher organizations, the Mothers' League, the League of Women Voters of Little Rock, and the Women's Emergency Committee crowded the room. Open to the public, the meeting was being reported on the radio.[28]

Prior to the meeting, Superintendent Terrell Powell had whispered to Everett Tucker, one of the three "moderate" members of the school board, that he planned to resign because the three radical segregationist members of the board had told him they did not plan to renew his contract. Tucker had asked Powell not to resign and promised his own support and that of Russell Matson and Ted Lamb. During the morning session, the moderates moved to rehire Powell, and the board vote was three/three. When they moved to rehire all the personnel recommended by the superintendent, the vote was again three/three. Every vote during the morning session ended in a three/three split before the group adjourned for lunch.[29] Frustrated by the conflict and seeing no immediate solution, the three moderates returned to the meeting and, on advice from lawyers, announced that they were leaving and that as a consequence a quorum no longer existed. They were confident that the remaining three men—Ed McKinley, Robert Laster, and Ben Rowland, the same three who had voted "no" on each issue presented during the morning—could not legally take any further action. At that point, however, McKinley declared the remaining three members a quorum and continued the meeting with the vote on teacher contracts. Observers left to make phone calls to share news of the dramatic events. The radio carried the session live, and Lola Dunnavant's diary tells of teachers at Central High huddled around the radio, listening to the afternoon's events.[30] The session after lunch was punctuated with open and closed sessions of the board as the McKinley faction systematically fired forty-four of the LRSD's best employees, later describing all of them as "integrationists." By 6:17 P.M., the remaining board members had failed to renew contracts for the three top administrators at Central High and the principal of Horace Mann High. In all, they fired five blacks and thirty-nine whites. Of these, twenty-seven were from Central High and seventeen were from ten other schools. In addition, this group included three secretaries, along with the thirty-four classroom teachers and seven principals.[31] At the same meeting, Superintendent Terrell Powell lost his job to Tom. H. Alford, the father of Second District congressman Dale Alford. The elder Alford had once served as the superintendent in Jacksonville, Arkansas.[32]

Shirley Stancil, a counselor at Central High, was in a carpool after school with other young teachers when she heard that three people had met and fired them: "The radio came on and names were given of teachers who were being fired. Later we received a letter signed by the three men who fired us."[33] Jo Ann Henry (Royster), a young math teacher from Central, was also in the car. She says she was honored to be in the purged group: "I was young and new, but I was honored to be in the company of Mrs. Elizabeth Huckaby, and my mentor Mrs. Christine Poindexter, and others." Soon Royster wondered how they had come up with the list of people to be fired: "I wondered about the teachers who were not from Central High."[34]

Stancil believes that two reasons might have landed her on the purge list. "It could have been my state police interview that we had to give in the spring of 1958. I tried not to let them make me say anything that I didn't believe," she recalls. "I felt the interview was an imposition and an inquisition, I didn't like the entire thing, and I couldn't believe they came to my home." Stancil says another reason she might have been fired was that she had failed to sign her contract with the private school group and relinquish her contract with the LRSD when those options were offered early in the Lost Year. "It wasn't hard for other teachers to tell how I felt about integration. During the crisis year, as a counselor, I tried to place the nine black children with faculty that were kind and with people who would support and protect them," she says.[35]

"I probably didn't realize how serious the situation might become during that time," recalls Jo Ann Royster. She realizes with the distance of time that her youth and the fact that she was a "new" teacher might have protected her. Like Huckaby and Stancil, Royster was among the fifteen teachers who had not signed a contract with the private school corporation in September 1958. She recalls: "I was probably purged because I made no secret of being for integration. When the legislature mandated the state police interviews, I made my position clear." Another reason Royster thinks she was labeled an enemy of the segregationists was that she had a student in her class whose parent was a CCC officer, and that student had not earned a very high grade in her class. "I think some of us were singled out for those reasons," she says.[36]

During the LRSD board meeting, some of the observing WEC members called from the building to Adolphine Terry's home to report events to the WEC executive board, which was holding a regular meeting. This group was the first to grant a vote of confidence for the purged teachers. Almost immediately, the Parent Teachers Association of Little Rock followed, with public statements supporting teachers, as did the Arkansas Education Association, the League of Women Voters, and the greater Little Rock Ministerial Alliance. The Little Rock Chamber of Commerce also spoke out against the firings, as did the *Arkansas Gazette* in a May 7 editorial.[37] A few individual members of the WEC also acted the evening after the purge within another organization, the Forest Park Elementary PTA, to help launch what was to become a very public and vocal campaign to save the teachers.

Forest Park Elementary School's principal, Frances Sue Woods, was one of the persons purged. She may have been a target because she was the sister of Irene Samuel, a WEC leader who had done much to organize voters during the year. Another elementary principal, Opal Middleton, was also fired, and teachers in both their schools met to make public statements of support for all who had been purged. On Wednesday evening, May 6, after a telephone campaign by the WEC, four hundred people crowded into Forest Park's auditorium. This group resolved not only to support Mrs. Woods but to begin a recall campaign targeting the three members of the LRSD board who had voted for the purge. Using the recently passed Arkansas Act 9 (intended as a segregationist measure), this group hoped to recall Ed McKinley, Robert Laster, and Ben D. Rowland. Drew Agar, vice president of the school's PTA, presided over the meeting. The following day, Agar appointed a three-woman committee to plan and direct the circulation of recall petitions.[38]

The purging of the teachers was shocking to everyone in the community, but it hit Jess Matthews especially hard. He had led Central High through the Crisis Year and through the Lost Year, and now his own firing and the firings of his employees were too much. Huckaby's diary entry the morning after the purge reads: "A very upset day at school. Jess at rockbottom, whipped. Announced substitutes and then he said he was a failure at leading us.[39] If Matthews was despondent over the school board's actions, then the backlash among the city's voters surely buoyed his spirits. Huckaby noted as much the following day: "Morning paper reported cheering news of public indignation of purge attempt. To our advantage that other than Central High teachers included. Jess feels much better—back at helm."[40]

Segregationists in the legislature had passed Act 9 during the extraordinary summer session of 1958, and they had planned to use it as security against any school board member who was not cooperative with them. Arkansas had no other recall law on the books, and this one applied only to school board members, not any other elected officials. The signatures of 15 percent of the voters were necessary for each recall petition, which would require about sixty-three hundred names of qualified voters in Little Rock. Segregationist plans were now backfiring, as the supporters of the purged teachers thought to use the new law against the segregationists themselves. Two days after the purge, on May 7, as the Little Rock Chamber of Commerce was passing its resolution asking for the reversal of the purge, the LRSD board members who had conducted the purge were defending their actions. Ed McKinley said publicly that he was surprised by the public outcry and called the dismissals an "extraneous academic issue."[41]

Opposition to the purge rose quickly in the community. A cluster of young men met at Brier's Restaurant to form an umbrella organization to further the idea of the recall of the segregationist board members. The group included Edward Lester, Robert Shults, and Maurice Mitchell, all lawyers. An *Arkansas Gazette* reporter named Gene Fretz came up with the acronym STOP for Stop This Outrageous Purge. Soon William S. Mitchell became the spokesperson for the group, and eventually, Henry Woods, a law partner of former governor Sid McMath, acted as its political strategist.[42] On May 7, then, 179 men met at the Union Bank to form the STOP organization and sign the first petitions. The *Arkansas Gazette* published every name on the petition in the morning paper.[43]

The atmosphere in Little Rock was changing rapidly. The meeting of parents and teachers at Forest Park Elementary on Wednesday night was followed by larger crowds at Forest Heights Junior High on Thursday night and Williams Elementary on Friday night. Each group protested the firings of the teachers and administrators.[44] Overflow crowds on Friday night endorsed Everett Tucker Jr., Russell Matson, and Ted Lamb with standing ovations, while they vocally opposed the LRSD board members who had purged the teachers.[45] As early as March, Tucker and Matson had visited with Central High faculty to assure them that they and Lamb would not vote to terminate teachers' contracts. That visit was during the legislative session, when the rumors of a teacher purge were just beginning.[46] Now, on May 9, it was the Central High faculty's turn to endorse Matson, Lamb, and Tucker, and they did so with unanimous resolve.[47]

The segregationists were not silent during these meetings. Amis Guthridge, the lawyer for the Capital Citizens' Council, made a public statement that "communist fronters were in Little Rock helping the Chamber of Commerce and the Women's Emergency Committee to Open Our Schools put on a race-mixing campaign." He said that "rigged communist-like demonstrations" had been held at five PTA meetings the week before.[48] Guthridge promised to "name names" among the purged teachers and "reveal the subversive organizations to which some belong.[49] On May 13, the *Gazette* ran a transcript of proceedings at another meeting of approximately eight hundred at the Pulaski Heights Elementary–Junior High PTA meeting, where the attorney Riddick Riffel, acting as moderator, offered Guthridge twenty minutes to speak against the group's resolution protesting the teacher purge. A court reporter kept a record of all comments during the evening, but Riffel later explained to reporters that while he had "done his best to give him [Guthridge] an opportunity to speak . . . he declined to do so. I don't know why."[50]

Most of the early well-attended meetings in school settings were held in western Little Rock, the newer and wealthier section of the city. Faubus thus labeled the men who formed STOP and the WEC members part of the "silk stocking brigade," again stressing the issue of class division among whites in the city.[51] Historian Irving Spitzberg explains an even finer class distinction when he carefully describes those men who joined STOP as "second rank executives: the vice presidents, junior partners, young ministers, and young professionals" rather than the department store owners, bank presidents, utility executives, and real estate developers.[52] Spitzberg praises the work of William S. Mitchell, a senior lawyer, and B. Finley Vinson, a younger man who was the executive vice president of First National Bank.[53] Historian Elizabeth Jacoway labels Mitchell "one of the most respected men in the city."[54]

STOP worked closely with the networking and telephone skills of the well-organized WEC to pull together a twenty-day campaign that utilized hundreds of tactics. The primary job involved circulating petitions for signatures, which members handled with door-to-door work and drive-up signings at War Memorial Stadium. The STOP volunteers collected more than nine thousand signatures in fewer than seven days, checking each signature against names in the official poll-tax book before they delivered the petitions to the offices of the county clerk.[55] They organized telephone campaigns and letter writing by precinct and voting wards. They prepared advertisements for the newspapers featuring purged teachers' photos and biographical information. Huckaby mentions being contacted by various WEC members and a young news reporter regarding setting up the photos and interviews of some purged teachers.[56] Many STOP advertisements featured telling statistics regarding the forty-four purged school employees, listing 579 years of service to the LRSD and 809.5 total years of teaching experience. Those who did not vote to remove the purgers, the ads said, would be losing the collective experience of highly seasoned and respected teachers.[57] The extremist LRSD board members had finally overstepped their bounds when they chose to attack these longtime teachers and administrators.

Only five black teachers were purged. Two of these were from Horace Mann: Principal LeRoy Christophe and B. T. Shelton. The other three were teachers from Dunbar Junior High. One common trait among the purged black teachers was their longevity of service: they had been in the district, respectively, for twenty-seven, twenty-six, eleven, ten, and fourteen years. Shelton had filed a lawsuit against the district and had been involved in another lawsuit for equal pay for black teachers back in the 1940s, while Christophe was Little Rock's highest-ranking black administrator. When asked why he believed the five black teachers were targeted, Leon Adams, the black band director at Horace Mann, replied in one word: "leadership."[58] William Walker, a black English teacher, mentioned several of the purged teachers by name, describing them as "outspoken activists" who might "stir up the rest of us." Walker continued: "If you can kick the leader in line then you get the rest of them. . . . It didn't surprise me that they came after Principal Christophe because he was our hero.[59]

The fact that most of the fired teachers were white demonstrates the division in the community. The Lost Year and the Central High crisis did not divide blacks from whites because years of de jure segregation had already done that. Only a few vocal and active blacks were targeted and vilified by name in the press, such as Daisy Bates and L. C. Bates, and only a few black teachers were purged. What the crisis and the Lost Year did was divide the white community, splitting the few whites who took a courageous stand for desegregation from the majority white segregationists. Those who were purged were widely perceived to be supporters of integration; with the publication of their names, it was apparent that some teachers had always been among those few leaders, the small but crucial number who could be identified with the cause of desegregation. The firing of the teachers offered the new STOP campaign the opportunity to move away from racial integration to the new issue of fairness to teachers—something many people could embrace. This allowed a blending of new moderates—now willing to accept token integration as the LRSD administration had proposed in 1957—with those few courageous individuals who had worked actively against segregation the previous year.

No teachers from Hall High were purged. Some interviewed teachers suspected that the school board had not finished firing personnel. The three-member board that fired teachers on May 5 had actually recessed its meeting a little after six P.M., scheduling its continuation for the following afternoon at three P.M. This later meeting was then canceled early in the afternoon of May 6.[60] Shirley Stancil, the purged white guidance counselor at Central, says: "One of the stories . . . and I believe it . . . that I heard at the time was that when the purge happened Faubus was out of town. . . . Many of us believe that they had not finished firing everyone. Their intention was to fire enough of us that they couldn't open the schools if they didn't have teachers."[61] Stancil adds that they "took care of first things first with those they really needed to get rid of." Then she explains why she believed that the school board members had finally overstepped. "I heard that Faubus called them and asked, "What are you doing to me? Little Rock will not stand for this."[62] Even the headline of the *Arkansas Gazette* the following day read, "Teacher Purge *Begun* by 3 Board Members," indicating the paper's expectation of a renewed meeting.[63] Whether Faubus knew of the plans of the segregationist board members is in question. The following day, he was quoted as saying: "The School Board impasse is strictly up to the Board. They haven't consulted with me or I with them."[64] After relating a long anecdote about his own early teaching career, when his contract had not been renewed, he said defensively, "You can't say a 'mass firing' when you are talking about 40 or so out of 800 school teachers."[65] Faubus was clearly distancing himself from the events of the previous day and downplaying the purge.

Former students of purged teachers sent letters of support from around the state and nation. One such letter, shared with all the teachers at Central High, was signed by 936 former students, voicing their protest against what they felt was a "malicious and unjustified reprisal of our teachers."[66] A junior STOP group registering one thousand members provided student volunteers for duty with the parent organization. Irene Samuel of the WEC phoned Irving Spitzberg, a displaced student from Hall High, asking him to head the junior workers. Both were from the Jewish community, which turned out to be very active in the campaign. Spitzberg enlisted the help of former classmate and friend Chris Barrier, and together they were able to organize hundreds of students for late-night and after-school work. Spitzberg, though too young to drive alone, had a 1948 Dodge that he used to round up many of the student workers.[67]

The youth helped the adults with various duties, but WEC and STOP members contacted over twenty-three thousand people by phone or in person. One technique credited to WEC organizer Irene Samuel featured making typed cards from the voting records. Those who had supported the WEC in the past were marked as "saints." Those who belonged to the Mothers' League or the CCC were labeled as "sinners." Those who were somewhere between the extreme views were labeled as "savables" and were contacted by phone or in person to solicit their support.[68]

Support for teachers came from various other groups. The American Association of University Women (AAUW) hosted a luncheon on the Saturday before the Monday recall vote. Mrs. Ladd Davies, a spokesperson for the Little Rock Branch, addressed the thirty-one white women teachers in attendance. Photos of the honorees wearing corsages, hats, and white gloves appeared later in *Life Magazine*, and Davies's measured but emotional words were later copied for all those in attendance: "I know that if the adversity that has been yours can bring the people of Little Rock to their senses, can stir them to action, can make them realize that no one else can do for them the job they must do for themselves—then you, too will feel that it has indeed served a purpose. We honor you today in your adversity. We pledge to you not sympathy but action."[69]

Another show of support came at an enormous public rally held on May 19 at Robinson Auditorium, with approximately 350 white teachers attending. The purged teachers were seated on the stage facing the 2,000 in attendance to hear the remarks of the many speakers supporting them and the recall effort. All members of STOP had received invitations, and the WEC telephone chain had also promoted attendance. However, Malcolm Taylor, the president of the CCC, hoped to complicate these plans by giving a statement to newsmen the day before claiming that "many Negroes, including Negro teachers, are planning to attend the integrationist rally. . . . These Negroes will be seated alongside the whites in all parts of the auditorium."[70] Drew Agar, a STOP leader, responded that police would be present to "gently" turn away any Negroes seeking to attend. A local black minister announced that a separate rally for Negroes would be held in a different location the same night as the white gathering.[71] Thus, on the same evening as the STOP rally, the five black purged teachers and principals were honored at the Dunbar Community Center in a rally attended by 75 teachers and 500 others. After two hours of oratory, those in attendance were encouraged to vote in the recall election. Onstage was an enlarged replica ballot with instructions to "Mark your ballot like this," showing attendees that they needed to recall McKinley, Laster, and Rowland.[72]

On May 16, eleven days after the purge and more than a week after the formation of STOP, M. L. Moser, the pastor of Central Missionary Baptist Church, announced the existence of the Committee to Retain Our Segregated Schools (CROSS). Moser said that its purpose was to recall the three moderate members of the school board who had walked out prior to the teacher purge. On May 21, Moser ran an advertisement in the *Arkansas Democrat* stating that the teachers had been fired for "teaching alien doctrine, incompetence, breaking and entering, trespassing on private property, invasion of privacy, punishment, intimidation of students and immorality."[73] The teachers promptly brought a $3,900,000 libel suit against Moser and LRSD board president Ed McKinley. Eugene Warren, an attorney for the Little Rock Classroom Teachers Association, represented the white purged teachers. Each of the teachers asked for $100,000, alleging that he or she had been libeled by Moser's advertisement. The suit said the advertisement "openly and maliciously charged the plaintiffs with immorality, incompetence, want of professional capacity and unprofessional conduct." This advertisement probably strengthened the resolve of purged teachers, as well as their supporters.[74] The five purged black teachers belonged to a different teachers' association and were not parties to this particular suit.

The same day that the advertisement ran, Elizabeth Huckaby managed to deliver her parents' absentee ballots for the recall election. She played a more direct role in the recall campaign than some other teachers did, assisting both the AAUW and the WEC with contact information and materials regarding the purged teachers.[75] Indeed, Huckaby was a whirlwind of activity throughout the twenty-day period between the purge and the recall vote. In those same weeks, she and her brother Bill, on behalf of their aging parents, made a down payment on the house next door to her own. She went by her parents' home on Scott Street almost daily, but after her father's hospitalization in the spring and at the suggestion of her husband, Glen, they decided to move them in next door. In the midst of the purge, in other words, Elizabeth Huckaby was not only going to work every day, helping different groups gather information, joining in lawsuits, and gathering ballots for her parents, but completing legal documents for a home purchase, filling out forms to change her parents' address, cleaning the house next door, and helping her parents pack, while her husband did yeoman's work in the yard and on the structure of the house next door.[76]

LRSD board president Ed McKinley said publicly that he was completely unfamiliar with the *Arkansas Democrat* ad and that he "had nothing to do with the contents," even though Eugene Warren had notified him previously by letter. McKinley added that "the LRSD board was ready to tell any teacher who asked why his contract had not been renewed."[77] B. T. Shelton decided to take him up on the offer. As one of the five purged black teachers, Shelton worked through his attorneys to ask Judge J. Smith Henley permission to see materials pertaining to his dismissal. Because Shelton had brought suit in federal district court just the month before to have Acts 10 and 115 declared unconstitutional, his attorney, Thad Williams, asked to see the minutes of the May 5 school board meeting and the employment recommendations made by Superintendent Terrell Powell. He hoped "to see if the reason for the dismissal was because of *Act 10* or *115*."[78] Judge Henley allowed Williams to see only that portion of the records pertaining to Shelton, but the attorney declined to comment on what he had learned. Williams also attempted to see records regarding the other four black purged teachers—Zerita Tate, Mary Gaines, Roland Smith, and LeRoy Christophe—but Judge Henley denied this request, saying that none of the four were plaintiffs in the lawsuit over Acts 10 and 115.[79]

Author Henry Alexander reports that the segregationist group CROSS had "a founder and chairman, a name, a headquarters, an advertising agency, the support of Faubus and little else."[80] The Mothers' League performed most of the group's work, and its leadership came from the Capital Citizens' Council. Though CROSS began later than STOP, it collected over seven thousand signatures for its petitions to recall the three more moderate members of the LRSD board.[81] Alexander estimates that CROSS expenditures were $10,000 and reports that STOP was more than adequately financed at over $36,000.[82] These funds were raised and spent in fewer than twenty days, between the purge of the teachers and the recall election.

Immediately after the announcement of CROSS's formation, the group quickly arranged its own rally, inviting Wesley A. Swift, the California state director of the Anti-Communist League and the pastor of a well-known church. The rally was planned for May 16, but Swift left Little Rock several days later without speaking. Reverend Moser explained that some CROSS leaders had decided it was "unwise to have an outsider as a speaker," so Moser spoke at the rally, saying "there is no such thing as token integration."[83] Board member Robert Laster also spoke at the rally, predicting that if the schools opened on an integrated basis, it would "make the Civil War look like a picnic."[84] Congressman Dale Alford spoke at another CROSS rally, and Governor Faubus spoke on television on May 22, endorsing CROSS's work and again stressing the issue of class. He said that "prominent and wealthy leaders of Little Rock were attempting to force integration on the Negroes and the honest white people of the middle and lower classes."[85] The moderates of STOP followed the agenda set by the WEC and claimed that their campaign was not about integration but public education and the teacher purge.

The personal relationships among some Central High teachers had been uneasy since early in the school year, when the LRPSC offered contracts. At that time, teachers had learned more about each other's views on race and on whether they were willing to work for a segregationist institution. Now, with the purge, these difficult relationships brought emotions surging to the fore. In the minds of the purged teachers at Central High, the names listed with theirs belonged to like-minded people, those who were moderate to enthusiastic regarding integration—with one exception. Elizabeth Huckaby noticed that at least one teacher from Central High didn't seem to belong. This same teacher, she wrote, had approached segregationist school board president Ed McKinley when he spoke at the recent Bale School dedication, stating that her name had been put on the wrong list.[86] The division among the teachers in the building was now obvious. Among the teachers, those who supported STOP and those who supported CROSS were now less restrained in their remarks to one another. Huckaby recorded just three days after the purge, "Most people have stopped being cautious in what they say."[87]

Within three days of the firings, news emerged that the Arkansas State Police interviews conducted with teachers in the spring of 1958 for the Legislative Council of the Arkansas General Assembly might be the source for the purge list.[88] A news article quoting an unnamed purged Central High teacher gave a possible tie between those interviews and the three members of the LRSD board who had fired the teachers. This teacher quoted a statement made by McKinley—that "certain teachers on the list had said that integration at Central High would have gone better if more Negroes had been enrolled." She said she had made such a statement to the state police investigators the previous year but had not said this to anyone else. She strongly suspected that someone had leaked the interview contents to the segregationists.[89]

A few days before the recall election, Faubus stated that he had never given the Arkansas State Police investigation materials to McKinley, who had quoted statements from the police reports that very week, in both a televised statement and a radio address. Other members of the ALC also denied passing along the information, Chairman Paul Van Dalsem defensively commenting that any member of the ALC could have shared the documents. He also pointed out that Attorney General Bruce Bennett had access to the materials.[90]

On the Sunday before the Tuesday recall vote, three Central High teachers issued a statement to the press entitled "To Set the Record Straight," saying that none of the three had "authorized the use of their names or statements to Mr. Ed McKinley on his TV and radio broadcasts." Emily Penton, the American history teacher who had continued to teach on early-morning television because of public demand, Earnestine Opie, Central's registrar, and Vivian Daniel, another American history and government teacher, made this public disclosure. These three teachers had not been purged. It appears that their words, recorded by the state police in interviews in the spring of 1958, were now being used by and for the segregationist cause. Despite their denial that they had provided permission to use their words, they did not deny what they had said on the record a year before: McKinley had quoted them as saying that "Negro students who had attended Central High School in 1957–58 were not A or B students."[91] After McKinley's public comments, Huckaby was upset with the three: "Before I went to school Adgie Williams called to tell me Miss Opie, Miss Penton and Miss Daniel cited as 'good teachers' by Mr. McKinley because of affidavits about integration. I hated to go to school."[92] On the morning of the vote and the release of Penton's, Opie's, and Daniels's statement, Huckaby wrote of "their tepid disclaimer."[93] Though by the spring of 1959, most faculty members at Central High felt relatively sure of other teachers' feelings regarding race and desegregation, the self-restraint that previously marked their interactions with one another now fell away.

The day of the recall election, May 25, 1959, was an anxious one for Elizabeth Huckaby, who went to work at Central High. In addition to her anxiety over the vote, she was still agitated by the remarks her three colleagues had made in the press. Apparently, Jess Matthews was equally anxious about the vote: Huckaby noted that he had lost his substitute book in his own desk drawer. She waited until the noon hour to cast her ballot, describing her whole day as "restless." That evening, she sat with Glen on their porch, "resolved to listen till the bitter end." The radio station KLRA reported the trend for STOP candidates throughout the evening, but the Huckabys felt that the vote was still "too close for comfort." At twelve-thirty A.M. only two boxes of 4A still had not been reported, and KLRA went off the air: "We went to bed—not too hopeful knowing the 4th ward." The following day, Huckaby wrote: "Glen rushed in with paper, grabbed me, we had won! Everyone at school gay." Many of the female teachers who had been purged, and who had been honored on Saturday by the American Association of University Women, wore their corsages from the event to school that day in celebration.[94]

The vote came less than three weeks after the firing of the public school teachers and administrators. The three moderate members of the LRSD board retained their offices by very slim majorities: Lamb by 431 votes, Matson by 651, and Tucker by 1,224. The losers, McKinley, Laster, and Rowland, were recalled from the board and had to step down. A breakdown by voting district reveals that the STOP victory rested upon support in high-income precincts and predominately black precincts. About 20 percent of all votes polled were cast by residents in high-income white precincts, 53 percent by voters in middle-income white precincts, 10 percent by voters in low-income white precincts, and 17 percent by voters in predominantly black precincts.[95]

Because the results of this election are so significant, an examination of the voting statistics is important. Twenty-four percent of the city's 106,000 citizens were black.[96] A poll tax was necessary for voting in Arkansas at this time, and the number of eligible voters based on those receipts was 35,620 whites and 6,273 blacks. The count of votes was complicated, since the ballot allowed voting either "for removal" or "against removal" of each of the six board members. Thus, each board member could receive a different tally for his removal or for his retention. Of the eligible 41,893 voters, 60 percent —or 25,457 people—cast a ballot in at least one category. This figure in the May recall election allows comparison to the voting numbers in September 1958, when 27,031 people had gone to the polls to support or deny "complete integration" of all Little Rock schools. Only this time, their vote recalled the extreme segregationists who had been endorsed by Governor Orval Faubus.[97] Even before the June 18, 1959, ruling of the U.S. District Court, denying the constitutionality of Arkansas's school-closing law and its funds-withholding law, the people of Little Rock voted for public education, knowing full well that public schools would include some degree of racial integration.[98]

This vote meant many things. First of all, a politically charged period that had shaken the very foundations of many young lives was coming to an end. It meant that the voters of Little Rock—25,457 of them—were vitally interested in their public schools. Further, the vote demonstrated that the majority of Little Rock voters—when their children lost their right to a free public education and when their respected teachers, both black and white, lost their jobs and their fundamental civil liberties—were willing to act. This public stand proved that Little Rock voters could be guided by intrinsic values rather than court orders. Many in Little Rock now dared to hope the vote also meant that the majority of citizens wanted public schools open with the condition of limited racial integration.

The coalition of white and black Little Rock voters that won a victory for the STOP forces on May 25, 1959, had existed since Orval Faubus's first run for the Democratic nomination for governor in 1954, against Francis Cherry. Neither their numbers nor their influence had been great enough to defeat Faubus's racial policies in statewide elections, but they had grown in number, rallying for open schools and some degree of desegregation in Little Rock in 1959.

CHAPTER SEVEN

The Community Rallies— Some Leaders Do Not

There was no one outcome for everyone in Little Rock.
—Sybil Jordan (Hampton), Central High student

LITTLE ROCK, MAY 25—SEPTEMBER 15, 1959

MAY 25. STOP wins the LRSD board recall election.

JUNE 11. The Pulaski County Board of Education appoints three new LRSD board members.

JUNE 18. Federal district court rules Arkansas Acts 4 and 5 unconstitutional.

JULY 10. Baptist High graduates twenty-eight seniors and announces a change in its status.

JULY 20. Trinity Interim Academy announces inactive status.

JULY 21. The LRSD board plans to use Act 461 (1959), Arkansas's second pupil-placement law, for high school students.

JULY 21–24. Registration of Little Rock high school students begins—earlier than normal.

JULY 25. Registration at Raney High reaches 1,226 students.

AUGUST 4. The LRSD board announces that high schools will open early, on August 12. The same day, T. J. Raney announces that Raney High will not reopen for a second year.

AUGUST 12. All four public high schools open; Hall and Central are desegregated on a token basis.

AUGUST 12. Segregationists march from the State Capitol to Central High but are turned away by local police and fire hoses.

LABOR DAY. Segregationists bomb the LRSD board meeting room and do other damage to public property.

SEPTEMBER 15. The LRSD board selects three additional black students to enter Central High after appeals using the pupil-placement acts. (Act 461 passed in the 1959 regular session.)

It would take a little time for Little Rock to understand what had happened on May 25, 1959. The words of Will Mitchell, the STOP campaign chairman, resonated with a slight majority of the population. At an eleven P.M. rally at the Marion Hotel on the night of the vote, he stated: "This is a great awakening of our home town. This is an occasion when the people of our home town have risen up and taken our own affairs into our own hands. I've never seen such a wonderful demonstration of community spirit."[1] From that night until the present, differing interpretations of the recall vote have been forwarded. One WEC leader labeled her organization's work and STOP's grassroots victory as "educat[ing]" the citizens that the racist leadership of a governor and his fellow segregationists "was leading the city down a dark alley of hate and fear. By refusing to follow, Little Rock had killed its dragon and reclaimed it conscience and dignity." A more recent historian's version quotes Everett Tucker as saying that he "did not think the community had suddenly decided to be in favor of integration." No matter which interpretation one chooses, however, the vote cannot be interpreted as a win for Orval Faubus or for the segregationists he had endorsed.[2]

Governor Faubus made no statement the day after the election. He was reported to be fishing near Stuttgart but promised to make himself available at the capitol to reporters on May 27.[3] On that day, he called a press conference and was photographed smiling jovially as he said that he perceived no shift in the community's sentiment regarding the basic segregation-integration issue. Instead, he clung to the idea that "the only election squarely to the point came last September when Little Rock voters by 3 to 1 opposed total school integration." But he had carefully crafted that vote around his promise of private segregated education in public school buildings and with public school teachers—a promise he could not keep when the courts acted on September 29, 1958, with restraining orders. On May 27, he continued by saying that there was no clear-cut issue in the recent recall election, which was being "heralded as a victory by those who favor integration." Despite the fact that he had publicly supported the three recalled members of the LRSD board, at the end of the press conference he admitted that "quite likely some mistakes were made. . . . It [the teacher purge] was used as an emotional issue."[4] The popular governor was not about to embrace defeat and could be counted on to interpret events in his own way.

The Pulaski County Board of Education, a group that in the past had held only the routine duty of allotting money to school districts, faced a new public responsibility. Prior to the special session of the Arkansas General Assembly in summer 1958, the county judge held the authority to fill vacancies on local school boards, but now this was the responsibility of the little-known Pulaski County Board of Education. The five elected board members held the power of appointment, despite the fact that only one lived in the city of Little Rock and two were known supporters of Governor Faubus. The WEC leadership attempted to pass along the suggested names "of citizens who would support the schools," according to WEC leader Vivion Brewer's memoir.[5] Sixteen days after the May 25 recall vote, this board met on the fourth floor of the county courthouse and announced the new members of the LRSD board: J. H. Cottrell, a state representative; B. Frank Mackey, a retired Little Rock detective then employed by Pyramid Life Insurance Company; and H. L. Hubbard, a building contractor. When reporters asked county board chair J. B Morgan of Wrightsville what had guided the board members in their choices, he said they had chosen "people who were capable of serving, who were not radicals and who were substantial citizens of Little Rock."[6] Huckaby's diary of the same day reflects her belief that the teacher purge would now be reversed: "P.M. papers give three new school board members. One or two good ones to add to the three already there. We are safe."[7]

Four days after his appointment, H. L. Hubbard resigned, saying he realized that he was ineligible to serve. Though he did not say why, the *Arkansas Gazette* printed that he had been convicted of a felony in 1938, which deprived him of his vote. This news contradicted Morgan's description of the new appointees as "substantial citizens of Little Rock." Hubbard was later replaced by W. C. McDonald, the manager of Western Paper Company, who pleased the WEC with his first public statement: "I believe in public education and I believe our schools should be opened in spite of our feelings about integration and segregation."[8] The day of Hubbard's resignation, June 15, the remaining five members of the new LRSD board met for the first time as a group and elected Everett Tucker as president, Russell Matson as vice president, and Ted Lamb as secretary. All three officers were the LRSD board members who had successfully weathered the recall vote.[9] At this same meeting, they rehired Terrell Powell as superintendent, replacing T. H. Alford. The reshaped LRSD board voted to expunge from the record the purge of forty-four teachers and all actions of the rump LRSD board meeting on May 5, when the purge had occurred. Then it voted unanimously to rehire thirty-nine of the forty-four purged teachers. Five of the forty-four had refused to comply with Act 10, which required them to list their organizations and donations. The board gave these five, and one other who was not on the purge list, until June 25, 1959, to submit an affidavit.[10] Only one of the six people who refused to sign Act 10 and whose contract was not renewed by the LRSD agreed to sign—Ernest Gephardt, the industrial education teacher at Central High.[11] Several of the black teachers would soon leave the state, some following Principal LeRoy Christophe to Wilmington, Delaware, where he became principal at Howard High School.[12] The vice principal of Central High, J. O. Powell, refused to sign Act 10; left the state with his WEC member wife, Velma; and in later years wrote a manuscript that was highly critical of Little Rock school administrators.[13] Using official personnel directories of the LRSD system for 1958–59 and comparing those to the 1959–60 records reveals an enormous loss of teachers who did not return to Little Rock's senior high schools. From Central High, thirty-two out of ninety-two did not return. From Hall High, twelve out of forty-three did not return, and from Horace Mann High, five out of thirty-five did not return the year high schools reopened. These numbers easily add another important category when the many losses from the Lost Year are assessed.[14]

In the eyes of most Little Rock high school teachers, June 18, 1959, turned out to be a doubly good day. First, they received their fall teaching contracts. Elizabeth Huckaby writes that hers arrived by mail that day and that she signed it and sent her husband to the post office to return it immediately.[15] Second, on the same day, a three-judge federal district court overruled the Arkansas Supreme Court and declared the Arkansas school-closing law and funds-withholding law unconstitutional. Arkansas Acts 4 and 5 were thus no longer valid, and the court ordered the new LRSD board to proceed with its original desegregation plan.[16] Finally, the federal courts were ruling on the legality of the state laws created by Faubus and the segregationists in the summer of 1958. Without a doubt, these rulings reinforced the board and the moderates in the community. However, without the recent recall election, with its demonstration of the public attitude within the Little Rock community, these two rulings would be only that—another federal mandate that might be at least temporarily delayed, just as the Supreme Court ruling of September 12, 1958, had been ignored for a time. Before May 25, 1959, the leadership and voters of Little Rock had not yet embraced both open schools and some degree of racial integration in public schools. The new state laws passed in the summer of 1958 had served to keep schools closed and delay desegregation. Faubus and the segregationists had placed state laws between the school board and the federal courts—the historically refuted idea of interposition. For a time, the earlier LRSD board was frustrated by these laws, Little Rock voters responding in September 1958, when they believed that Faubus could deliver private segregated schools open for everyone. Even more significant now, in the summer of 1959, was that the community had found a new voice—and they were embracing what Irving Spitzberg calls a new, undivided leadership on the school board, with the emergence of new leaders in the community.[17] Elizabeth Jacoway states that at that time "a consensus began to emerge among Little Rock's social and business leadership."[18]

On June 25, the new LRSD board announced that it would open all four secondary schools by the fall of 1959. Historian Ben Johnson proposes that this new LRSD board and the new business establishment had found a way of appeasing the many sides of divided Little Rock—namely, by opening the schools but legally keeping any meaningful degree of desegregation at bay. This use of the state's pupil-placement law would become more public in early June.[19]

Though it was apparent from the announcement that the board intended to open the high schools, there was no assurance that the extreme segregationists and the governor would not again use state powers or violence to interfere. Faubus actually announced his intention to appeal the federal court's ruling on Acts 4 and 5 to the U.S. Supreme Court.[20] Evidence of the uncertainty in the community is also clear in the decisions being made by the various private academies that were finishing out their late school year. Writer Roy Reed describes the new LRSD board members at this point as "far less confident than they sounded in public," noting that they privately worried that reopening schools would bring violence.[21]

As the adults of Little Rock moved forward under the new elite consensus or continued to cling to the Faubus strategy, Elizabeth Huckaby wrote letters of thanks to organizations that had supported teachers, telling the WEC that although the STOP campaign had enjoyed major credit, their efforts would not have been successful without the WEC having worked for so many months, "defending the schools, educating the public, and assembling the workers who were so effective in STOP."[22]

At the same time, displaced high school students from around the state and nation were coming home for the summer. Almeta Lanum (Smith) and her sister had been able to ride to Pine Bluff, a city fifty miles south of Little Rock, with a classmate whose father commuted to work there. All three girls were able to enroll at St. Peter's Catholic School, a black Catholic facility that served a small community in Pine Bluff. Almeta was a junior, her sister a sophomore. The school was small and not well balanced. Almeta recalls that she was one of only six juniors, while the school had twenty-five seniors. School officials thus combined the two groups into one class of thirty-one, and the juniors had to take twelfth-grade history and English. Almeta was a good student and did well in her studies. She came home daily and worked at the Ivory Branch Library in the evenings. When the summer of 1959 came, she was glad to be back in Little Rock, wondering how she would make up her junior classes as a senior when Horace Mann opened in the fall.[23]

Mary Dennis (Ragston), a Horace Mann senior, had spent her year in North Little Rock at Scipio Jones High School. Her mother had originally planned to send her to Chicago to live with older relatives and attend Wendell Phillips High School. Several of her closest girlfriends had, in fact, gone to Chicago. Ragston's mother had at one time been the school librarian at Jones High before transferring to Horace Mann High when it opened, becoming the first librarian at the new black high school. Mary's mother had called upon the principal at Jones High, hoping to enroll Mary there rather than send her off to Chicago. She arranged for Mary to live with the Dokes family, who were personal friends, during the week and spend the weekends at home. The Dokeses had many children in school in North Little Rock, and Mary walked to high school with them. She still calls them her sisters and brothers, and they remain close friends. Mary remembers that two other former Horace Mann students managed to get into Jones High, one a fellow senior and the other, her cousin, a junior—a small number of transfers since the North Little Rock system demanded a home address within the city for any student to transfer that year. The irony was that Mary's mother, as a faculty member of Horace Mann, reported for work every day at the closed high school from which Mary had always thought she would graduate. Instead, her high school diploma reads "Scipio Jones High."[24]

Local private school seniors were graduating from the varied educational facilities they had attended across the city. On May 29, Raney students held a prom at the Marion Hotel, where Johnny Roberts and the Rebels, a band of young musicians, performed their favorite dance tunes. Bob Lawrence remembers that after the prom, he and his friends drove through Snappy's, a favorite fast-food hangout at Sixth and Broadway. His aunt, an obstetrical nurse, had borrowed her boss's Porsche for Bob to drive, and he remembers driving everywhere he could that night so all his friends could see him.[25]

The 190-member Raney senior class graduated at Robinson Auditorium on June 26, wearing burgundy gowns with gray collars and gray tassels on their mortarboards. Their diploma covers held the insignia of a rebel Confederate hat with crossed swords, students required to pay $3.50 for the gowns and $1.75 for the covers.[26] Governor Faubus, the commencement speaker, addressed the graduates' historic role—telling them that the name of their school might become as significant as "Valley Forge," "Gettysburg," or "Omaha Beach."[27] Philip Moore, a graduating senior from T. J. Raney High, remembers the graduation ceremony and notes that afterward he and his friends celebrated at several local spots in town before a late-night breakfast and early-morning games at a bowling alley on Asher Avenue.[28] David Scruggs also graduated from Raney High that night and remembers the ceremony vividly because his parents found Governor Faubus's speech "quite appalling. They thought he had made a political speech rather than one that celebrated us as young graduates or one that spoke of our future."[29]

Soon after graduation, Raney High announced that its administrators planned to open again in the fall but would be charging tuition of fifteen dollars a month per student, something that had not been required of the 827 students from 1958–59. That year, Raney High had received about $72,000 in state aid, in accordance with Arkansas Act 5, before federal courts stopped the payments. Additionally, donations from supporters of private segregated education from across the nation made up part of the private school's budget.[30]

On July 10, Baptist High graduated a class of twenty-eight after the school solved its financial difficulties with a contribution of $6,000 from the Little Rock Private School Corporation. This money—part of the funds donated to the founders of Raney High—was shared with Baptist High on May 7 to help that school meet financial obligations lingering from its original capital outlay for equipment and its somewhat generous number of scholarship students. T. J. Raney said that passing the money along was his idea and that the Raney board agreed because "we felt a responsibility for those kids."[31] After graduation ceremonies, Baptist High announced that it would no longer operate on a temporary basis and would become a permanent Christian academy if demand existed the following school year. Its plan to charge $250 per year for tuition, with a minimum of seventy-five students to be registered by July 22, failed. Only twenty-two students had signed up by that date, and the school returned their money and stored its desks and equipment.[32] Trinity Interim Academy did not hold a graduation ceremony because at midterm it had advised all enrolled seniors to transfer to accredited schools in order to insure their admission to college the next year. This left twenty juniors and sophomores to finish the year at Trinity. On June 18, 1959, Mrs. James B. Gates, the school's director, announced that Trinity would not open for a second year unless public schools were again closed.[33]

The Central Baptist Academy had an enrollment of thirty-six Little Rock students by spring and graduated a class of twelve in June. At that time, the school's president, Reverend A. R. Reddin, said that plans for a second year of operation were indefinite. Another year of operations would depend on need, as well as what the sponsoring organization and the churches wished to do.[34] The Anthony School had operated for sophomores and juniors only—just as Trinity Academy had—so there was no need for a graduation ceremony. Like Raney, the Anthony School planned a second term. Because the Anthony School had operated for fourteen years as a kindergarten with some elementary grades, Mr. and Mrs. Allen Anthony announced on August 16 that they planned to offer both a senior year and the two lower high school grades, beginning on September 15, 1959.[35]

Events in late June began to point to a split among the victors of the May 25 recall election. This split, which would separate the liberal WEC leadership and the NAACP from the new elite business leaders and the new LRSD board, became public soon after the June 18 federal court announcement on the unconstitutionality of Arkansas Acts 4 and 5. Within days of that public decree, the LRSD board announced registration plans for all high school students later that month, using the new Arkansas Act 461, the more recent of two Arkansas statutes calling for a pupil-assignment screening system. In preparation, board president Everett Tucker, Superintendent Terrell Powell, and the attorney Herschel Friday went to Charlotte, North Carolina, and Norfolk, Virginia, to observe their use of pupil-assignment laws.[36] Although WEC leaders, by virtue of their intense work to open the closed high schools throughout the 1958–59 school year, had been given what Sara Murphy calls "a seat at the table" with the new business leadership when the post-STOP campaign held debriefing meetings in July, they soon learned that the "seat at the table proved to be a not altogether comfortable one," the male leadership criticizing some of the women's plans to be proactive in the fall opening of schools.[37] The liberal leadership of the WEC desired more integration and strategies to promote biracial cooperation, something that both the new group of businessmen leaders and the LRSD board ignored.[38] When the president of the LRSD board, Everett Tucker, returned from the "fact-finding" mission to other southern states, he announced that he had "greater confidence" in the pupil-placement laws, since the team had met with leaders in other states who had successfully implemented similar methods. As a matter of fact, the new Arkansas Act 461 was modeled almost word for word on a similar Alabama document.[39] Some white attorneys viewed pupil-placement laws as a way to achieve "voluntary segregation," because white students were allowed to choose white schools, and black students black schools, with the law spelling out procedural appeals for assigning those students who chose to cross the color line. Another aspect of the assignment law worked against the black students. Unlike previous arrangements, this new law did not lend itself to "class-action lawsuits," meaning that an individual student who wished to appeal his status and was denied would have to sue for himself alone, rather than for all persons in the same situation. Prior to this, students had been able to file class-action suits.[40] The May 9, 1958, federal ruling by the Northern District of Alabama's three-judge panel in the case of *Shuttlesworth v. Birmingham Board of Education* affirmed that school district's use of pupil placement, and the November 24, 1958, affirmation of the U.S. Supreme Court encouraged the LRSD board in its plans to move forward with the legal yet most drastically limited degree of desegregation.

Some additional statements of the newly constituted board clearly reflect segregationist thinking. Though moving forward with opening the schools with some degree of racial desegregation, board members soon made a collective statement addressed to Governor Orval Faubus. They said that each member of the board "personally prefers segregation but if no choice is offered, we will not abandon free public education in order to avoid desegregation." They were not fans of integration, but they opposed closing the public schools again, and they did not wish to be found in contempt of federal court.[41]

In July, Governor Faubus released his own new plan for integration of Little Rock schools in what he claimed was a response to the LRSD board. His bizarre plan included voluntary segregation in two high schools and voluntary integration in two others. He added that the integrated schools would be segregated by gender so that either Hall High or Mann High would be for females and the other school for males. Central High and Little Rock Tech would be segregated and coeducational. The LRSD board said it would take his suggestion under advisement but doubted that the courts would approve it and also stated that Faubus's suggested degree of integration was more than they had planned on, hinting at just how limited their own plan might be.[42]

On July 31, the new LRSD board not only returned to the status quo of 1957 but stepped back even further, undercutting the number of black students it would admit to previously white high schools. WEC member Sara Murphy declared that the new board "proved not to be much better than the deposed members" removed by the May recall vote.[43] During high school registration, sixty black students applied for admission to white high schools, including one at Little Rock Tech, five at Hall High, and forty-nine at Central High. The board at first limited the number accepted to three at Central and three at Hall, using the pupil-assignment law. Murphy reported that the WEC found it "unbelievable that the board they had worked so hard to elect would go backward instead of forward.[44] This early proposal that six black students be admitted into two high schools would be three fewer than the nine admitted in 1957. The board officially enrolled three black girls at Hall High for 1959–60, one in each grade, after redrawing the boundary lines to include about twenty-five black families within that zone. These three girls—Effie Jones, Elsie Robinson, and Estella Thompson—all lived within the redrawn boundaries of Hall High, a formerly all-white high school. Their assignment to Hall High was undoubtedly in response to criticism of the old Blossom Plan for not integrating the wealthier "silk-stocking" districts of western Little Rock, coming after several letters to the editor in local newspapers suggested plans to take desegregation beyond Central High.[45] Of the fifty-four black students denied admission, nineteen filed protests, while eighteen decided to stay out of school until they were admitted to either Hall or Central High.

What the LRSD board did next can be well described as purposeful evasion, if not subterfuge: it denied admission to two former members of the Little Rock Nine, Thelma Mothershed and Melba Patillo. Russell Matson later shared the board's reasons for these two denials: "Mothershed had a heart problem, and Mann was a one story building while Central has five floors." The board now suggested that it was choosing to look after the health interests of young Thelma, despite the fact that Mothershed had attended Central in 1957, at the high point of racial turbulence, with this same heart condition. Regarding Patillo, Matson said that "while not a trouble-maker herself, she seemed to attract trouble and the board thought it better to return her to Horace Mann."[46] The actual pupil-placement law allowed the board to use any or all of sixteen criteria for the assignment of a student to a particular school, but race was supposedly not one of these. Instead, criteria such as "scholastic aptitude, mental energy, psychological qualifications, morals, conduct, health, and personal standards" were included in the new law.[47] Students unhappy with their placement would have the opportunity to appeal.[48]

There was no mention in the press regarding the board action on Mothershed or Patillo. In her memoir, *White Is a State of Mind,* Patillo does not mention the pupil-assignment laws or any interaction she had with the LRSD board. She mentions only that she did not attend school anywhere during the Lost Year because she believed that attending elsewhere would remove her from the court case. The following year, she went to Santa Rosa, California, to live with the McCabes, a white Quaker family, attending one semester at Montgomery High School and entering San Francisco State College in spring 1960, where she eventually earned her bachelor's degree.[49] Mothershed attended summer school in St. Louis and earned enough credits to receive her diploma by mail from Central High. She went on to attend Southern Illinois University in Carbondale.[50]

Of the remaining Little Rock Nine, the LRSD board admitted only three to Central High for the 1959–60 school year. Carlotta Walls and Jefferson Thomas attended Central, but Elizabeth Eckford learned that she had enough credits from correspondence courses to graduate and did not need that year's work.[51] At this point, the NAACP, which had not spoken out against pupil placement, now sought a restraining order to prohibit the school board from using Arkansas Act 461. Lawyers Wiley Branton and Thurgood Marshall viewed the law as a scheme allowing the state to avoid giving black students their constitutional right to education, granted by the Supreme Court, and asked that students be assigned only on the basis of attendance zones. Black leaders strongly objected to the screening techniques applied to black students, but not to white students. The LRSD board asked Judge Miller to dismiss the case as premature, since the black students had not asked for the administrative remedies that the law provided.[52] Only after the opening of the high schools and well into September would the board honor the requested transfers, with individual hearings and with disappointing results for applying black students.

With the announcement of the early opening of the high schools, Elizabeth Huckaby, as a top Central High administrator, was required to appear at the LRSD administration office at nine A.M. on Monday, July 20. There she met with Superintendent Terrell Powell, board president Everett Tucker, and attorney Herschel Friday. Her frustration with these leaders is evident in her journal as she follows "Mr. Friday "with the question, "Whose side is he on?" She had reason to be annoyed, as much from her personal life as from their decisions to limit desegregation. Her father had begun to have medical problems in late June and was hospitalized from June 26 to July 8. This only added to the many responsibilities that Huckaby had assumed, including tending to her invalid mother next door and spending nights in an aluminum lawn chair at her father's side. Even when her sister Clara arrived from New York to help, Huckaby still had to cook meals for everyone and transport her sister to and from their health care duties. She had not had a restful summer vacation when she returned to her school duties.[53] Her first mention of the consequences of using the pupil-placement restrictions does not appear in her journal until July 30: "Mr. M. stated at noon that *after all,* if the five Negroes formerly attending Central were assigned to us, we would have our quota. He stated that all white students would be assigned to their respective districts and would have to apply for transfer."[54]

The first official day of registration was Tuesday, July 21, Huckaby reporting that "only 166 pupils" registered. Though Mr. Matthews and the new vice principal for boys, Delmar Hart, were pallbearers for a funeral that morning, she felt that she had "plenty of backing": "police cars outside, a plainclothes man inside and Gene Smith [the police chief] was there a good while, especially from 11:30–11:45 when photographers and reporters were admitted." Probably worrying about safety, she mentions the parents of former Little Rock Nine students: "We got Mr. Eckford, and Mr. Mothershed out before they [the press] came." She also mentions Mrs. Patillo and Mrs. Thomas coming in the afternoon. She makes no mention of any of these former Little Rock Nine students being there with their parents.[55]

On July 25, Raney High began registering students with plans to continue their enrollment through Monday, August 3. By that date, 1,226 students had signed up at the private white high school. But the next day, August 4, the LRSD board surprised the city, the students, and parents with its announcement that the public high schools would open early, on August 12, well before the traditional opening date assigned for the lower grades. Publicly, the board stated that the earlier date, with nineteen extra class days, was needed for "orientation" because the schools had been closed for a year. However, LRSD board member Ted Lamb later confirmed that their motive was to foil the governor if he tried to call a special session of the legislature, as he had on August 26, 1958.[56] The same day as the public school announcement, T. J. Raney shocked the city with news that Raney High would not reopen for a second year. Though the school had operated for a year with no obvious financial difficulties, had purchased property, and had engaged in a building program, the reason given for closing was a "lack of funds." The news came as a surprise to students, school supporters, staff, and even the roofers working on the new addition to the facilities at Sixteenth and Lewis streets.[57]

Unknown to most was the fact that the LRSD board had voted to approach Governor Faubus with a proposed merger of Raney High with the public school system. The majority of the board feared that the large white enrollment at Raney would hurt the public school system. This plan had been proposed by insurance executive Herbert Thomas as a solution he felt would satisfy the most people by keeping Raney High as a segregated facility. The LRSD board drafted a letter to be delivered by J. H. Cottrell, who, as a member of the legislature, was close enough to the governor to start some quiet negotiations. At the capitol, Cottrell heard about Raney's closing, and he turned around, never delivering the proposal.[58] WEC leader Vivion Brewer describes this as a "comedy" that only narrowly escaped the label of "tragedy."[59] This was a close call: had the plan been carried out, the entire landscape of public education in Little Rock would undoubtedly have been quite different. This plan further demonstrates that five of the six LRSD board members (Ted Lamb voted no) were willing to squander the victory of May 25, in a fashion far more to the liking of Orval Faubus and the segregationists than to the more liberal leaders of the WEC. At this point, Vivion Brewer wrote, "We took another look at the School Board."[60]

Elizabeth Huckaby canceled her dental appointment for the morning of August 5, "since I knew the rush would be on. Jess not there." She called the administration office, asking for help, and Central High ended up turning away a few students in the morning and fifty-six in the afternoon since they were shorthanded for registration duties. The new plan for registration included giving identification cards to all registered students, as well as filling out extended forms for each student. On Friday, August 7, she described a very busy day, demonstrating her frustration with "the flood of students" who poured in, including fifty-five in one hour. She reported that "many were bitter because of not being able to go to Raney" and because they had to sign the pupil-placement waivers. She adds, "I couldn't help mentioning that sending white kids to Horace Mann had been suggested only by Faubus and that Pupil Placement was sponsored by him." In Huckaby's mind, there was no question that the new LRSD board was willing to use legislation endorsed by Faubus during the regular session of the Arkansas General Assembly in early 1959. Despite her concerns, she was pleased when teachers from Hall High and Central High were called to hear Everett Tucker read a firm statement about discipline on the morning of August 10. That same day, she worked on a committee at Central High, planning "2½ hours of orientation through the homerooms for students on Wednesday, Thursday, Friday." They also planned a student handbook study and a test over the material each afternoon and an assembly of all students on Friday. Students arrived at noon every day that first week, the count on the first day 74 percent of those registered. Most students, she observed, seemed "eager to get going," and despite the fact that she had to twist Jess Matthews's arm to hold the Friday-afternoon assembly, she happily reported "no disturbances of any nature," declaring that the assembly had "worked perfectly." Again, however, her frustrations show: "Jess's only comment, 'It was too stiff.'" Still, she added, "Well we can break the ice later but we can't stiffen after thawing—and we need it stiff now."[61] She did not want a repeat of the 1957–58 disciplinary problems with some white students.

Though the moderate winners of the recall election were now divided, the Capital Citizens Council and the segregationists continued their opposition to any sort of desegregation, no matter how minimal. Their lawyer, Amis Guthridge, spoke of the six black students who had been accepted into the white schools: "If six Negroes can force their entrance unnecessarily into two white high schools, then 600 have the same right."[62] Another ploy of the segregationists came just days before the early opening of the high schools, when Malcolm Taylor, an osteopath and a CCC leader, protested the early opening of schools in the summer heat, saying that it would unnecessarily expose Little Rock youth to a polio outbreak.[63] The LRSD board had solicited affirmative statements from thirty-five local doctors, saying that "opening schools now would not create an additional danger of polio."[64] When the LRSD board met to discuss this health issue, Ted Lamb, the board member most enthusiastic in his support of school integration, read a telegram from Jonas Salk, the discoverer of the famed polio vaccine, which stated that "the early opening was not likely to increase the risk of polio and that advanced students of epidemic diseases had long abandoned the use of isolation, quarantine, or closing of public places for control of polio epidemics."[65] In his personal memoirs, Lamb said that Salk had told him on the phone that opening schools early "wouldn't have a damn thing to do with it" and that the "only way to keep those kids from coming down with polio was to shoot their butts full of my vaccine."[66]

All four high schools opened as planned on August 12, but not without attempts by some segregationists to thwart the day. The night before, Faubus spoke on television, attacking the LRSD board but also opposing violence. The morning of the school opening, approximately 1,000 screaming segregationists rallied at the state capitol building with signs, flags, and anti-integration placards to listen to segregationist speeches by Governor Faubus and others. After the rally, a man pointed in the direction of Central High and encouraged the group to march to the school for a "peaceful assembly."[67] Approximately 250 "belligerent demonstrators" walked or drove behind four men carrying American and Confederate flags. Little Rock police met the marchers a block from Central High and told them to disperse. When the crowd turned into an unruly mob, firemen used high-pressure hoses on them, and police arrested twenty-four people.[68]

At Hall High, there was no violence or threat. City authorities were better prepared and more willing to stop the mob than they had been two years before. Vivion Brewer reported that "everyone: WEC, parents, sympathizers, feared renewed violence." Many, she noted, hoped for the involvement of the U.S. marshals, but neither the school board nor the city directors made any move to ask for their help.[69] She was correct to worry, because segregationists were not finished: less than one month later, on Labor Day, September 8, segregationists tossed dynamite into the LRSD board administrative building, the private business office of Mayor Werner C. Knoop, and the city-owned station wagon of Fire Chief Gann L. Nalley. Police Chief Eugene Smith welcomed the help of the FBI in the investigation, and police guards assumed positions at the homes of school board members and major city officials. Chief Smith also asked that school officials turn on the lights at all school buildings. The blasts had come in rapid succession beginning at 10:20 P.M. Judging from the targets, it was clear that they were related to school integration.[70] The following day, the police said that the bombers had tried and failed to blow up a fourth target, the business office of Letcher Langford, a member of the City Manager Board. The police found sixty-five sticks of dynamite in the woods in the western part of the city and more dynamite, fuses, and several feet of fuse wire in the backyard of one of the suspects.[71] The LRSD board had been routed from a meeting less than two weeks before by two tear-gas bombs tossed in the front lobby by two unidentified women. Fire Chief Nalley probably became a target after his men used fire hoses on demonstrators on August 12 near Central High. Mayor Knopp may have become a target after the City Manager Board, which he headed, told the Little Rock police to keep the peace and put down violent demonstrations related to the opening of school.[72] By September 10, one prominent member of the Capital Citizens' Council, E. A. Lauderdale Sr., and a truck driver, J. D. Sims, had been charged with the Labor Day bombings.[73] The following day, three more were charged, while Malcolm Taylor, the president of the CCC, praised Lauderdale, calling him a "hard working Christian patriot." Taylor added that "if he [Lauderdale] could be selected as the scapegoat and railroaded to prison then no American can dare voice his honest resentment to police state tactics nor hope to find refuge in the time honored laws and constitutional rights of this once great land."[74] Eventually, five men were convicted, all linked to the Ku Klux Klan. Governor Faubus commuted Lauderdale's sentence, and he served less than six months. Two other bombers served even less time, and only one, who admitted his guilt, served two years.[75]

Only after the opening of all Little Rock schools, and weeks after the high schools had opened, did the LRSD board hear the appeals of some black students and a few white students who were not satisfied with their assignments. The LRSD board began to hear such appeals on September 8, when seven black and two white students appeared before them. The black students who were interviewed at that time included Sandra Johnson, the daughter of Warren Johnson, a bricklayer. The school board interviewed her in an open session where the press was allowed. She reported that she had attended school in California the previous year, and she felt comfortable attending an integrated school. The remaining six black students, who had their sessions in private, were William L. Crout, Alice Louise Flakes, John Emanual Gray, Sybil Jordan, Jane Lee Hill, and her brother Lee Andrew Hill.[76] Among this group, Lee Hill had applied to Little Rock Technical High, the only black student to make such a request. Jane Hill (Williams) had appeared in early September 1957 with the Little Rock Nine, attempting to enter Central High. The National Guard had turned her away with the group, and she later enrolled at Horace Mann High for the 1957–58 school year. Now in 1959, her senior year, she and her younger brother were trying to attend majority-white schools.[77]

On September 9, the board interviewed additional black students in private session: Merriam Lupper, William Massie, John Dickey Miller, Margetta Motley, William Henry Norwood, Carmella Sells, and Llona Marjarie Weaver.

Among those interviewed, only Norwood sought a transfer to Hall High, while most wanted to attend Central High. The board denied a transfer to John Albert Jones, whom they had seen the week before.[78] On September 15, the board announced that among all the black student appeals, they had selected only three more to attend Central High: James Franklin Henderson Jr., a sixteen-year-old junior and the son of Reverend J. F. Henderson Sr., the pastor of the Allison Memorial Presbyterian Church; Sandra Johnson, a junior and the daughter of Warren Johnson, now listed as a building contractor; and Sybil L. Jordan, fifteen, a sophomore and the daughter of Leslie W. Jordan, a letter carrier for the Little Rock Post Office.[79] This action brought the total number of black students attending previously white high schools to eight, three at Hall and five at Central. Perhaps the recently announced hearing scheduled for September 30 with Judge John E. Miller in the federal district court at Fort Smith had encouraged the board to add a few more blacks to the token number allowed among the large white population. But clearly, the LRSD board was not moving forward with integration enthusiastically.

Sybil Jordan (Hampton) recalls that her screening to become the only black sophomore at Central High in 1959–60 was a process. There was "psychological testing by someone in the Little Rock Public School system which included the Rorschach test followed by personal interviews with the school board members." She believes that her tests revealed that she was upbeat and positive and that her personal strengths would lend a balance to the challenges of the new year's schooling. She remembers two LRSD board members in particular: Everett Tucker, because he was the board president and orchestrated her interview, and Ted Lamb, because his questions were kind and he looked into her eyes. She says the conference made it quite clear that they were looking for black students who could be good role models for those who would come behind them in the integration process. She believes that the school board, influenced by the white business community, worked hard to control the setting for orderly integration to keep the Little Rock situation off the front pages—something they wished to avoid, based on the image the city had fostered in 1957. Her three-year experience at Central High is best summed up with her remark that "all is not perfect when people are struggling, but I know I helped pave the way for other black students who came behind me. There was no one outcome for everyone in Little Rock—but for many people it was a springboard to higher attainment."[80]

The morning after the transfers were announced, the *Arkansas Gazette* revealed that two members of the LRSD board had not voted to reassign the three black students to Central High: J. H. Cottrell and B. Frank Mackey had opposed the reassignments based on what they considered the inappropriate actions of the two black girls and because they thought Henderson would be "better off" at Horace Mann, where he could participate in athletics. As for the girls, Sandra Johnson and Sybil Jordan, the men said that they had violated "the Board's published administrative procedures" by not attending school while the school board was considering their transfer requests.[81] On the other hand, Ted Lamb, who had become the spokesman for those in the community most interested in moving forward with integration, remarked on the issue of "good faith," defending the actions of the majority of the board, which was under a federal court order to desegregate. He and Russell Matson stressed that they believed that the pupil-assignment laws would be preserved so long as school boards acted in good faith. Lamb said, "I believe they can act in good faith and effectively limit the degree of integration by using the laws."[82] This was the statement of the most liberal member of the board and the one most often targeted by segregationist outrage, causing him to lose much of his advertising business.[83] And so it went with pupil-assignment laws in Little Rock and across the South, local school board members walking the narrow dividing line between integrating a number of black students large enough to satisfy the federal courts but small enough to satisfy the reluctant and vocal whites in the community. It was another dance of one step forward and two steps back.

■ ■ ■

Public high schools in Little Rock remained open with no reported violence for the remainder of the school year. Token racial integration continued in the city and across Arkansas over the next few years. Compared to states in the Deep South at the time, Arkansas's limited progress outpaced Alabama, the District of Columbia, Florida, Georgia, Louisiana, Mississippi, North Carolina, South Carolina, Tennessee, and Virginia, with eight of the state's school districts integrated to some degree.[84] The LRSD board controlled the tempo of desegregation, making sure the process remained methodical, slow, and controlled by whites. Desegregation using the pupil-placement laws continued until the Eighth Circuit Court of Appeals ruled that the LRSD board had discriminated against black students and ordered the board to stop discriminating.[85] In 1965, Sergeant Roosevelt and Delores Clark, whose four children were assigned to all-black schools, filed suit with the help of the Legal Defense Fund of the NAACP, challenging the constitutionality of the pupil-assignment scheme. Even before the ruling in the *Clark* case, the LRSD drew up a "freedom of choice plan," a strategy many other southern cities had also adopted. In 1966, the appeals court upheld the district's new approach, despite the fact that only 621 out of Little Rock's 7,341 black students were attending majority-white schools.

Historians Ben Johnson and John A. Kirk document a concerted effort on the part of white business elites, combined with the LRSD board, to limit racial desegregation by controlling "racial topography," producing well-segregated neighborhoods.[86] By 1970, the U.S. Eighth Circuit Court of Appeals ruled freedom of choice and pupil assignments based on zones unconstitutional. The response of the LRSD was to implement busing of all students across the entire district, prompting white flight to the suburbs and the mushrooming of private academies across the city (based on a Supreme Court ruling in *Swann v. Charlotte- Mecklenburg Board of Education*). By 1976, Little Rock schools held a majority of black students for the first time.[87] In 1982, the LRSD sued in federal court to consolidate the existing school districts in Pulaski County—Little Rock, North Little Rock, and the Pulaski County School District. However, in 1985, the U.S. Court of Appeals ruled against this plan and allowed only an expansion to the city limits. The black majority increased steadily until 1986, when it reached 71 percent. In 1987, the LRSD expanded its footprint to overlay almost the entire city, bringing in three additional high school populations and boosting enrollment figures, but the black population remained above 60 percent even after the addition of the new high schools. Since that time, a majority-black population has continued.[88] Within these new boundaries, a new student-assignment plan called "Controlled Choice" was implemented by the LRSD but has been described as "an administrative nightmare and public relations fiasco" by Judge Robert L. Brown. In his 1988 report on desegregation, written for the Winthrop Rockefeller Foundation, Brown concluded that there was a growing attitude among blacks that "busing their children across town to white neighborhoods and to schools skewed in favor of white students may not be in their best interest." He wrote that some in the black community favored a nurturing environment with black teachers and principals in students' own neighborhoods, particularly in the early grades. Additionally, Brown called upon the business community to totally commit to public schools by enrolling their children and grandchildren in them. He asked for attitudinal changes from whites and blacks and for an end to segregated housing patterns. He stressed the need to provide quality education to all Little Rock children and to attempt to end federal court oversight of the LRSD.

In spring 2006, Brown wrote an article for the *Arkansas Historical Quarterly* entitled "The Third Little Rock Crisis," lamenting the fact that Little Rock appeared to be continuing "experimentation . . . the federal courts not yet declaring the LRSD to have unitary status.[89] On February 23, 2007, almost fifty years after the 1957 Central High Crisis Year, U.S. district judge William R. Wilson declared the LRSD unitary, releasing it from court oversight and monitoring. More important, he pointed out that historians should begin to fully examine school desegregation in Little Rock after 1957, believing they will note the "failure of the citizens to fulfill constitutional obligations" and the upper-class effort in the late 1960s, intent on "reserving for their children safe, nearby schools with modern facilities and solid instruction as a racially neutral right." He predicted that such a study might "well conclude that this adaptation represented little more than the gentrification of segregation."[90]

At present, the LRSD has five public high schools, but their combined enrollment in 2007 was 4,092 students. This figure is an increase of a mere 500 students since 1959. The racial breakdown in 1959 was 20 percent black, and today it is 68 percent black. This is not a case only of upper-class whites leaving the district, but total enrollment numbers do demonstrate the loss of broad public support for public schools. Little Rock's population has steadily increased, but this has not mirrored the growth across all of Pulaski County, which grew from a population of 196,685 in 1950 to 349,660 in 1990. With the present Little Rock demographic of 55 percent white, 40 percent black, and 2.7 percent Latino, the public school system clearly does not reflect the city's racial breakdown.[91] Little Rock's figures are not unique, of course, reflecting those of urban settings across the country, with thriving parochial and private schools for people of means and underfunded public schools for the rest.

Little Rock tried private and segregated education in 1958–59, financed with private funds and, for a time, with state monies. The courts and, more importantly, the citizens of Little Rock proved willing to stand up for public education and public school teachers. Today's figures provide a sad commentary on current conditions when compared to the all too brief moment on May 25, 1959, when a coalition of black and white voters in Little Rock championed public schools. For one inspiring but brief time, in spite of desegregation, school patrons acted together for a worthwhile and common cause. Irving Spitzberg, Lost Year classmate and author, has said: "It is worrisome that today in most cities across the country, all families are not a part of the public school system. Decisions made without a stake in the life of the common community can lead to ones that are not rational and in which we lose the moral crunch. Today's parents are simply not invested. If today the governor closed the public high schools in Little Rock, I am afraid that the public reaction might be a yawn and an 'oh isn't that too bad? And, that is a very sad situation indeed."[92]

Afterword

And all of that hate just left me
—Edie Garland (Barentine), Lost Year student

The loss of part or all of the 1958–59 school year was more than an inconvenience for 3,665 students, 177 teachers and administrators, their families, and their community. Both race and class brought disproportionate suffering to displaced black and some poor white students. Public schools lost support in the segregationist community. Public school teachers lost their civil liberties at the hands of the legislature and the governor. School closure for these teenagers was a life-changing event, often to their personal detriment. More important than the disruption of their physical world was the molding of their identities, their egos, and their views on race and desegregation within a cauldron of racial turmoil. The general tendency of historians to dismiss the Lost Year as a footnote to the media-drenched Little Rock desegregation crisis of 1957–58 obscures its true significance. Beyond the public tragedy for the community and the schools, the personal stories remain. For the students, the private victims, the consequences of this year have been playing out quietly over lifetimes. Students were separated from friends and families, and parents watched as their aspirations for their children dissipated, young people delaying or deferring their young dreams. There was no one outcome for these young people—some became bitter over their loss and bitter toward those of another race, but some redirected themselves toward personal achievement and a higher vision.

Dick Gardner, who lived near Central High and was a sophomore during the 1957 crisis, now runs a successful heating and air-conditioning company. When schools did not open in 1958, Gardner asked his parents for permission to join the U.S. Navy. He served four years and earned his GED. He now looks back on how his life and career were affected by closed schools and denied access: "I think things would have been different if I had not left home. . . . I know I would have finished high school at Central. I'd have gone to college, my daddy would have seen to that. He would have seen to it." Gardner mentioned several times that his father wanted him to be an engineer: "The navy was better than what so many others were doing. So many didn't go to school, they didn't have a job, they were just kicking the gravel around. It wasn't a good situation. Daddy was scared I would get into trouble . . . kids all over the place with nothing to do, seventeen-year-old kids loose on the streets. He always wanted me to be an engineer, to get an education, and I did, not like what he wanted. . . . It just didn't work out that way."[1]

P. H. Gilkey, a black junior who did not return to school, also remarks on the Lost Year: "Well, it separated me from the people I knew and loved. I was seventeen years old, and I was away from home. I had not completed high school and was having to depend on the military to complete it. I was suddenly thrust among people from all over the world who had no idea what I was even thinking and who didn't really care."[2]

Shirley Collier Stephens, a black eleventh-grader who after three months finally left town to attend another Arkansas school, felt betrayed. She and so many other students spent weeks in anticipation, hoping that with the passing of time their schools might open. Her experience living with an aunt out of town was not a particularly good one, but the following year she refused to return to Horace Mann: "I would never go back to Horace Mann. I told my mother I could not. I told my father that I could not go there after what they did. I felt so violated and rejected. There was probably a lot more pain within me that even I didn't realize because when they opened the school my mother was just so anxious for me to come back and I said, 'No.'" Denied access, she summed up her feelings about the Lost Year: "I lost everything, I lost friends. I lost my home and my family for a time. I lost my community. It wasn't just about school, I lost everything."[3]

Edie Garland (Barentine), from Hall High, was sent to Oklahoma to live with relatives for her senior year. Prior to that, she had been active in her church, served as a white counselor at an all-black Methodist camp, and participated in mixed-race discussion groups at the YWCA and in private homes. She remembers saying: "If I ever come face to face with Orval Faubus, he will hear what I think of him. I wanted someone to blame for what happened in the Lost Year and what happened at Central High. Many, many years later I ended up alone on an elevator with him. He was much older. I noticed his suit was ill-fitting and his shoes were dirty. We made no eye contact and in that short ride, I thought, this is a man and he is vulnerable, and he is old and tired. And all of that hate just left me. His shoes were dirty, and I had never stood in his shoes. As he exited the elevator, I looked at him and was able to say, 'It's good to see you, Governor.'" Though her statement appears to absolve Faubus, she can now forgive the person so many in the community blamed for their loss only through her own personal moral growth.[4]

P. H. Gilkey, who went on to serve for over twenty years in the U.S. Navy before earning his undergraduate and graduate degrees, was the principal of the Step One Alternative School operated by Pulaski County within the juvenile justice system for twelve years before his retirement. He was able to use his own history to inspire the incoming students, telling them that they had been given a second chance at getting an education, something he was denied. If a student made it through the Step One program, his expulsion would become null, he would receive credit for the semester, and he would be allowed to return to school. Gilkey, now, is proud of the 86 percent success rate this school had under his leadership and feels his example played an important part in its achievement.[5]

Faye Perry (Russ) remained in Little Rock after her graduation from Horace Mann in 1960, earning her LPN degree and working at the Veterans' Administration Hospital from 1966 to 1973. But when the second of her three sons entered preschool within the LRSD, she quit her nursing job and volunteered with the public school's pre-K program. Soon she was offered a position to work in the program and became its home school coordinator. In that capacity, she gained even more interest in cultural diversity and heard of the work of the Panel of American Women, which chose her as its facilitator and coordinator of culturally diverse teams. The Panel, started by WEC member Sara Murphy in 1963, consisted of about thirty women representing different religious and racial groups who talked informally about how prejudice had affected their lives and the lives of their children. Each team included a Catholic, a Jew, a black, sometimes another minority, and a white Protestant and appeared by invitation to speak before organizations in public settings. By 1979–80, when Faye joined the group, the Panel received federal funding that allowed it to work with all sixth-graders in the LRSD. Russ stated: "That was the best job I've ever had in my life, I believe. I could see so much growth from our work." Sadly, the funding ended in 1980, but Russ mentioned that some of those young people, now grown, live in her neighborhood and still talk to her about the program.[6]

John Taylor was a sixteen-year-old junior at Little Rock Central High during the 1957–58 school year. He describes himself during that time as a "science nerd" who was brand new to Little Rock and just trying hard to fit into his new surroundings. His father, a psychiatrist, was the new clinical director at the Arkansas State Hospital, and the two drove into the city on the weekend of August 31 from Alexandria, Louisiana. The family was to have a house on the grounds of the hospital, but he and his dad were to "bach" it in smaller temporary quarters until his mother arrived within six weeks. Taylor was small in size, and he recalls now that for sixteen-year-old boys "all that matters is going to school, doing your job of learning, earning good grades, and trying to be something you are not—an athlete. So I played in the band and did science instead." His experiences during the first year of integration revolved around his own new world, his classes, and the new white friends he had made. In 1997, as a longtime college professor of chemistry, he began to tell others about "some of those dark memories of eleventh grade. How I was in the wrong place at the wrong time. How I was part of the silent minority as my father talked equality for all. . . . I was ashamed for never speaking up. Too scared. Too stupid, just a kid being a teenager wanting a normal school year." As for the Little Rock Nine, he says: "I did not even know their names. They kept to themselves, and we kept to ourselves. I did learn one of the Nine's name early in the year, Minnijean Brown, as she was a target for a group of white students. At graduation, I learned the name of Ernest Green, as I was in the band playing that evening. . . . I did not know who Martin Luther King [Jr.] was or that he was in the stands. Just that Ernest was in danger of being shot at the ceremony and security was high at the stadium." The following year, when schools were closed, he kept his two summer jobs "to make more money for school which certainly would begin soon." He started two correspondence courses, one in English and one in solid geometry. After six weeks had gone by, he says, the hope of school starting was fading, and reality was setting in: "There was no school. There would be no senior year." In October, he went with his mother to southern Louisiana, where two former classmates and their mothers offered to allow him to live with them. His father refused, offering him the possibility of living with the family of one of his former patients: "I didn't know them, but I should have gone. I didn't want to leave home. . . . I wanted to be with the moms of my friends, not someone I didn't know." When Raney High opened, John enrolled in physics and trigonometry for the second six weeks. Then he dropped out to go to college, after taking his College Boards. He began at Little Rock University as a college freshman at just seventeen years of age, one of 64 of Central High's 535 "seniors." He went from being an honor student in high school to a struggling B/C college freshman, attempting to survive without the proper preparation. He did well in chemistry, but he knew he did not have the conceptual understanding to continue in engineering. Since that time, he says, "I have devoted my life to education, especially community college education, where underprepared adults come for a second chance to attempt postsecondary education in a caring environment." John has just completed his forty-fourth year as an educator. In recent years, he has begun speaking in public venues during Black History Month, telling his story of life in Little Rock. He spoke in April 2008 at the eighteenth International Conference on Teaching and Learning. He begins each talk with the following: "When you lose your health, you understand what you have taken for granted. When they take school from you, you realize the value of education, that education is a privilege and should not be taken for granted or wasted."

Robert L. Brown has been an Arkansas Supreme Court justice since 1991; has had a career in the legal profession; and has published extensively in journals such as *Arkansas Lawyer, Arkansas Business,* and *Arkansas Times.* He was scheduled to be a senior at Hall High in 1958–59. His father, Robert R. Brown, the Episcopal bishop of Arkansas, had called for the integration of Little Rock Episcopal churches in 1957 and been roundly criticized by many for doing so. Brown recalls that his father lost friends because of his principled stands. In some cases, old friends would cross the street to avoid speaking to him, and he received harassing telephone calls. Brown was sent away to an Episcopal high school in Texas during the 1958–59 year, but even from that distance he knew that "the fiery glow of racial hatred continued to burn unabated in Little Rock. . . . Raised in this crucible of racial ferment, my personal views began to take shape. I supported integrated schools in 1958–59, and my commitment was strengthened by a trip to Morehouse College in Atlanta my senior year in college, the 1963 March on Washington, the 1966 race riots, and the assassinations of Martin Luther King Jr. and Bobby Kennedy in 1968. Through it all, I recognized that affording equal education was the only chance for our multicultural society to survive and prevail and that it would take several generations for progress to be truly obtained and gauged."

In 1982, when his only child, Stuart, entered the Little Rock public schools, it was at the height of white flight and much turmoil. His desire to understand these problems led to his 1999 report for the Winthrop Rockefeller Foundation entitled "The Second Crisis of Little Rock."[7] From researching that report, he says now, "I concluded that much remained to be done." Today Brown says: "No doubt, my personal history and my participation and connection with the Little Rock public schools gave me a unique perspective when the issue of public school funding for adequate and equal education was raised to my court in 2002 in the *Lake View* case. The future of this state and, indeed, this country, rests on the education of all of our children. Our state constitution requires adequacy and equality in education. And my court did not shrink from this challenge in the *Lake View* cases. I am convinced that the seeds of what we sowed will bear fruit in the succeeding generations for all races in this state."[8]

The voices of the Lost Year still resonate—if we will only listen. Those who remain bitter warn us to never take away the right to a free public education for all. The voices of those who have gone on to higher personal achievement or to a higher vision inspire us in their triumph.

APPENDIX

Document One

This proclamation signed by Gov. Orval Faubus on September 12, 1958, closed the four public high schools in Little Rock locking out 3,665 black and white students. Notice that the document was a response to the federal court order of the same day demanding that the LRSD Board open the high schools "on a racially integrated basis." Arkansas Act 4 allowed state power to close the schools but required a referendum by the voters of the district. In this document Faubus scheduled that vote on October 7, 1958 but later moved the election to September 27, a Saturday before new poll taxes went into effect. Appendix 1, Brief for Women's Emergency Committee to Open Our Schools, as Amicus Curiae Supporting Appellee *Garrett v. Faubus*, Governor, 230 Ark. 445 (1959) (No. 5–1824). *Courtesy of the National Park Service, Little Rock Central High School National Historic Site.*

A-1

STATE OF ARKANSAS
EXECUTIVE DEPARTMENT

PROCLAMATION

TO ALL TO WHOM THESE PRESENTS SHALL COME - GREETINGS:

WHEREAS,   Act No. 4 of the Acts of the Second Extraordinary Session of the Sixty-first General Assembly, approved September 12, 1958, provides that the Governor: (A) order any or all schools of a school district to be closed immediately; and (B) call a special election within thirty days thereafter at which special election all qualified electors of the school district shall have an opportunity to vote for or against the proposition of racial integration of all schools within the school district, whenever the Governor shall determine that such action is necessary in order to maintain the peace against actual or impending domestic violence in the school district, or shall determine that a general, suitable, and efficient educational system cannot be maintained in any school district because of integration of the races in any school of the district; and,

WHEREAS,   the Little Rock School Board has fixed Monday, September 15, 1958, as the date for convening of classes in the senior high schools of said district and has been ordered by a federal court to operate same on a racially-integrated basis; and,

WHEREAS,   I have determined that domestic violence within the Little Rock School District is impending, and that a general, suitable, and efficient educational system cannot be maintained in the senior high schools of the Little Rock School District because of integration of the races in such schools;

NOW, THEREFORE,   I, Orval E. Faubus, Governor of the State of Arkansas, acting under the applicable provisions of the aforementioned Act No. 4 of the Acts of the Second Extraordinary Session of the Sixty-first General Assembly, approved September 12, 1958, do hereby order by public proclamation that:

(A) The public senior high schools of the Little Rock School District are hereby ordered closed pursuant to said Act, effective at 8 o'clock A. M., Monday, September 15, 1958.

(B) That a special election be held in the Little Rock School District on Tuesday, October 7, 1958, in the manner provided by law in said Act No. 4.

IN WITNESS WHEREOF, I have hereunto set my hand and caused the Great Seal of the State of Arkansas to be affixed. Done in office on this 12th day of September, 1958.

Orval E. Faubus
GOVERNOR

SECRETARY OF STATE

590

Document Two

This "Proclamation: Notice of Special Election" was signed by Gov. Orval Faubus on September 16, 1958 and carefully outlined for voters how their referendum ballot would be worded. Based upon Arkansas Act 4 passed in the extraordinary session of the Arkansas General Assembly in August 1958, voters were asked to vote "for racial integration of ALL schools within the Little Rock School district or for racial segregation" of these same schools There was no mention of opening or closing the four high schools that Governor Faubus had closed beginning on September 15, 1958. Appendix 2, Brief for Women's Emergency Committee to Open Our Schools, as Amicus Curiae Supporting Appellee *Garrett v. Faubus*, Governor, 230 Ark. 445 (1959) (No. 5–1824). *Courtesy of the National Park Service, Little Rock Central High School National Historic Site.*

A-2

STATE OF ARKANSAS
EXECUTIVE DEPARTMENT

PROCLAMATION

N O T I C E   O F   S P E C I A L   E L E C T I O N

NOTICE is hereby given that a Special Election will be held in the

LITTLE ROCK SCHOOL DISTRICT

on Saturday, September 27, 1958, between the hours of 8 a.m. and 6:30 p.m., at

which all qualified electors within the district shall have an opportunity to vote

on the following proposition:

FOR RACIAL INTEGRATION OF ALL SCHOOLS WITHIN THE
    LITTLE ROCK SCHOOL DISTRICT . . . . ▱

AGAINST RACIAL INTEGRATION OF ALL SCHOOLS WITHIN
    THE LITTLE ROCK SCHOOL DISTRICT . . . . ▱

    The County Board of Election Commissioners shall designate all polling

places, provide the election supplies, appoint the judges and clerks for holding

the election, and shall otherwise have supervision over the conduct of the

election. At the close of the election, the judges at each polling place shall

make a return of the votes, certified by the clerks of the election, and file it

in the office of the County Clerk of the County in which said district is

administered, for immediate delivery to the County Board of Election Commissioners,

which said Board shall immediately, but not later than the fifth (5th) day next

following the election, proceed to ascertain and declare the result of the

election and certify its findings to the Governor.

    This notice of Special Election is given pursuant to the provisions

of Act 4 of the Acts of the Second Extraordinary Session of the Sixty-first

General Assembly approved September 12, 1958.

                      IN WITNESS WHEREOF, I have hereunto set
                      my hand and caused the Great Seal of the
                      State of Arkansas to be affixed. Done in
                      office this _16_ day of September, 1958.

                      Orval E. Faubus
                              G O V E R N O R

Document Three

A newspaper announcement of the referendum to be held on September 27, 1958. The voting places are listed by ward and precinct. The predominant black precincts were 1B, 1E, 2D, 2E, and 3C. The high-income white precincts were 4E, 5C, 5D, 5E, 5F, and 5G. In many elections in the 1950s, these two diverse groups had voted alike. The outcome of this referendum was a three to one vote for segregation, with only the black precincts fully supporting integration. Notice that voters needed a 1957 poll tax receipt for this 1958 vote. *Arkansas Democrat,* page 6, September 23, 1958. *Courtesy of the* Arkansas Democrat-Gazette *and Special Collections, University of Arkansas Libraries, Fayetteville, Virgil Blossom Papers, Manuscript Collection 1364, Box 29, Folder 6.*

NOTICE OF
SPECIAL SCHOOL ELECTION
LITTLE ROCK SCHOOL DISTRICT
SEPTEMBER 27, 1958

Pursuant to the Proclamation of the Governor of Arkansas, dated September 12, 1958, as amended by his Proclamation of September 16, 1958, all as authorized and provided by Act No. 4 of the Acts of the Second Extraordinary Session of the Sixty-first General Assembly, NOTICE is hereby given that a Special School Election will be held in the Little Rock School District on —

SATURDAY, SEPTEMBER 27, 1958

between the hours of 8 o'clock a. m. and 6:30 p. m. at which all qualified electors of said school district shall have an opportunity to vote on the following proposition:

—For Racial Integration of All Schools Within the Little Rock School District.

—Against Racial Integration of all Schools Within the Little Rock School District.

The voting places within the boundaries of said district shall be as follows:

FIRST WARD—
A—Ponder's Drug Store, 16th and Park Avenue
B—Fire Station, 14th and Pulaski
C—Assembly of God Church, 15th and State
D—Methodist Church, 28th and Wolfe
E—Fire Station, 23rd and Arch

SECOND WARD—
A—First Lutheran Church Basement, 316 East 8th
B—Fire Station, MacArthur Park, 12th and Commerce
C—Frick's Drug Store, 424 East 21st
D—Fire Station, East Roosevelt and Vance
E—Fire Station, East 6th and Fletcher

THIRD WARD—
A—Court House
B—Pine Crest Offices, 1116 West Markham
C—Collins Temple Baptist Church, 11th and Ringo
D—1st Nazarene Church (Bldg. North), 9th and Battery
E—Vocation Building, Arkansas Deaf School
F—Woodruff School, 7th and Johnson
G—Mallory Building Material Co., Cantrell Road

FOURTH WARD—
A—First Assembly of God Church, 4523 West 12th
B—Fire Station, 3515 West 12th
C—Garland School, 24th and Maple
D—Fire Station, 22nd and Peyton
E—Methodist Church, Broadmoor
F—Guy Storey D-X Station, 5624 Hwy. 67, Meadowcliff

FIFTH WARD—
A—Fire Station, Markham and Elm
B—Masonic Hall, Kavanaugh and Beech
C—Masonic Lodge, Cantrell and Pierce
D—Fire Station, Kavanaugh and Harrison
E—Vacant Store Building, 2316 Durwood Road
F—Cantrell Drug Company, 7524 Cantrell Road
G—St. Mark's Church, 1000 Mississippi

CAMMACK VILLAGE—Community Hall

WILSON SCHOOL—Old Hot Springs Hwy. (now No. 5)

1. Qualified electors of the Little Rock School District are urged to bring RECEIPT FOR POLL TAX FOR 1957, issued prior to October 1, 1957, to polling place, and

2. Any person who has obtained the age of 21 years since October 1, 1957, and prior to September 27, 1958, will be eligible to vote in this election as a "maiden voter" by executing the necessary affidavit with the election officials at the voting precinct.

TOM GULLEY, Sheriff
Pulaski County, Arkansas

Document Four

The contract offered by the Little Rock Private School Corporation to white public high-school teachers on Monday, September 29, 1958. Mrs. Jo Ann Henry, math teacher at Central High, did **not** sign her contract, joining only fourteen others in refusing to sign on with a segregationist institution. *Courtesy of Mrs. Jo Ann Henry Royster, mathematics teacher from Central High.*

THE LITTLE ROCK PRIVATE SCHOOL CORPORATION

TEACHER'S CONTRACT

(For Certified Personnel Teaching Three or More Hours Per Day)

1958-59

STATE OF ARKANSAS   Classification   B-2
COUNTY OF PULASKI   School Central High

    This contract and agreement between The Little Rock Private School Corporation,

Pulaski County, Arkansas, and   Mrs. Jo Ann Henry   a legally qualified teacher.

WITNESSETH:

    The Corporation, by a majority vote at a legally held meeting on September 29,

1958, offers to employ_____ Her _____ to teach in The Little Rock

Private School Corporation for a term of nine months and one day beginning on

September 30, 1958, and ending June 19th, 1959.

    The salary to be paid the employee for the period of employment is $ 3109.58 .

    It is agreed that if the revenues of the Corporation be increased or decreased beyond the amount anticipated at the time this contract is made, the terms herein stated shall be revised in accordance with provisions of law that govern other school facilities of the state.

Pay dates shall be as follows:

		January 16	10 days
		January 29	10 days
		February 27	20 days
October 27	20 days	March 27	20 days
November 24	20 days	April 24	20 days
December 23	21 days	May 22	20 days
		June 19	20 days

    Holidays with full pay are to be observed in accordance with the laws of Arkansas and the established policies of the Corporation.

    Both parties hereto agree that all steps taken under the terms of this contract shall be in accordance with all laws and regulations governing the employment and compensation of teachers, and the conduct of said teacher during the effective period of the contract.

        The teacher shall file in the office of the Superintendent of The Little Rock Private School Corporation an official transcript of college training, an acceptable proof of date of birth, and shall register a valid teaching license of highest grade attainable with college credits, unless heretofore filed with his or her immediate prior employer.

All school employees shall present annually, to the superintendent's office, a certificate, from a regularly licensed physician, showing condition of physical and mental health, as required by the laws of Arkansas, and by the rules and regulations of the State Board of Health.

All teachers who have been residents of Arkansas for one year must present a poll tax receipt before drawing their salaries.

If the schools are dismissed for any reason over which the Corporation has no control, the teacher agrees to make up, without pay, such part of the time as the Corporation deems necessary.

The teacher agrees that the Corporation, as the employing agency, is authorized to make such deductions from the salary specified herein as may be required by Law for Teacher Retirement and taxes to the Government of the United States.

Both parties hereto agree that this contract may be cancelled by mutual consent upon written notice by either party duly presented at least 30 days before the effective date of such cancellation.

This offer terminates if not accepted by returning two signed copies to The Little Rock Private School Corporation, 14th & Park Streets, Little Rock, Arkansas, within one (1) day of the date shown in the next paragraph.

Signed this _____29th_____ day of _September_____, 1958

THE LITTLE ROCK PRIVATE SCHOOL CORPORATION
OF LITTLE ROCK

By _____ Accepted this_____ day of _____, 1958
         President

By _____   _____
         Secretary   Teacher

RELEASE AND CONTRACT

STATE OF ARKANSAS

COUNTY OF PULASKI

I, _____Mrs. Jo Ann Henry_____, hereby tender my resignation to the Little Rock School District, saving any and all rights and privileges as authorized by Act 4 of the Second Special Extraordinary Session of the 61st General Assembly, and the Little Rock School District, acting in accordance with resolution adopted on the 29th day of September, 1958, hereby signifies its acceptance of same by endorsement hereon, and the said Little Rock School District further agrees that should The Little Rock Private School Corporation be dissolved or discontinue the operation of any and/or all of the schools leased from the Little Rock School District, then said Little Rock School District hereby agrees to reinstate Mrs. Jo Ann Henry to his or her previous status including salary and classification on the day immediately following his or her termination with The Little Rock Private School Corporation.

This agreement between Mrs. Jo Ann Henry and the Little Rock School District is made in consideration of the mutual promises herein enumerated.

Signed this 29th day of September, 1958.

BOARD OF DIRECTORS
SCHOOL DISTRICT OF LITTLE ROCK

By _____ Executed this 29th day of September, 1958
         President

By _____   _____
         Secretary   Employee

Document Five

The temporary restraining order issued on September 29, 1958 by the U. S. Eighth Circuit Court in the case of *Aaron v. Cooper*. This document prevented the LRSD Board from leasing to the newly formed Little Rock Private School Corporation the public high-school buildings and prevented public-school teachers from working for the LRPSC. Federal marshals delivered documents to all teachers who had been offered contracts earlier the same day. State officials and board members of both the LRSD and the LRPSC were also restrained. *Courtesy of Mrs. Jo Ann Henry Royster, mathematics teacher from Central High.*

UNITED STATES COURT OF APPEALS

FOR THE EIGHTH CIRCUIT

JOHN AARON ET AL)
  Appellants)
)
v.   :   App. No. _____
)
WILLIAM G. COOPER ET A L.)
  Appellees)

TEMPORARY RESTRAINING ORDER

This cause having been heard on the application of appellants for a temporary restraining order to preserve, insofar as their integrated status is concerned, the operation of the senior high schools of the Little Rock School District, pending hearing and disposition of appellant's motion for an injunction pending appeal; and it appearing that appellees will, unless restrained, immediately transfer possession, control, and operation of the senior high schools of the Little Rock School District to a private corporation for operation as schools on a segregated basis and thereby impair the effectiveness of this court's jurisdiction over the pending appeal; and it appearing that appellees have already executed a lease of the senior high school properties to a private corporation and contemplate delivering possession of such properties to said private corporation on the morning of September 30, 1958, so that time does not permit the giving of the notice prescribed by this court's rules;

NOW, THEREFORE, IT IS HEREBY ORDERED that appellees William G. Cooper, Harold Engstrom, Wayne Upton, Dale Alford, R. A. Lile, and Virgil T. Blossom, their officers, agents, servants, employees, and attorneys, and all persons in active concert or participation with them, are hereby restrained from taking any further action to transfer possession, control, or operation, directly or indirectly, of the senior high schools of the Little Rock School District, or from in any way further altering the status quo of such senior high schools insofar as their integrated status is concerned, existing at the time of the issuance of the Order of the District Court of September 25, 1958, which is the subject of the present appeal.

This Order shall be effective until the hearing and disposition of appellant's motion for a writ of injunction pending appeal, which hearing is set before the Court at the United States Court House and Custom House, St. Louis, Missouri, at 10 o'clock a.m. Monday, October 6, 1958.

Appellants shall give a surety bond in the amount of $1,000.00 as security for the payment of such costs and damages as may be incurred or suffered by any party who is found to have been wrongfully enjoined or restrained.

JOSEPH W. WOODROUGH
United States Circuit Judge

Issued at 4:10 p.m.
September 29, 1958.

Document Six

The affidavit required by Arkansas Act 10. All public-school administrators, teachers, and college professors were required to list all organizations to which they belonged or to which they had paid dues for the previous five-year period. Mrs. Bernice McSwaim, a black teacher at Gibbs Elementary, added a note at the end of her sworn document, claiming that all information she had supplied was "complete and correct, relying solely on memory." In this way, she could hide her membership in the NAACP, which was illegal according to Arkansas Act 115. *Courtesy of Mrs. Bernice McSwaim.*

AFFIDAVIT
(Certified Personnel - Little Rock School District)

STATE OF ARKANSAS

COUNTY OF _Pulaski_

I, _Bernice McSwain_, being an applicant for the position of _Teacher_ at _Gibbs Elementary_ School, being first duly sworn, do hereby depose and say that I am now or have been within the past five years a member of the following organizations and no others: (names and addresses of organizations)

1. National Education Association - Washington, D.C.
2. Arkansas Teachers' Association - 924 Ringo
3. Arkansas Ed. Assn. Investment Corporation - 1500 W. 4th
4. Classroom Teachers
5. City Teachers' Assn.
6. Little Rock Negro P.T.A. Council
7. Gibbs Parent Teacher Association - 16th + Cross
8. A.M. + N. College Alumni Assn., L.R. Branch - 16th + Izard
9. Maids + Matrons Club - Mt. Zion Bapt. Church
10. Mt. Zion Baptist Sunday School Dept. - 908 Cross

and further, that I am now paying, or within the past five years have paid, regular dues or made regular contributions to the following organizations and no others: (names and addresses of organizations)

1. Union A.M.E. Church - Wright Ave. Pulaski
2. Mt. Zion Baptist Church - 908 Cross
3. Community Chest - Little Rock, Ark.
4. American Red Cross - 2nd + Gaines
5. Ark. Division American Cancer Assn. - 239 Gaines
6. March of Dimes - Boyle Bldg.
7. Florence Crittenton Home - Sweet Home Pike
8. Pulaski County Tuberculosis Assn. - Glover Bldg.
9. Phillis Wheatley Y.W.C.A. - 924 Gaines

The above information is complete and correct, relying wholly on memory.   _Bernice McSwain_
                                                    (Signature of Affiant)

Subscribed and sworn to before me this _13_ day of _April_, 19_59_.

Mamie S. Jackson   Notary Public
Signature and Title of Official

Document Seven

All forty-four purged employees of the Little Rock School District received letters by registered mail, dated May 5, 1959, when three members of the six-member Little Rock School Board fired them without cause. Mrs. Grace Dupree taught home economics for twenty-nine years in Arkansas schools and was employed at Central High when she was purged. *Courtesy of nephew of Grace Dupree.*

ADMINISTRATIVE OFFICES

LITTLE ROCK PUBLIC SCHOOLS

8th and Louisiana   Phone FRanklin 5-4465

LITTLE ROCK, ARKANSAS

May 5, 1959

Mrs. Grace Dupree
1100 Schiller Street
Little Rock, Arkansas

Dear Madam:

You are hereby notified that your contract with the Board of Education, Little Rock School District has not been, and will not be, renewed for the 1959-60 school year.

Very truly yours,

Ed I. McKinley, Jr.
President, Board of Education
Little Rock School District

Ben D. Rowland, Sr.
Secretary, Board of Education
Little Rock School District

Judge R. W. "Bob" Laster
Member, Board of Education
Little Rock School District

Document Eight

On May 5, 1959, after a year of closed public high schools, three members of the six-member LRSD Board fired forty-four public school employees in an illegal session. Thirty-nine whites and five blacks were fired, including principals, teachers, and three secretaries, all of whom were suspected of being in support of racial integration. *Document created from Arkansas Gazette, May 10, 1959, Sec A, "Here's Background Data on 44 Purged from School Jobs by Three Directors."*

Purge List (*Arkansas Gazette,* May 10, 1959)

* Denotes a refusal to sign Act 10
† Denotes reassignment

CENTRAL HIGH SCHOOL

J. W. Matthews	Principal
J. O. Powell*	Vice Principal for Boys
Elizabeth Huckaby	Vice Principal for Girls
Juanita Brietz	Secretary
Alice Ann Coffman	Secretary
Harriet Dietz	Secretary
Helen Conrad	Mathematics
Pauline Dunn	Biology
Grace Dupree	Home Economics
Abby Foster	Latin
Ernest Gephardt*	Vocational/Printing
Doris Glenn	English
Irene Harrell	Spanish
Orlana Hensley	Guidance
Alma Jeffries	Mathematics
Nyna Keeton	Distributive Education
Loreen Lee	Latin
Shirley McGalin	Speech
Cassie Moren	Physical Education
Jennie Perkins	History
Christine Poindexter	Mathematics
Frances Rudd	Home Economics
Shirley Stancil	Guidance
Margaret Stewart	Social Science/Guidance
Kathleen Taylor	English

Donna Wells	English
Susie West	English

FOREST HEIGHTS JUNIOR HIGH

J. Harvey Walthall	Principal
Donald Bratton	Latin

SOUTHWEST JUNIOR HIGH

Alice Glover	English

WEST SIDE JUNIOR HIGH

Lois Grimmett	Physical Education
Eugene Keeton	Physical Education
Margaret Reiman†	Mathematics
Harvey F. Milner†	Biology

CENTENNIAL SCHOOL

Imogene Hines	Principal

FOREST PARK SCHOOL

Frances Wood	Principal

FRANKLIN SCHOOL

Opal Middleton	Principal

PARHAM SCHOOL

Sidney Reid	Principal

WILLIAMS SCHOOL

Jo Ann Henry†	Mathematics

MANN HIGH SCHOOL

LeRoy Christophe	Principal
B. T. Shelton*	Bricklaying

DUNBAR JUNIOR HIGH

Mary Gaines*	Home Economics
Rowland Smith	Social Sciences
Zerita Tate*	Mathematics

Document Nine

This advertisement by the Mothers' League, a segregationist group, for the May 25, 1959, recall vote, solicited support for the recall of the three more moderate members of the Little Rock School District Board and asked for votes against the removal of the more avowed segregationists from the six-member public school board. The vote narrowly recalled McKinley, Rowland, and Laster, and was a victory for the STOP campaign and the moderates. *Courtesy of the Arkansas History Commission.*

DO YOU WANT NEGROES IN OUR SCHOOLS?

IF YOU <u>DO NOT</u> THEN GO TO THE POLLS THIS COMING MON-
DAY AND

VOTE

FOR REMOVAL — AGAINST REMOVAL

LAMB	McKINLEY
MATSON	ROWLAND
TUCKER	LASTER

THIS IS THE SIMPLE TRUTH. IF THE INTEGRATIONISTS WIN THIS SCHOOL BOARD FIGHT, THE SCHOOLS <u>WILL BE INTEGRATED THIS FALL</u>. THERE WILL BE ABSOLUTELY NOTHING YOU OR WE CAN DO <u>TO STOP IT</u>.

PLEASE VOTE RIGHT!!!

*Join hands with us in this fight—
send your contributions to*

THE MOTHERS' LEAGUE

P. O. BOX 3321 • LITTLE ROCK, ARKANSAS

Ad Paid for by Margaret C. Jackson, President; Mary Thomason, Secretary

Document Ten

The statement signed by 936 former Central High students in support for their purged teachers, distributed with a cover letter from Principal Jess Matthews on June 2, 1959.
Courtesy of Jo Ann Henry Royster, mathematics teacher from Central High.

DECLARATION

We, as former students of Little Rock Central High School, join in protest of what we feel to be the malicious and unjustified reprisal of our teachers:

(1) Because, they are directly responsible for having built over a period of years one of the top thirty-eight high schools in America;
(2) Because, they have produced more than twenty National Merit Scholars for each of the last two years;
(3) Because, they have unselfishly given many years of loyal and devoted service to both their students and the community of Little Rock as teachers and as citizens;
(4) Because, regardless of their personal opinions during the integration controversy, to which they are entitled as Americans, they have, without qualification or exception, acted only with their students' welfare and interest as their primary concern;
(5) Because, these teachers have made it possible for us, as their former students, to share a feeling of pride, honor, and privilege to have attended their classes;
(6) Because, these teachers, with whom we have been personally associated, have dedicated their lives to molding our character and developing us as future citizens of this, our free and democratic America;

We firmly pledge our support to their cause, and give our unqualified endorsement to these teachers, who have exhibited unimpeachable character as teachers and as citizens of Arkansas.

With abiding faith in our democratic principles . . .

This petition was signed by nine hundred and thirty-six (936) of your former students.

Document Eleven

Based on the official personnel directories of the Little Rock School District for 1958–59 and 1959–60, the persons listed did not return the second year to the LRSD. The numbers indicate a greater loss by percentage at the two white high schools than at the all-black, Horace Mann High. *Personnel Directories were copied from the LRSD in 1995 by Selma Hobby for the author.*

High School Teachers from the LRSD Who Did Not Return for the 1959–60 School Year

CENTRAL HIGH SCHOOL (32 out of 92 did not return)

J. O. Powell	Vice Principal for Boys
Judith Armstrong	English
Thelma Casteel	Business Education/Math
Marguerite Chappel	English/Social Studies/ Special Education
Bertha Cotton	Kindergarten
Vivian Daniel	Social Science
Bobbye Free	Business Education
Naomi Hancock	Vocal Music
Allen Howard	Coach/Physical Education
William P. Ivy	Mathematics
Alma Jeffries	Mathematics
Miller King	Chemistry
Carol Ann Lackey	Business Education
Mary Long	English
John McCullars	Mathematics
Robert McDonald	Art
Kay McSpadden	English
Edna Middlebrook	Journalism
Harvey Milner	Biology
Cassie Moren	Physical Education
Jennie Perkins	Social Science
Kenneth Ritchie	Instrumental Music
Frances Rudd	Home Economics
Sara Shanks	Speech
Harriet Stegeman	Social Science/French
James Stewart	Special Education
Margaret Stewart	Social Science/Guidance
Charles Tobler	Vocational Printing

Donna Wells	English
Susie West	English
Mary Wheeler	Physical Education
Betty Jane Young	English/Guidance

HALL HIGH SCHOOL (12 out of 43 did not return)

Terrell Powell	Principal
Earnest Trickey	Vice Principal for Boys
Annette Carter	English
Edith Chapman	Social Science
Jeanette Eason	Business Education
Jim Fulmer	Mathematics
Johnnie Hixson	American History
Frances Johnson	Physical Education
Bill Kessinger	Coach
J. D. McGee	Physical Education
Myrna Peterson	Chemistry
Bud Swift	Biology

HORACE MANN HIGH SCHOOL (5 out of 35 did not return)

LeRoy Christophe	Principal
Otis T. Harris	Vice Principal for Boys
Leon L. Adams Jr.	Band
Treopia Gravelly	Counselor
John I. King	Foreign Languages

NOTES

INTRODUCTION: BEFORE THE LOST YEAR

1. The first black students to integrate the school were called the Little Rock Nine. There were three boys and six girls: Ernest Green, Jefferson Thomas, Terrence Roberts, Carlotta Walls, Elizabeth Eckford, Melba Pattillo, Minnijean Brown, Thelma Mothershed, and Gloria Ray.

2. John William Graves, review of *Redefining the Color Line: Black Activism in Little Rock, Arkansas, 1940–1970,* by John Kirk, *Journal of Southern History* 69, no. 4 (2003): 978.

3. Tony A. Freyer, *Little Rock on Trial:* Cooper v. Aaron *and School Desegregation* (Lawrence: University Press of Kansas, 2007), 210–11.

4. Numan Bartley, *The Rise of Massive Resistance (*Baton Rouge: Louisiana State University Press, 1969), 275 n23.

5. John A. Kirk, *Beyond Little Rock: The Origins and Legacies of the Central High Crisis* (Fayetteville: University of Arkansas Press, 2007), 8–9.

6. Elizabeth Jacoway, *Turn Away Thy Son: The Crisis That Shocked the Nation* (New York: Free Press, 2007), 325–27.

7. Ben F. Johnson III, "After 1957: Resisting Integration in Little Rock," *Arkansas Historical Quarterly* 66, no. 2 (2007): 258, 262.

8. Virgil T. Blossom, *It HAS Happened Here* (New York: Harper and Brothers, 1959), 195.

9. Jacoway, *Turn Away Thy Son.*

10. Elizabeth Jacoway, "Taken by Surprise: Little Rock Business Leaders and Desegregation," in *Southern Businessmen and Desegregation,* ed. Elizabeth Jacoway and David R. Colburn (Baton Rouge: Louisiana State University Press, 1982); "Richard C. Butler and the Little Rock School Board: The Quest to Maintain 'Educational Quality,'" *Arkansas Historical Quarterly* 65, no. 1 (2006): 24–38.

11. George C. Iggers, "An Arkansas Professor: The NAACP and Grass Roots," in *Little Rock USA,* ed. Wilson Record and Jane Cassels Record (San Francisco: Chandler Publishing Company, 1960), 283–91.

12. John Kirk, *Redefining the Color Line: Black Activism in Little Rock, Arkansas, 1940–1970* (Gainesville: University Press of Florida, 2002).

13. Kirk, *Beyond Little Rock.*

14. Karen Anderson, "The Little Rock School Desegregation Crisis: Moderation and Social Conflict," *Journal of Southern History* 70, no. 3 (2004): 603–37.

15. Bartley, *Rise of Massive Resistance.*

16. Corrine Silverman, *The Little Rock Story,* rev. ed. (Indianapolis : Inter-University Case Program Bobbs-Merrill Co., 1959); Record and Record, *Little Rock USA.*

17. Colbert Cartwright, "Lessons from Little Rock," *Christian Century* 74, Oct. 9,

1957, 1193–94; "The Improbable Demagogue of Little Rock, AR," *Reporter* 17, Oct. 17, 1957, 23–25.

18. Robert R. Brown, *Bigger Than Little Rock* (Greenwich, Conn.: Seabury Press, 1958).

19. Thomas Pettigrew and Ernest Q. Campbell, *Christians in Racial Crisis: A Study of Little Rock's Ministry, Including Statements on Desegregation and Race Relations by the Leading Religious Denominations of the United States* (Washington, D.C.: Public Affairs Press, 1959).

20. Pettigrew and Campbell, *Christians in Racial Crisis*, 129.

21. Brooks Hays, *A Southern Moderate Speaks* (Chapel Hill: University of North Carolina, 1959).

22. Dale Alford and L'Moore Alford, *The Case of the Sleeping People (Finally Awakened by the Little Rock School Frustrations)* (Little Rock: Pioneer Press, 1959).

23. David Chappell, *A Stone of Hope: Prophetic Religion and the Death of Jim Crow* (Chapel Hill: University of North Carolina Press, 2004).

24. Carolyn Gray LeMaster, *Corner of the Tapestry: A History of the Jewish Experience in Arkansas, 1820s–1990s* (Fayetteville: University of Arkansas Press, 1994), 374–79.

25. Irving Spitzberg, *Racial Politics in Little Rock 1954–1964* (New York: Garland Publishing, 1987).

26. Mark Newman, "The Arkansas Baptist State Convention and Desegregation 1954–1968," *Arkansas Historical Quarterly* 56, no. 3 (1997): 294-313.

27. Jane Dailey, "Sex, Segregation, and the Sacred after Brown," *Journal of American History* 91, no. 1 (2004): 119–45.

28. V. O. Key, *Southern Politics in State and Nation* (New York: Alfred Knopf, 1949), 183–204.

29. Boyd Alexander Drummond, "Arkansas Politics: A Study of a One Party System" (Ph.D. diss., University of Chicago, 1957).

30. Daisy Bates, *The Long Shadow of Little Rock: A Memoir* (New York: David McKay & Son, 1962).

31. Grif Stockley, *Daisy Bates: Civil Rights Crusader from Arkansas* (Jackson: University Press of Mississippi, 2005).

32. Orval Faubus, *Down from the Hills I* (Little Rock: Pioneer Press, 1980); Orval Faubus, *Down from the Hills II* (Little Rock: Democrat Printing and Lithographing Co, 1986).

33. Roy Reed, *Faubus: The Life and Times of an American Prodigal* (Fayetteville: University of Arkansas Press, 1997).

34. Elizabeth Huckaby, *Crisis at Central High: Little Rock 1957–58* (Baton Rouge: Louisiana State University Press, 1980); *Crisis at Central High*, dir. Lamont Johnson (CBS Entertainment, 1980).

35. Elizabeth Huckaby Diary, 1959, Elizabeth Huckaby Collection, A-122, box 2, file 11, Archives and Special Collections, University of Arkansas at Little Rock (UALR).

36. Lola Dunnavant and J. Eison, eds., "Steel Helmets under a September Sun, Little Rock Central High 1957–58," *Pulaski County Historical Review* 37 (1989): 22–

35; Lola Dunnavant, "Long Halls Growing Darker, Little Rock Central High 1958–59," *Pulaski County Historical Review* 38 (1990): 46–59.

37. J. O Powell, untitled manuscript, J. O. Powell and Velma Powell Collection (MC 1367), box 1, folders 4 and 5, Special Collections, University of Arkansas Libraries, Fayetteville.

38. Henry M. Alexander, *The Little Rock Recall Election* (New York: McGraw Hill, 1960).

39. Vivion Brewer, *The Embattled Ladies of Little Rock, 1958–63: The Study to Save Public Education at Central High* (Fort Bragg, Calif.: Lost Coast Press, 1999).

40. Sara Murphy, *Breaking the Silence: Little Rock's Women's Emergency Committee to Open Our Schools 1958–63,* ed. Patrick C Murphy II (Fayetteville: University of Arkansas Press, 1997).

41. Lorraine Gates, "Power from the Pedestal: The Women's Emergency Committee and the Little Rock School Crisis," *Arkansas Historical Quarterly* 55 (1996), rpt., 66, no. 2 (2007): 194–223.

42. Spitzberg, *Racial Politics in Little Rock.*

43. Neil McMillen, "The White Citizen's Council and Resistance to School Desegregation in Arkansas," *Arkansas Historical Quarterly* 30 (1971): 95–122.

44. David Chappell, *Inside Agitators: White Southerners in the Civil Rights Movement* (Baltimore: Johns Hopkins University Press, 1994); David Chappell, "Diversity within a Racial Group: White People in Little Rock 1957–1959," *Arkansas Historical Quarterly* 54, no. 4 (1995): 444–56.

45. Graeme Cope, "A Thorn in the Side? The Mother's League of Central High School and the Little Rock Desegregation Crisis of 1957," *Arkansas Historical Quarterly* 57, no. 2 (1998): 160–90; Graeme Cope, "Honest White People of the Middle and Lower Classes," *Arkansas Historical Quarterly* 61, no. 1 (2002): 37–58; Graeme Cope, "'Marginal Youngsters' and 'Hoodlums of Both Sexes'? Student Segregationists during the Little Rock School Crisis," *Arkansas Historical Quarterly* 63, no. 4 (2004): 380–403.

46. Freyer, *Little Rock on Trial; Little Rock Crisis: A Constitutional Interpretation* (Westport, Conn.: Greenwood Press, 1984); Tony Freyer, "The Past as Future: The Little Rock Crisis and the Constitution," in *Understanding the Little Rock Crisis,* ed. Elizabeth Jacoway and C. Fred Williams (Fayetteville: University of Arkansas Press, 1997).

47. Sources for this time line include all of the following: Bartley, *Rise of Massive Resistance;* Huckaby, *Crisis at Central High;* Record and Record, *Little Rock USA;* http://www.ardemgaz.com/prev/central/wcentral04.html; http://www.ardemgaz.com/prev/central/CHSmain.html.

CHAPTER ONE: THE SUMMER OF RELIEF TURNS TO ANXIETY

1. Elizabeth Paisley Huckaby, journal, vol. 2, May 27, 1958, Elizabeth Paisley Huckaby Personal Records (MC428), series 1, box 1, folder 3, Special Collections, University of Arkansas Libraries, Fayetteville.

2. Huckaby, *Crisis at Central High,* 209. See also Jack Schnedler, "What Happened after Central High Crisis," *Arkansas Democrat-Gazette,* Oct. 4, 1997 (http://www.ardemgaz.com/prev/central/CHSmain.html).

3. Huckaby journal, May 27, 1958.

4. Huckaby journal, May 25, 1958.

5. Huckaby, *Crisis at Central High,* 209. See also Schnedler, "What Happened after Central High Crisis."

6. Huckaby, *Crisis at Central High,* 217.

7. Huckaby, *Crisis at Central High,* 217.

8. Huckaby, *Crisis at Central High.* See also Sondra Gordy, "Through the Eyes of a Heroine," *Arkansas Historical Quarterly* 67, no. 2 (2008): 141–67.

9. Huckaby journal, May 27, 1958.

10. Elizabeth Paisley Huckaby to William M. Paisley, May 4, 1958, Huckaby Personal Records.

11. Huckaby journal, May 23, 1958.

12. Huckaby journal, May 23, 1958.

13. Huckaby journal, May 28, 1958.

14. Elizabeth Paisley Huckaby, interview with author, Dec. 18, 1995.

15. "Gazette and Editor Win Two Pulitzer Prizes for Race Crisis Stand," *Arkansas Gazette,* May 6, 1958.

16. Murphy, *Breaking the Silence,* 61–63.

17. Adolphine Terry's personal journal, quoted in Murphy, *Breaking the Silence,* 62.

18. Michael B. Dougan, *Arkansas Odyssey: The Saga of Arkansas from Prehistoric Times to the Present* (Little Rock: Rose Publishing Company, 1994), 502.

19. "Large and Applauding Crowd Honors Gazette and Editors," *Arkansas Gazette,* June 4, 1958.

20. Huckaby journal, June 3, 1958.

21. Winthrop Rockefeller was Arkansas's governor from 1966 to 1970—the first Republican governor since Reconstruction. He served as head of the Arkansas Industrial Development Commission under Faubus but split with him over the Central crisis.

22. "Large and Applauding Crowd."

23. Huckaby, *Crisis at Central High,* 170–72.

24. Iggers, "Arkansas Professor," 283.

25. Iggers, "Arkansas Professor," 284.

26. Iggers, "Arkansas Professor," 283–91. This statement was prepared by Iggers in 1959 for Record and Record, *Little Rock USA* (1960).

27. Kirk, *Redefining the Color Line,* 94; Blossom, *It HAS Happened Here,* 15–24.

28. Ben F. Johnson III, *Arkansas in Modern America, 1930–1999* (Fayetteville: University of Arkansas Press, 2000), 160. See also George C. Iggers, "A Study on Equality under Segregation in the Little Rock Public School System," National Park Services, Little Rock Central High School National Historic Site Collections, Little Rock.

29. Freyer, *Little Rock on Trial,* viii, 13–14.

30. Iggers, "Arkansas Professor," 287.

31. *Aaron v. Cooper*, Aug. 28, 1958, Civ. No. 3113, U.S. Dist. Ct. E. Ark. Aaron was the first listed student, and Cooper was president of the school board at this time.

32. "Segregationist Rally, March 20, 1956," reprinted from *Southern School News* (Apr. 1956): 8, in Record and Record, *Little Rock, U.S.A.* These numbers differ from those Blossom gives: 426 whites, 533 blacks in the Mann area; 213 whites, 516 blacks in the Central area; and 700 whites, 6 blacks in the Hall area gives (*It HAS Happened Here*, 17).

33. According to Blossom, the original number of blacks for Central was 80, later reduced to 32. Through Blossom's interviews the applicants were reduced even further, to 17. According to Blossom, "When tensions became great the 17 who had been selected withdrew for reasons of their own" (*It HAS Happened Here*, 21).

34. Kirk, *Redefining the Color Line*, 90–96, 106–8. Kirk also mentions the grueling interview process that Blossom used to dissuade black applicants from attending Central High.

35. Reed, *Faubus*, 195.

36. Public resistance to desegregation had emerged in Little Rock in 1956 with the formation of the Capital Citizens' Council, a branch of the White Citizens' Council formed during Faubus's first term as governor. The Gallup Poll conducted in May 1955 had found that only 20 percent of southern citizens viewed the *Brown* decision favorably. This percentage increased to 22 percent in early 1956 and to a high of 27 percent in Jan. 1957. But the Aug. 1957 poll marked an all-time low, with only 16 percent of southerners favoring the *Brown* decision.

37. Reed states that both Upton and Miller saw this as a possible delaying tactic, not a serious challenge to final federal authority (*Faubus*, 195).

38. Reed, *Faubus*, 196.

39. Reed, *Faubus*, 199. See also Faubus, *Down from the Hills I*, 201.

40. Reed, *Faubus*, 199.

41. Blossom later explained the change, writing that the judgeship of Eastern Arkansas had been vacant for a while and that Davies was temporarily assigned to the vacancy (*It HAS Happened Here*, 161).

42. Reed, *Faubus*, 196.

43. Huckaby journal, June 2, 1958.

44. Huckaby journal, June 3, 1958.

45. Ray Moseley, "Waiting for the Next Governor, School Board President Tells Court," *Arkansas Gazette*, June 5, 1958.

46. Ray Moseley, "School Officials Describe Chaos in Central High," *Arkansas Gazette*, June 4, 1958.

47. Moseley, "Waiting for the Next Governor."

48. Moseley, "Waiting for the Next Governor."

49. Moseley, "Waiting for the Next Governor."

50. Moseley, "Waiting for the Next Governor."

51. Blossom, *It HAS Happened Here*, 179.

52. Blossom, *It HAS Happened Here*, 176.

53. Kirk, *Beyond Little Rock*, 96.

54. Moseley, "School Officials Describe Chaos."

55. Huckaby journal, June 4, 1958.

56. Huckaby journal, June 6, 1958.

57. Moseley, "Waiting for the Next Governor."

58. Huckaby journal, June 6, 1958.

59. Huckaby, *Crisis at Central High,* 218.

60. Huckaby journal, June 5, 1958.

61. See Powell account, 1958–1979, Powell and Powell Collection. J.O. and his wife, Velma, were activists in the community, Velma serving as a founding member of the WEC and as a member of the interracial Arkansas Human Relations Council. J.O., a native of Little Rock and a graduate of Little Rock High School, held views on race that were more than rare for the time period. One of J. O. Powell's teaching colleagues said that the couple was truly "color-blind." William Lincoln, the photography teacher from Central, recalled that J.O. had made some statements "concerning the rights of different cultures, and I think that's what got him frustrated, because he didn't get much backing" (William Lincoln, interview with author, Mar. 3, 1996). Lincoln also said that the Powells used Dr. Jerry Jewell, a black dentist in the community, as their dental professional—something truly rare in the South during this time period.

62. Moseley, "Waiting for the Next Governor."

63. "They Wanted to Integrate, But—: Why School Superintendent Blossom Now Seeks a 2? Year Delay," *U.S. News and World Report,* June 20, 1958, 74–86. Excerpts from the June 4, 1958, transcript of the hearing under Judge Harry J. Lemley were reprinted in this article.

64. Three anti-integration proposals were passed in the general election of Nov. 6, 1956. Amendment 47 nullified the Supreme Court's desegregation decisions. Initiated Act 1 was intended to assign pupils to schools based on factors other than race. The final proposal was a resolution of interposition, which became Amendment 44, asserting that the state could block the decisions of the U.S. Supreme Court.

65. Ray Moseley, "Board Was Too Lenient in Dealing with Trouble, N.Y. Educators Declare," *Arkansas Gazette,* June 6, 1958.

66. In the small community of Lawrence County in northeast Arkansas, when threats of violence were launched in response to the school board's plan to integrate twenty-five black students into all-white schools, the board and superintendent obtained a federal court injunction preventing further interference with the planned desegregation. This made Hoxie, Arkansas, the first southern case to involve federal officials.

67. Moseley, "Waiting for the Next Governor."

68. Anderson, "Little Rock School Desegregation Crisis."

69. Anderson, "Little Rock School Desegregation Crisis."

70. "Dr. Alford Says He Opposed Board Report," *Arkansas Gazette,* June 20, 1958.

71. Howard Bell, unpublished memoir (Summer 1959), 12 (in author's possession).

72. "School Board Rips Governor's Version of Crisis at CHS," *Arkansas Gazette,* June 18, 1958.

73. "School Board Rips Governor's Version."

74. "Dr. Alford Says He Opposed."

75. "Negroes File Appeal Plea with Lemley," *Arkansas Gazette,* June 22, 1958.

76. Elizabeth Paisley Huckaby to William M. Paisley, June 22, 1958, Huckaby Personal Records (MC428), series 1, box 1, folder 3.

77. Huckaby journal, June 3–30, 1958.

78. Huckaby journal, July 29, 1958.

79. "Faubus Sweeps to Third Term—Landslide Margin 2 to 1," *Arkansas Gazette,* July 30, 1958.

80. The *Bulletin* campaign brochure, July 18, 1958, 3.

81. See "The Special Election: Saturday, Sept. 27," *Arkansas Gazette,* Sept. 15, 1958; *Arkansas Gazette,* July 31, 1958.

82. Voting records of the Arkansas Secretary of State for the Democratic summer primaries of 1954, 1956, 1958, Arkansas History Commission (microfilm). Also see B. F. Johnson, "After 1957," 261–62. Historian Ben Johnson traces the voting coalition of blacks and upper-class whites back to at least 1950. See also *Arkansas Gazette,* July 31, 1958.

83. Huckaby journal, July 30, 1958.

84. "Faubus Sweeps to Third Term."

85. See Huckaby journal, Aug. 4, 29, 1958, regarding her comments about the importance of saving materials. Also see the total collection of materials Huckaby saved from Central High administrative minutia (Huckaby Personal Records).

86. Huckaby journal, June 9, 1958.

87. Huckaby journal, June 19, 1958.

88. Huckaby journal, June 28, 1958.

89. Huckaby journal, Aug. 18, 1958.

90. Huckaby journal, Aug. 18, 1958.

91. Huckaby journal, Aug. 19, 1958.

92. Huckaby journal, Aug. 19, 1958.

93. Huckaby journal, Aug. 22, 1958.

94. "Board Bars Negroes after Stay Granted—Time Allowed to Take Case to Higher Court," *Arkansas Gazette,* Aug. 22, 1958.

95. Ernest Valachovic, "Prompt Approval Expected for Governor's Package—Radio & T.V. Stations to Cover Session," *Arkansas Gazette,* Aug. 26, 1958.

96. "Full Tribunal to Tackle School Crisis in Rare Move," *Arkansas Gazette,* Aug. 26, 1958. Though the *Arkansas Gazette* reports that this was the fifth time the Court had met in four decades, Michael Dougan, in *Arkansas Odyssey* (502), indicates that it was only the third special term in the Supreme Court's history.

97. "All Schools in City Open Sept. 8," *Arkansas Gazette,* Aug. 26, 1958.

98. Huckaby journal, Aug. 25, 1958.

99. Text of address by Faubus, *Arkansas Gazette,* Aug. 27, 1958.

100. Text of address by Faubus, Aug. 27, 1958.

101. "Six Bills to Block School Integration Offered by Faubus—Legislators Act Quickly on Proposals," *Arkansas Gazette,* Aug. 27, 1958.

102. "Six Bills to Block School Integration."

103. For a fuller treatment, see Jeff Woods, *Black Struggle, Red Scare: Segregation and Anti-Communism in the South, 1948–1968* (Baton Rouge: Louisiana State University Press, 2004), 72.

104. Ernest Valachovic, "Faubus' Bills Get Final Okay of Legislature," *Arkansas Gazette*, Aug. 29, 1958.

105. "Final Ruling on CHS Set by September 15," *Arkansas Gazette*, Aug. 29, 1958. See also Silverman, *Little Rock Story*, 25.

106. Huckaby journal, Aug. 29, 1958.

107. "Plans for Enforcement Fully Co-ordinated, Cobb Asserts," *Arkansas Gazette*, Sept. 10, 1958.

108. Huckaby journal, Aug. 29, 1958.

109. Huckaby journal, Sept. 2, 1958.

110. Huckaby journal, Sept. 8, 1958.

111. Ernest Valachovic, "Faubus Closes CHS after Court Denies Delay of Integration. Segregation Bills Signed: 4 Schools Out," *Arkansas Gazette*, Sept. 13, 1958.

112. Huckaby journal, Sept. 14, 1958.

CHAPTER TWO: NOTHING BUT CONFUSION

1. Bill Lewis, "Exchange Student Anxious to Begin Studies at CHS," *Arkansas Gazette*, Sept. 25, 1958.

2. "Faubus Sees Quick Opening," *Arkansas Gazette*, Sept. 23, 1958.

3. Huckaby journal, Sept. 15, 1958.

4. Huckaby journal, Sept. 15, 1958. See also Ray Mosely, "High School Bands, Football Cancelled: Deadlock Continues: Stopgap Moves Are Advanced for Instruction," *Arkansas Gazette*, Sept. 16, 1958.

5. Moseley, "High School Bands, Football Cancelled."

6. Jerry McConnell and Charley Thornton, "Tigers, Warriors to Stick Together," *Arkansas Gazette*, Sept. 16, 1958.

7. Ray Moseley, "Board Asks Faubus' Will on Football," *Arkansas Gazette*, Sept. 16, 1958.

8. Blossom, *It HAS Happened Here*, 185.

9. Ray Moseley, "Board Okays Resumption of Football," *Arkansas Gazette*, Sept. 18, 1958.

10. Faustine Childress Jones, *A Traditional Model of Educational Excellence: Dunbar High School of Little Rock, Arkansas* (Washington D.C.: Howard University Press, 1981), 2–7.

11. Maude Woods, interview with author, Nov. 10, 1995. See also Jerome Muldrew, interview with author, Dec. 1, 1995.

12. M. Woods, interview, Nov. 10, 1995.

13. Leon Adams, interview with author, Mar. 19, 1996.

14. "School Board Member Quits during Confusion to Obey U.S., State Rulings," *Arkansas Gazette*, Sept. 13, 1958.

15. Silverman, *Little Rock Story,* 23.

16. Silverman, *Little Rock Story,* 23.

17. Murphy, *Breaking the Silence,* 69.

18. Pat Deaton Perry, letter to author, Oct. 1, 2006.

19. "School Board Member Quits during Confusion."

20. "School Board Rips Governor's Version." See also "School Board Statement," *Arkansas Gazette,* June 18, 1958.

21. Blossom, *It HAS Happened Here,* 47.

22. See Cope, "Thorn in the Side?" 176. See also H. M. Alexander, *Little Rock Recall Election,* 6.

23. Spitzberg, *Racial Politics in Little Rock,* 78.

24. See Cope, "Thorn in the Side?" See also H. M. Alexander, *Little Rock Recall Election,* 6.

25. "Mothers Say Recall Petitions Still Not Ready," *Arkansas Gazette,* Sept. 25, 1958.

26. H. M. Alexander, *Little Rock Recall Election,* 6.

27. "High School Classes on Television Starting Monday September 22," *Arkansas Gazette,* Sept. 21, 1958.

28. "TV Teaching Gets a Tryout," *U.S. News and World Report,* Oct. 3, 1958, 73–75.

29. Nancy Popperfuss, interview with author, Mar. 9, 1996. The state of Arkansas did not provide free textbooks for high school students until the late 1960s. At this time white and black high school students had to purchase them, so black schools often used older texts that were sometimes out of date. Horace Mann High had a bookstore where black students purchased textbooks.

30. Bell, unpublished memoir, 10.

31. "TV Teaching Gets a Tryout," 75.

32. U.S. Census Bureau, *Characteristics of the Population,* vol. 1, part 5, Arkansas Table 47 (Washington, D.C.: Government Printing Office, 1970), 175.

33. Barry Cook, telephone interview with author, Feb. 11, 2000; Nielsen Media Research, *Number of Homes,* Sept.–Dec. 1958, 22.

34. Advertisement, *Arkansas Gazette,* Nov. 10, 1957.

35. "3,500 Students, 15 Teachers in Little Rock's T.V. School," *Arkansas Gazette,* Sept. 21, 1958.

36. Orville Henry, "Tulsa Grinds Up Razorbacks 27–14 in Hogs' Backyard," *Arkansas Gazette,* Sept. 28, 1958.

37. "Faubus Sweeps to Third Term."

38. "The Special Election Saturday September 27," *Arkansas Gazette,* Sept. 18, 1958.

39. "Special Election Saturday September 27."

40. Sherri Daniel (Evans), video interview with author, June 27, 2005.

41. "3,500 Students, 15 Teachers."

42. Murphy, *Breaking the Silence,* 73.

43. "Women Organize Campaign for Opening High Schools," *Arkansas Gazette*, Sept. 18, 1958. See also H. M. Alexander, *Little Rock Recall Election*, 6–7.

44. Murphy, *Breaking the Silence*, 72–73. See also Harry Ashmore, *Civil Rights and Wrongs* (New York: Pantheon Books, 1994), 130

45. L. Gates, "Power from the Pedestal," 26–57. See also Jacoway, *Turn Away Thy Son*, xi–xiii.

46. Murphy, *Breaking the Silence*, 74. Faubus often called the group part of the silk-stocking brigade. Henry Alexander describes their leadership as elite, focusing on their efforts to contact "influentials" in the community (*Little Rock Recall Election*, 7).

47. "Charter Is Granted for Private School: Incorporators Hope to Lease Four Buildings," *Arkansas Gazette*, Sept. 18, 1958.

48. Huckaby journal, Sept. 18, 1958.

49. "Here Is Text of Speech by Governor Faubus," *Arkansas Gazette*, Sept. 19, 1958.

50. See Jacoway, *Turn Away Thy Son*, 132, regarding Faubus's belief that Miller had betrayed him. See Freyer, *Little Rock on Trial*, 110, on Miller's equivocation.

51. "NAACP Asks Injunction against Leasing Schools," *Arkansas Gazette*, Sept. 28, 1958.

52. "71% at Hall Say 'Open,'" *Arkansas Gazette*, Sept. 21, 1958.

53. "CHS Students Ask Opinion on Opening," *Arkansas Gazette*, Sept. 25, 1958.

54. Silverman, *Little Rock Story*, 28.

55. Ray Moseley, "200 Students Demonstrate with Anti-Integration Chant," *Arkansas Gazette*, Sept. 23, 1958.

56. "60 Per Cent of Displaced Students Find Means to Continue Schooling," *Arkansas Gazette*, Oct. 23, 1958.

57. Little Rock School District Transfer Records, National Park Services, Little Rock Central High School, National Historic Site Collections.

58. Toshio Oishi, emails to author, Mar. 13, 14, 17, 18, 2003. See also Mrs. Virginia Brown Alexander, interview with author, Mar. 14–21, 2003.

59. On Feb. 13, 1943, the Arkansas state legislature passed the Alien Land Act "to prohibit any Japanese, citizen or alien, from purchasing or owning land in Arkansas." This act was later ruled unconstitutional.

60. Oishi, email.

61. Moseley, "200 Students Demonstrate with Anti-Integration Chant."

62. Mary Fletcher Worthen, *The History of Trinity: The Cathedral of the Episcopal Diocese of Arkansas* (Little Rock: August House Publishers, 1996), 211, 216.

63. "Episcopal Interim Academy Opens for Duration," *Arkansas Gazette*, Sept. 29, 1958. See also Moseley, "200 Students Demonstrate with Anti-Integration Chant."

64. Mrs. James Gates, telephone interview with author, May 22, 2006. Teachers included Egbert, Gates, Kilbury, Mrs. Joe Hardin, Mrs. Robert Bowling, Miss Jean Anderson, Mrs. Dwight Gillidette, Mrs. Ronald May, and Miss Carolyn Bell.

65. Bill Lewis, "Big Question: What about Next Year?" *Arkansas Gazette*, Apr. 19, 1959. See also Mrs. J. Gates, interview, May 22, 2006.

66. Deane Anthony Newell, telephone interview with author, June 12, 2006.

67. Chris Barrier, emails to author, June 24, 27, 2006.

68. Barrier, email, June 24, 2006.

69. Lily Major, telephone interview with author, Sept. 18, 2006.

70. Barrier, email, June 24, 2006.

71. Faye Perry Russ, interview with author, Sept. 28, 1998. See also Murphy, *Breaking the Silence,* 236–53, on the work of the Panel of American Women.

72. "The Special Election: Saturday, Sept. 27," *Arkansas Gazette,* Sept. 18, 1958.

73. Huckaby journal, Sept. 27, 1958.

74. Huckaby journal, Sept. 28, 1958.

75. Bartley, *Rise of Massive Resistance,* 275 n23.

76. *Arkansas Democrat,* Sept. 28, 1958.

77. See earlier discussion regarding Faubus's third-term primary victory in the summer of 1958 and accompanying footnotes regarding the records of the Arkansas Secretary of State, housed in the Arkansas History Commission. See also B. F. Johnson, "After 1957," 260–61. For the precinct records, see "Vote by Precincts," *Arkansas Democrat,* Sept. 28, 1958. See also "Table," *Arkansas Gazette,* Sept. 28, 1958.

78. Huckaby journal, Sept. 29, 1958.

79. Huckaby journal, Sept. 29, 1958.

80. Dunnavant, "Long Halls Growing Darker."

81. Little Rock Private High School Corporation Teacher's Contract, 1958–59, Sept. 29, 1958. See the appendix for a copy.

82. Bell, unpublished memoir.

83. Moseley, "Board Okays Resumption of Football."

84. Huckaby journal, Sept. 29, 1958.

85. Jo Ann Henry (Royster), interview with author, Oct. 25, 1995.

86. United States Court of Appeals for the Eighth Circuit, Temporary Restraining Order, *John Aaron et al. v. William G Cooper,* Sept. 29, 1958. See appendix for a copy. See also Jacoway, *Turn Away Thy Son,* 274–80; Freyer, *Little Rock on Trial,* 169–204.

87. Bell, unpublished memoir.

88. Huckaby journal, Sept. 29, 1958.

89. Elizabeth Paisley Huckaby to William M. Paisley, Oct. 5, 1958, Huckaby Personal Records (MC428), series 1, box 1, folder 3.

90. "U.S. Marshals Serve Papers: 175 Copies of Order on List for Delivery," *Arkansas Gazette,* Sept. 30, 1958.

91. Ray Moseley, "Restraining Orders Served on Officials," *Arkansas Gazette,* Sept. 30, 1958.

92. Margaret Frick, "Orso Cobb Directed Orders," *Arkansas Democrat,* Oct. 1, 1958.

93. Bell, unpublished memoir.

94. Huckaby to Paisley, Oct. 5, 1958.

95. Huckaby, interview, Sept. 18, 1995; Henry (Royster), interview, Oct. 25, 1995; Jo Ann Henry (Royster), video interview with author, June 29, 2005. In the appendix see a copy of the contract offered to white teachers at Central High. Notice whether or not there is a signature on the document that was returned to teachers at a later time.

CHAPTER THREE: WHERE SHALL WE GO?

1. George Douthit, "Board Solicits Private School Buildings, Funds," *Arkansas Democrat,* Oct. 1, 1958.

2. Douthit, "Board Solicits Private School Buildings."

3. Faubus, *Down from the Hills I,* 453. See also Ray Moseley, "Faubus Plan Fails, Schools Still Closed: He Vows to Fight On," *Arkansas Gazette,* Oct. 1, 1958.

4. Moseley, "Faubus Plan Fails."

5. "Misspelled Signs Blaming U.S. Go Up at 4 Schools," *Arkansas Gazette,* Oct. 1, 1958.

6. Huckaby journal, Sept. 29, 1958. See also Huckaby to Paisley, Oct. 5, 1958.

7. Faubus, *Down from the Hills I,* 457–58.

8. Faubus, *Down from the Hills I,* 457–58.

9. Faubus, *Down from the Hills I,* 458.

10. Jerry McConnell, "What's This? Tigers Fall from Top Spot?" *Arkansas Gazette,* Oct. 1, 1958.

11. McConnell, "What's This?"

12. Gene Hall, interview with author, Apr. 2, 1996.

13. Jerry McConnell, "AAA Spells Tight Rule for Tigers, Warriors Who Might Transfer," *Arkansas Gazette,* Sept. 17, 1958. See also *Time,* Nov. 3, 1958, 67–68.

14. Bill Sigler, video interview with author, June 21, 2005.

15. "Murchison Runs Horace Mann over Texas Team 12–7," *Arkansas Gazette,* Oct. 12, 1958.

16. "Lack of Money Only Problem by Private Schools, Dr. Raney Says," *Arkansas Gazette,* Oct. 3, 1958.

17. Douthit, "Board Solicits Private School Buildings."

18. "Two Accept Offer of Memphians," *Arkansas Democrat,* Oct. 1, 1958. See also Sue Phelps (Bushey), email to author, June 18, 2006.

19. "Two Accept Offer"; Phelps, email, June 18, 2006.

20. Henry Moon, photograph captioned "In School a Month Late," *Arkansas Democrat,* Oct. 1, 1958. Pictured are Carl McDaniel, Bill Orsburn, Betty Hervey, and Judy Caxson.

21. "Raney's Goal to Open School by Next Week," *Arkansas Gazette,* Oct. 3, 1958.

22. Katherine Pearcy Raines, interview with author, June 12, 2006.

23. "Faubus Opens Mass Appeal for Funds for City's Private School," *Arkansas Democrat,* Oct. 8, 1958.

24. "Negro Spokesman Expresses Doubt Schools to Open," *Arkansas Gazette,* Oct. 3, 1958.

25. "Negro Spokesman Expresses Doubt."

26. Huckaby to Paisley, Oct. 5, 1958.

27. Relman Morin, "US Court Extends School Lease Ban," *Arkansas Democrat,* Oct. 6, 1958.

28. "Retired Principal Hired to Serve as Private School Superintendent," *Arkansas Gazette,* Oct. 8, 1958.

29. "School Front to Shift Back to US Court," *Arkansas Gazette,* Oct. 12, 1958.

30. Huckaby journal, Oct. 14, 1958.

31. Huckaby journal, Oct. 15, 1958.

32. "Baptist to Open Academy," *Arkansas Democrat,* Oct. 7, 1958.

33. "Church Schools Open: 146 Students in Class," *Arkansas Gazette,* Oct. 13, 1958.

34. "Two Churches Open Classes for about 60," *Arkansas Gazette,* Oct. 13, 1958.

35. "Church Schools Open." See also "Two Churches Open Classes."

36. "Mann High Students Transfer," *Arkansas Democrat,* Oct. 15, 1958.

37. Goforth Coleman, interview with author, Sept. 22, 1998.

38. Illings—operated out of Sweet Home, Arkansas, by Horace Gillings—was listed under "Bus Service" in the 1958 Little Rock telephone book.

39. Coleman, interview, Sept. 22, 1998.

40. "Leasing Ban Is Extended as Court Debates Ruling," Oct. 15, 1958.

41. Jack Blalock, "700 White Pupils Register in Private & Baptist School," *Arkansas Gazette,* Oct. 21, 1958.

42. John C. Elkins, "Secondary Education in Little Rock, AR" (master's thesis, Arkansas State Teachers College, 1963), 19–22.

43. B. Lewis, "The Big School Question," *Arkansas Gazette,* Apr. 19, 1959. The members were Hardy L. Winburn, chair; Frank Shamburger, vice chair; Charles A. Bolton, secretary; and John Shamburger, A. B. Wetherington, Burt Treadway, and B. T. Harris.

44. Elkins, "Secondary Education," 19–22. On May 7, 1959, the LRPSC gave six thousand dollars of its donated money to Baptist High School. Donations to Raney had exceeded those to Baptist, but Raney's operators felt that the fund was intended for "all children of the closed schools." This generosity allowed Baptist to pay all outstanding debts to end the school year.

45. Lynn Nunnally Blagg, video interview with author, summer 2005.

46. Blagg, interview, summer 2005.

47. "Baptist School Accredited," *Southern School News* 5, no. 8 (1959): 14.

48. Gayle Singleton Gardner, interview with author, Feb. 12, 2003.

49. G. S. Gardner, interview, Feb. 12, 2003.

50. G. S. Gardner, interview, Feb. 12, 2003.

51. "Private Firm Says Senior Registration to Start Monday," *Arkansas Gazette,* Oct. 21, 1958.

52. Blalock, "700 White Pupils Register."

53. Elkins, "Secondary Education," 10.

54. Elkins, "Secondary Education," 11.

55. Elkins, "Secondary Education," 12. In Jan., eighteen students deemed slow learners who had applied for admission were being taught by Mr. M. L. Osment of the Highland Methodist facility

56. Faubus, *Down From the Hills I,* 466–69.

57. Faubus, *Down From the Hills I,* 466–69.

58. "Private School Starts Operation: Faubus Solicits Fund Contributions," *Southern School News* 5, no. 5 (1958): 8; "Baptist School Accredited."
        In Jan, the state of Arkansas granted Raney High accreditation with a class-A rating. Raney immediately applied for state funds based on Act 5, and $71,907.50 in state aid was received before a federal court ordered the distribution of funds to stop on Mar. 7, 1959, pending a decision on the constitutionality of the state law in *Aaron v. McKinley* (1958).

59. Carol Lynn Hallum, interview with author, Aug. 16, 1999.

60. Hallum, interview, Aug. 16, 1999.

61. Hallum, interview, Aug. 16, 1999.

62. Phillip Moore, video interview with author, June 28, 2005.

63. Phillip Moore, email to author, Apr. 1999.

64. Bobbie Forster, "Hazen Calls Meeting to Aid Students," *Arkansas Democrat,* Oct. 13, 1958.

65. "Corporation for White Seniors Expects 500 Today," *Arkansas Gazette,* Oct. 21, 1958.

66. Jerry Baldwin, interview with author, May 21, 2003. Today Baldwin credits his recruitment while at Hendrix College to referee intramural sports as changing his attitude regarding race. His training as a referee has given him a thirty-plus-year career as a basketball referee, in which he has learned that impartiality in calling high school games allows no preconceptions regarding the players. Through Baldwin's experience in athletics, he has learned to apply the same rules of fairness and equality in all aspects of his life—not just on the basketball court.

67. Bell, unpublished memoir, 10.

68. "Board to Use Idle Teachers for Vacancies," *Arkansas Gazette,* Oct. 24, 1958. For a list of Little Rock High School teachers who did not return in the 1959–60 school year, see the appendix.

69. Jo Evelyn Torrence Elston, interview with author, Mar. 19, 1996.

70. Henry (Royster), interview, Oct. 25, 1995.

71. Patricia Williams, interview with author, Mar. 22, 1996, 2–3.

72. Mary Ann Lofton Wright, interview with author, Mar. 18, 1996, 3.

73. Willie Brooks Johnson, interview with author, Jan. 11, 1996, 3–4.

74. Arceal Terry, interview with author, Dec. 18, 1995, 12.

75. Huckaby journal, Mar. 26, 1959.

76. Huckaby journal, Apr. 29–30, 1959.

77. Wright, interview, Mar. 19, 1996, 12–13.

78. "Corporation School for White Seniors Expects 500 Today," *Arkansas Gazette*, Oct. 20, 1958.

79. Jane Lewis (Huffman), email to author, June 19, 2006.

80. "Under Political Activity," *Southern School News* 5, no. 6 (1958): 12.

81. Silverman, *Little Rock Story*, 29. See also "School Board and Schoolmen," *Southern School News* 5, no. 5 (1958): 12; Dougan, *Arkansas Odyssey*, 502–3.

82. "Under Political Activity."

83. Sharon Priest, *Historical Report of the Secretary of State, Arkansas* (1998), 196–97.

84. "Faubus Is Easy Winner, GOP Foe Lags 5-to-1, *Arkansas Gazette*, Nov. 5, 1958.

85. "34 Commute to Conway's Baptist School," *Arkansas Gazette*, Nov. 4, 1958.

86. Myles Adams, interview with author, Mar. 31, 2003, 5.

87. M. Adams, interview, Mar. 31, 2003, 3. Adams learned about the schooling opportunity through his church and knew that his congregation would help pay the tuition fees. Myles, an active member of his church youth group, remembers, "They knew the situation about my father and they knew that we couldn't afford whatever it cost." He was an only child, and he and his mother took it quite hard when they learned that Myles's father had cancer. "We learned about it when I was in the tenth grade, and we lost him in 1961," Adams said. The Adams family were all faithful members of Temple Baptist Church on Wright Avenue, a congregation of the Baptist Missionary Association, a more conservative and fundamental branch of Baptists that had broken from the Southern Baptist Convention in 1924.

88. Melvin Bender, *She May Be Small . . . but There Are Those Who Love Her So: The History of Central Baptist College* (Conway, AR: River Road Press, 2001), 32.

89. Bender, *She May Be Small*, 31.

90. The delegates to the state meeting at Little Rock endorsed a "Resolution on Integration" that said in part: "Be it therefore resolved that we, the Arkansas Missionary Baptist Association, herewith voice our opposition to any force within or without our country, whether communistic, socialistic or other, which seeks to destroy our democratic and American way of life; that we reaffirm our faith in the whole counsel of God's Word; that we declare the integration of Negroes and whites in our schools and society to be a threat to the security of our nation and contrary to the teachings of God both in the Bible and in nature; and that we hereby describe the Supreme Court ruling . . . as being deplorable."

91. M. Adams, interview, Mar. 31, 2003, 7.

92. M. Adams, interview, Mar. 31, 2003, 11.

93. "38 Districts Ask Funds for Little Rock Transfer," *Arkansas Gazette*, Nov. 5, 1958.

94. "38 Districts Ask Funds."

95. Other students who attended were Lynda McClenney and Mandy Cannon, sophomores; Jean Pierce, Linda McClelland, Arlene Montgomery, and Jean McClenney, juniors; and Carolyn Harrell, Ray Gassaway, Tommy Porter, and Robert White, seniors. Information from yearbook of Lynda McClenney (Latham), email to author, July 30, 2007.

96. Robert White, email to author, Apr. 30, 2007.

97. "Appeals Court Directs Board to 'Accomplish Integration,'" *Arkansas Democrat,* Nov. 10, 1958.

98. Bobbie Forster, "Board Status Uncertain: All May Resign," *Arkansas Democrat,* Nov. 9, 1958. See also "Upton Blames Faubus: Says Board Tired of Being Whipping Boy," *Arkansas Democrat,* Nov. 14, 1958.

99. Forster, "Board Status Uncertain."

100. "School Directors' Children Enroll at Hot Springs," *Arkansas Gazette,* Sept. 28, 1958; Frank Shamblin Jr., telephone interview with author, July 24, 2006.

101. Forster, "Board Status Uncertain."

CHAPTER FOUR: WHOM SHALL WE BLAME?

1. Huckaby, *Crisis at Central High,* 181–82; Elizabeth Paisley Huckaby to William M. Paisley, Mar. 2, 1958, Huckaby Personal Records (MC428), series 1, box 1, folder 3.

2. Elizabeth Paisley Huckaby, Records Pertaining to the Integration of Central High School, Little Rock, Arkansas, 1957–1963, Huckaby Personal Records (MC428), series 2, box 2, folder 22.

3. Huckaby, Records Pertaining to the Integration.

4. Interviews between the state police and Central High teachers: Paul Magro, Everett Barnes, William Ivy, and Mrs. James E. Griffin, Orval Faubus Collection, box 497, folder 11, Special Collections, University of Arkansas Libraries, Fayetteville. Though these interviews were completed in the spring of 1958, several would come into play in the hands of segregationists as they purged teachers at the end of the 1958–59 school year.

5. Jerry Jones, "AEA Group Votes Fight to Preserve Public Education," *Arkansas Gazette,* Nov. 7, 1958.

6. J. Jones, "AEA Group Votes Fight."

7. Roy Reed, "Council Flings Budget Threat, Orders Probe," *Arkansas Gazette,* Nov. 8, 1958.

8. Reed, "Council Flings Budget Threat."

9. Editorial, *Arkansas Gazette,* Nov. 8, 1958.

10. Roy Reed, "ALC Cools Down on Poll of Teachers," *Arkansas Gazette,* Nov. 12, 1958.

11. "Board to Use Idle Teachers." See also Sondra Gordy, "Empty Classrooms, Empty Hearts," *Arkansas Historical Quarterly* 4, no. 4 (1997): 427–42.

12. Blossom, *It HAS Happened Here,* 194–95. See also Bobbie Forster, "Pay Checks Drawn as Board Time Runs Out," *Arkansas Gazette,* Nov. 14, 1958.

13. Bud Lemke, "Campbell May Not Fill Board," *Arkansas Democrat,* Nov. 13, 1958. The Pulaski County Board of Education would take on great significance after the May 25, 1959, recall elections removed three members of the LRSD board.

14. Blossom, *It HAS Happened Here,* 192–93. See also Forster, "Pay Checks Drawn."

15. Murphy, *Breaking the Silence,* 103–7. See also "Candidates Sought for Board: Bankers Asked to Serve as Holding Group," *Arkansas Democrat,* Nov. 13, 1958.

16. "Arkansas: Desegregation Top Issue in Hays Upset: School-Closing Crisis Unresolved," *Southern School News* 5, no. 6 (1958): 12.

17. Murphy, *Breaking the Silence*, 102.

18. Murphy, *Breaking the Silence*, 107.

19. Murphy, *Breaking the Silence*, 107.

20. See Jacoway, *Turn Away Thy Son,* chap. 14; Murphy, *Breaking the Silence,* chaps. 5, 6, 7; L. Gates, "Power from the Pedestal."

21. "Part of the Little Rock Public School System Is Beset by a Crisis," advertisement, *Arkansas Gazette,* Dec. 3, 1958.

22. Murphy, *Breaking the Silence*, 103–7; Laura Miller, *Fearless: Irene Gaston Samuel and the Life of a Southern Liberal* (Little Rock: Center for Arkansas Studies, 2002), 35–49; Jacoway, *Turn Away Thy Son,* chap. 14.

23. H. M. Alexander, *Little Rock Recall Election,* 9.

24. "CCC to Back School Board Slate of Six," *Arkansas Gazette,* Dec. 1, 1958.

25. Advertisement, *Arkansas Gazette,* Dec. 3, 1958.

26. "School Board Slate of 6 Uses Faubus' Name," *Arkansas Gazette,* Dec. 4, 1958.

27. "Faubus Off Fence, Calls Business Slate Integration Slate," *Arkansas Gazette,* Dec. 6, 1958.

28. "Faubus Off Fence."

29. "Meddling Shocks Lamb; Rector Shows His Check," *Arkansas Gazette,* Dec. 6, 1958.

30. Advertisement, *Arkansas Gazette,* Dec. 6, 1958.

31. Chappell, "Diversity within a Racial Group."

32. "Nelson High in County May Take Transfers," *Arkansas Gazette,* Nov. 9, 1958. See also Little Rock School District Transfer Records, 1958–59.

33. "5 CHS Negroes Taking Courses of UA by Mail," *Arkansas Gazette,* Nov. 28, 1958.

34. NAACP Papers, Dec. 5, 1958, group III, box A98, Manuscript Division, Library of Congress.

35. Daisy Bates Papers, State Historical Society of Wisconsin, box 4. See also Jerry Jones, "Wilkins Says Negroes Can't Set Up Schools," *Arkansas Gazette,* Nov. 3, 1958.

36. Bowman Burns, interview with author, Mar. 11, 2003.

37. John Dokes, video interview with author, June 28, 2005.

38. Myrthene Rowe (Wroten), telephone interview with author, July 30, 2007.

39. Little Rock School District Transfer Records, 1957–58.

40. Huckaby journal, Nov. 26, 1958.

41. Hall, interview.

42. "Private School to Be Known as Raney High," *Arkansas Gazette,* Dec. 3, 1958.

43. Huckaby journal, Dec. 7, 1958.

44. Huckaby journal, Dec. 7, 1958.

45. H. M. Alexander, *Little Rock Recall Election,* 9.

46. "Protests Hinted by 3 Losers in District's Strangest Race," *Arkansas Gazette,* Dec. 7, 1958.

47. "Protests Hinted by 3 Losers."

48. "Three on Each Side Win in School Race," *Arkansas Gazette,* Dec. 7, 1958.

49. "The School Board's Formidable Task," editorial, *Arkansas Gazette,* Dec. 13, 1958.

50. "School Board Vote Recount Fails to Change Any Outcome," *Arkansas Gazette,* Dec. 12, 1958.

51. "School Board's Formidable Task."

52. "Miller Sets School Hearing for Jan 6," *Arkansas Gazette,* Dec. 9, 1958.

53. "Miller Sets School Hearing."

54. "Miller Sets School Hearing."

55. "School Board Member Is Private Director Too," *Arkansas Gazette,* Dec. 13, 1958. The three new members who joined the original six-member private school board formed in Sept. came from a broad range of society. One was Dan T. Sprick, the former mayor of Little Rock; another was Carl E. Wright, a sales representative for a petroleum company.

56. "Temperature Due to Start Comeback," *Arkansas Gazette,* Dec. 16, 1958.

57. "Faubus Says Public Schools Not Necessity," *Arkansas Gazette,* Dec. 16, 1958.

58. See a complete treatment of these activities in J. Woods, *Black Struggle, Red Scare.*

59. J. Woods, *Black Struggle, Red Scare,* 2; "Public Phase of Red Hunt Begins Today," *Arkansas Gazette,* Dec. 16, 1958.

60. J. Woods, *Black Struggle, Red Scare,* 127–28. See also "Legislative Action," *Southern School News* 5, no. 7 (Jan. 1959): 14.

61. "Group Sending 'Little Rock Letter' with Yule Cards," *Arkansas Gazette,* Dec. 17, 1958.

62. "Dance at Hall High," *Arkansas Gazette,* Dec. 17, 1958.

63. Photo with cutline, *Arkansas Gazette,* Dec. 19, 1958.

64. "Vice Presidency Offered to Him, Faubus Asserts," *Arkansas Gazette,* Dec. 18, 1958.

65. "Legislative Action."

66. Murphy, *Breaking the Silence,* 129–33.

67. "58 School Closing Roused Them; Now Come Names," *Arkansas Gazette,* Mar. 13, 1998. Only in 1998, at a fortieth-anniversary celebration of the founding of the WEC, where its members were honored at a public ceremony at the Terry mansion, were the names released to the press. The antebellum structure—the home of the WEC founder, Adolphine Fletcher Terry—served as the backdrop for this belated event honoring the courageous group. Southwestern Bell paid to have each member's name etched into the glass windows of the sunporch of Mrs. Terry's home. Terry had given the structure to the city of Little Rock, and it has since been operated by the Arkansas Arts Center as the Decorative Arts Museum.

68. Brewer, *Embattled Ladies of Little Rock.*

69. George H. Gallup, *The Gallup Poll; Public Opinion, 1935–1971* (New York: Random House, 1972), 2: 1584.

70. Murphy, *Breaking the Silence,* 109–10. See also "Legislative Action."

71. Bartley, *Rise of Massive Resistance,* 288–89.

72. A. S. Fleming, "Effects of Closed Schools," *School Life* 41 (1958): 4–5.

73. Fleming, "Effects of Closed Schools," 4–5.

74. Fleming, "Effects of Closed Schools," 6.

75. Fleming, "Effects of Closed Schools," 4–5.

76. Dan Wakefield, "Lost Class of '59," *Nation,* Nov. 1958, 373.

77. "Board to Ask for More Time to Study Case," *Arkansas Gazette,* Jan. 6, 1959.

78. Roy Reed, "Delay Move Fails, School Case Edict Is Promised Soon," *Arkansas Gazette,* Jan. 7, 1959.

79. "Judge Tells Board to 'Move Forward' on Integration Plan," *Arkansas Gazette,* Jan. 11, 1959.

80. Text of Order, *Arkansas Gazette,* Jan. 11, 1959.

81. "Legislative Action."

82. "Virginia School Laws Killed: Faubus Says His Plan is the Answer," *Arkansas Gazette,* Jan. 20, 1959.

83. Freyer, *Little Rock on Trial,* 206.

84. "Negroes Ask School Opening New Laws Planned by Faubus," *Arkansas Gazette,* Jan. 13, 1959.

85. Shimon Weber, "How Has School Conflict Affected Jews in Little Rock," *Jewish Daily Forward,* Oct. 19, 1957.

86. LeMaster, *Corner of the Tapestry,* 374–79; Spitzberg, *Racial Politics in Little Rock,* 77, 93–94, 176.

87. Jane Franklin (Goff) and Joyce Franklin, video interviews with author, June 27, 2005.

88. Walthall was one of the forty-four teachers and administrators to be fired or purged in the spring of 1959 by segregationist members of the school board.

89. J. Harvey Walthall Jr., "A Study of Certain Factors of School Closing in 1958 as They Affected the Seniors of the White Comprehensive High Schools in Little Rock, Arkansas" (Ph.D. diss., University of Arkansas, 1963), 45, table 2. The six black students who entered college early all attended Philander Smith: Judith Freeman (Green), Paul Hatchett, Julia Suttle, Lonny McIntosh, Wadell Smith, and Betty Alford (Judith Freeman Green, personal correspondence with author).

90. Walthall, "Study of Certain Factors," 45, table 2.

91. Owen McMullen, interview with author, Mar. 29, 2003.

CHAPTER FIVE: ENTER THE POLITICIANS

1. "2873 Students from 4 Schools Still Studying," *Arkansas Gazette,* Jan. 7, 1959. Various sources have different figures for total enrollment, transfers, etc. But these were officially announced by the school district in Jan. based on Nov. figures.

2. "Raney High Due to Get State Funds," *Arkansas Gazette,* Jan. 3, 1959.

3. "Faubus Takes Oath 3rd Time, Second in Arkansas History," *Arkansas Gazette,* Jan. 14, 1959.

4. "Faubus Lists Objectives of Third Term Program," *Arkansas Gazette,* Jan. 14, 1959.

5. Ernest Valachovic, "Local Option Student Aid Key to Plan," *Arkansas Gazette,* Jan. 14, 1959.

6. "Now We Face the Tragic Last Resort," *Arkansas Gazette,* Jan. 14, 1959.

7. "Can't Deduct School Costs on State Tax," *Arkansas Gazette,* Jan. 15, 1959.

8. George Douthit, "Faubus Indicates Donations to Private School Funds May be Deducted from Tax Bill," *Arkansas Gazette,* Nov. 9, 1958.

9. "Can't Deduct School Costs."

10. Kirk, *Redefining the Color Line,* 135–36. See also Murphy, *Breaking the Silence,* 111–12. Murphy correctly points out that it was Williams's wife, a WEC member, who had encouraged his stand—something Murphy labeled a breakthrough.

11. "Time to Evaluate School Situation, Leaders Advised," *Arkansas Gazette,* Jan. 15, 1959. See also Murphy, *Breaking the Silence,* 112.

12. Murphy, *Breaking the Silence,* 112–13.

13. "Chamber of Commerce Backs School Board, Pledges Aid," *Arkansas Gazette,* Jan. 27, 1959.

14. Jacoway, *Turn Away Thy Son,* 301.

15. Roy Reed, "Board Asks to Open Segregated Schools While It Drafts Plan: Seeks to Scrap Old Program, Find Dignity,'" *Arkansas Gazette,* Jan. 22, 1959.

16. Spitzberg, *Racial Politics in Little Rock,* 98.

17. Spitzberg, *Racial Politics in Little Rock,* 99.

18. Reed, *Faubus,* 151.

19. Witt Stephens and his brother Jack controlled Stephens, Inc., the tenth-largest investment-banking firm in America by 1977. Witt Stephens invested in municipal bonds and eventually became the head of Arkansas Louisiana Gas Co., the forerunner of Centerpoint Energy. By the 1970s, state senators who served on the powerful Joint Budget Committee had obligations or ties to Stephen's, Inc. See Dougan, *Arkansas Odyssey,* 506–7, for a discussion of the Faubus political machine. See also footnote 32, this chapter.

20. Reed, *Faubus,* 151.

21. Reed, *Faubus,* 151.

22. "Negroes Contest School Board's Plea," *Arkansas Gazette,* Jan. 25, 1959.

23. "Arkansas: Propose New School Move Outside Federal Court Jurisdiction," *Southern School News* 5, no. 8 (1959): 14.

24. "Arkansas: Propose New School," 14.

25. "Arkansas: Propose New School," 14. See also Ernest Valachovic, "Racial Unrest in Arkansas Laid to Reds," *Arkansas Gazette,* Jan. 17, 1959.

26. "Faubus Wellwishing Crowd Inspects Raney High School," *Arkansas Gazette,* Jan. 19, 1959.

27. "Virginia School Laws Killed."

28. "Faubus Challenges Crisis Cost Survey, Notes Sales Upturn," *Arkansas Gazette,* Jan. 27, 1959.

29. Ernest Valachovic, "Legislator Heaps Scorn on Press, Would Clip Wings of Gazette Eagle," *Arkansas Gazette,* Jan. 30, 1959.

30. "Arkansas: New Anti-Segregation Lawsuit Starts: First Since Little Rock School Crisis," *Southern School News* 5, no. 9 (1959): 2.

31. "Tyler's Bill Derailed: Poll of Businessmen for School Opening; House Passes, Senate Tables Board Packing," *Arkansas Gazette,* Mar. 3, 1959.

32. Sid McMath, *Promises Kept: A Memoir* (Fayetteville: University of Arkansas Press, 2003), 292–94. The influence of AP&L came into play for any candidate for governor, including Faubus in his first run in 1954. Faubus's biographer, Roy Reed, explains that Faubus dared to run against "their man (Francis) Cherry," who had defeated McMath in 1952 and was planning a second term in 1954. The utility opposed Faubus and raised the company's rates during the election campaign. Faubus brought this up in every campaign speech, blaming his opponent, Cherry, for the increases. When Faubus defeated Cherry after his one-term stint as governor, it was sweet vengeance. It would take a little while to force AP&L to fully support Faubus, but he carefully orchestrated this support by playing Witt Stephens's gas utility against the electric monopoly. Faubus's Public Service Commission was "persuaded to give Stephen's newly acquired Arkansas Louisiana Gas Company two hefty rate increases in 18 months of Faubus's first term." Arkla sharply increased what it charged AP&L for gas to generate electric power. Reed explains that Arkla prospered while AP&L "was being hung out to dry" and that "the Stephens combine became the engine that drove the Faubus machine for twelve years."

33. Bob Trout, "Police Crack State-wide, Teen-age Vice, Dope Ring," *Arkansas Democrat,* Feb. 26, 1959.

34. Huckaby journal, Feb. 17, 1959.

35. Trout, "Police Crack . . . Dope Ring."

36. Joe Wirges and Jerry Jones, "Youth Marijuana Parties Told; Investigators Jail 6," *Arkansas Gazette,* Feb. 27, 1959.

37. Wirges and Jones, "Youth Marijuana Parties Told."

38. Wirges and Jones, "Youth Marijuana Parties Told." See Elizabeth Jacoway's full treatment of miscegenation in *Turn Away Thy Son.*

39. Wirges and Jones, "Youth Marijuana Parties Told."

40. Judy Fagan, telephone interview with author, Sept. 22, 2006.

41. Fagan, interview, Sept. 22, 2006.

42. Rodney Worthington, "Holt Queries Negroes in Marijuana Probe," *Arkansas Democrat,* Feb. 28, 1959.

43. Worthington, "Holt Queries Negroes."

44. Fagan, interview, Sept. 22, 2006.

45. "Pinball Operators Say Judge Set Up Payoff to *Democrat* Reporter," *Arkansas Gazette,* Feb. 27, 1959.

46. "Laster Says Whole Thing 'Ridiculous,'" *Arkansas Gazette,* Feb. 27, 1959.

47. George Douthit, "Faubus Ties Charge to Opening Schools," *Arkansas Democrat,* Mar. 3, 1959.

48. Douthit, "Faubus Ties Charge."

49. Jerry Jones, "Laster Ouster Attempted; Faubus Calls Payoff Charge Plot, but Won't Aid Judge: Integrationist Scheme Seen by Governor," *Arkansas Gazette,* Mar. 4, 1959.

50. Ernest Valachovic, "Governor Said to Back Bills to Abolish Job," *Arkansas Gazette,* Mar. 4, 1959.

51. "Pulaski Legislators in House Withdraw Laster Ouster Bills," *Arkansas Gazette,* Mar. 5, 1959.

52. Fagan, interview, Sept. 22, 2006.

53. "No Minimum Plan Approved by 819–245 Vote," *Arkansas Gazette,* Mar. 3, 1959.

54. "No Minimum Plan Approved."

55. Photo, *Arkansas Gazette,* Mar. 4, 1959.

56. "Gazette Backers Seek to Resurrect School Board Packing Bill," *Arkansas Gazette,* Mar. 4, 1959.

57. Roy Reed, "Howell Offers New Board Bill," *Arkansas Gazette,* Mar. 6, 1959.

58. "Windsor in Vigil over School Bill," *Arkansas Gazette,* Mar. 6, 1959.

59. "Purge Motive Is Uncovered in Tyler Bill," *Arkansas Gazette,* Mar. 5, 1959.

60. "The Teacher Purge," editorial, *Arkansas Gazette,* Feb. 10, 1959.

61. "Teacher Purge."

62. Huckaby journal, Mar. 3, 1959.

63. "Arkansas: New Anti-Segregation Lawsuit Starts."

64. "Purge Motive Is Uncovered."

65. Their entire statement was: "The Executive Committee of the Little Rock Council of Parent-Teachers Associations is strongly opposed to the passage of House Bill 546. We do not understand why the General Assembly would attempt to direct the affairs of any school district. This bill would abolish local control which should be the prerogative of each individual school district. We commend those members of the Pulaski County delegation who had the courage to speak out and vote against the passage of this bill" ("Purge Motive Is Uncovered").

66. "Board Election Bill Hits Snag in House, Reopening Okayed," *Arkansas Gazette,* Mar. 10, 1958.

67. Ernest Valachovic, "House Okays Plan to Elect Three More to School Board," *Arkansas Gazette,* Mar. 12, 1959.

68. Valachovic, "House Okays Plan."

69. "Arkansas: Legislature Adopts 32 Racial Bills, Only Two Stir Up Debate," *Southern School News* 5, no. 10 (1959): 10–12.

70. Huckaby journal, Mar. 2–15, 1959.

71. *Southern School News* 5, no. 10. The constitutional amendment proposed by Faubus in this session was soundly defeated in the Nov. 1960 general election. Faubus's proposed constitutional amendment allowing the closure of public schools by local option went down to a resounding defeat in Nov. 1960.

72. Cathie Remmel Matthews, telephone interview with author, Dec. 7, 2006; Cathie Remmel Matthews, video interview with author, June 20, 2005.

73. Matthews, interview, Dec. 7, 2006.

74. Dick Gardner, telephone interview with author, Dec. 8, 2006; Dick Gardner, audio interview with author, Feb. 14, 2003.

75. Paul Hoover, interview with author, Mar. 11, 2003.

76. Hoover, interview, Mar. 11, 2003.

77. Linda Collins (Newsome), interview with author, Nov. 3, 1998; Linda Collins (Newsome), telephone interview with author, Dec. 10, 2006.

78. P. H. Gilkey, interview with author, Mar. 29, 2003; P. H. Gilkey, telephone interview with author, Dec. 7, 2006.

CHAPTER SIX: WHY NOT BLAME THE TEACHERS?

1. J. Woods, *Black Struggle, Red Scare,* 50, 72–84; Jeff Woods, "Designed to Harass: The Act 10 Controversy in Arkansas," *Arkansas Historical Quarterly* 56, no. 4 (1997): 443–60; "Act 115 Has Served Purpose of Harassing, Bennett Says," *Arkansas Gazette,* June 9, 1959.

2. Huckaby journal, Apr. 7, 9, 1959.

3. See the appendix for a copy of this affidavit.

4. M. Woods, interview, Nov. 10, 1995.

5. Howard Bell, interview with author, Mar. 13, 1996.

6. "UA Dean Attacks Act 10 as McCarthyism Device, Predicts Faculty Exodus," *Arkansas Gazette,* Apr. 30, 1959.

7. J. Woods, *Black Struggle, Red Scare,* 72–84.

8. "Powell Blasts Teacher Act: Refuses to Sign Affidavit," *Arkansas Gazette,* Apr. 11, 1959; J. Woods, *Black Struggle, Red Scare,* 78–79; Jerrol Garrison, "US Court Upholds Act 10 but Rules NAACP Ban Illegal," *Arkansas Gazette,* June 9, 1959. By the time schools opened in 1959–60, J. O. Powell had left the state with his wife, Velma, an active WEC officer. B. T. Shelton was not granted his teaching position at Horace Mann that year either.

9. "Act 115 Has Served Purpose of Harassing."

10. T. E. Patterson, *History of the Arkansas Teachers Association* (Washington, D.C.: National Education Association, 1981), 112–15. Financing for the continuation of the lawsuit was provided in part by the black Arkansas Teachers' Association, using two thousand dollars from the reserve fund and a voluntary donation of five dollars per member. The case was a continuation of *B. T. Shelton v. McKinley* (1959). By Jan. 1960, months after public high schools had reopened, the Arkansas Supreme Court unanimously approved Act 10, saying that school boards had every right to look into teachers' backgrounds. It was spring 1960 before a combined AAUP and NAACP appeal reached the U.S. Supreme Court, and it took until Dec. 1960 for the U.S. Supreme Court to reach a 5–4 decision to overturn the Arkansas affidavit law. See also J. Woods, *Black Struggle, Red Scare,* 79–84.

11. Roy Reed, "NCA Asked to Drop Idled High Schools," *Arkansas Gazette,* Apr. 23, 1959. See also "3 Closed Schools Dropped from NCA," *Arkansas Gazette,* Apr. 25, 1959.

12. Dunnavant, "Long Halls Growing Darker" (journal entry for May 1, 1959).

13. Huckaby journal, Apr. 22, 1959.

14. Huckaby journal, Apr. 23, 1959.

15. Reed, "NCA Asked to Drop Idled High Schools."

16. Huckaby journal, Apr. 24, 1959.

17. "McCuiston Explains Reason for NCA Withdrawal Move," *Arkansas Gazette,* Apr. 26, 1959.

18. Alva J. Gibson, "Proceedings of the Commission on Secondary Schools," *North Central Association Quarterly* 34, no. 1 (1959): 52.

19. Popperfuss, interview, Mar. 9, 1996, 42.

20. Gibson, "Proceedings of the Commission on Secondary Schools," 52.

21. John Starr, "This Is Little Rock Today," *Arkansas Gazette,* Jan. 18, 1959; "Raney High Due to Get State Funds"; "Raney High School Asks for State Aid," *Arkansas Gazette,* Jan. 24, 1959.

22. Dunnavant, "Long Halls Growing Darker," 48–49.

23. L. Adams, interview, Mar. 19, 1996.

24. "Latest Report on Teachers Indicate 176 Won't Return," *Arkansas Gazette,* Apr. 30, 1959.

25. Listed by name in the appendix are high school teachers who did not return in 1959–60, according to LRSD personnel directories. The records are listed by the high school where the teachers were employed in 1958–59.

26. M. Woods, interview, Nov. 10, 1995.

27. Jacoway, *Turn Away Thy Son,* 313.

28. Roy Reed, "Teacher Purge Begun by 3 Board Members," *Arkansas Gazette,* May 6, 1959; Jacoway, *Turn Away Thy Son,* 314–16.

29. Reed, "Teacher Purge Begun."

30. Dunnavant journal, May 5, 1958.

31. H. M. Alexander, *Little Rock Recall Election,* 12. Copies of the purge letter and a list of forty-four purged teachers are included in the appendix.

32. H. M. Alexander, *Little Rock Recall Election,* 12.

33. Shirley Stancil, video interviews with author, June 27, 2005, Feb. 27, 1996.

34. Henry (Royster), Oct. 25, 1995; Jo Ann Henry (Royster), video interview with author, June 27, 2005.

35. Stancil, interviews, June 27, 2005, Feb. 27, 1996.

36. Henry (Royster), interviews, Oct. 25, June 27, 2005.

37. Miller, *Fearless,* 44–45.

38. H. M. Alexander, *Little Rock Recall Election,* 11–19; Murphy, *Breaking the Silence,* 161–65; Brewer, *Embattled Ladies of Little Rock,* 155–59.

39. Huckaby journal, May 6, 1959.

40. Huckaby journal, May 7, 1959.

41. H. M. Alexander, *Little Rock Recall Election,* 11–19.

42. Spitzberg, *Racial Politics in Little Rock,* 17–18.

43. "Here are 179 Who Signed STOP Pledge," *Arkansas Gazette,* May 8, 1959.

44. "Williams School Meeting Tonight," *Arkansas Gazette,* May 8, 1959.

45. Photo, *Arkansas Gazette,* May 6, 1959.

46. Huckaby journal, Mar. 16, 1959.

47. "CHS Faculty Endorses Matson, Lamb, Tucker," *Arkansas Gazette*, May 9, 1959.

48. "Citizens' Council Lawyer Attacks 'Communist-like PTA Objection to Purge,'" *Arkansas Gazette*, May 11, 1959.

49. "Citizens' Council Lawyer Attacks."

50. "Riffel Refutes Guthridge's Charges," *Arkansas Gazette*, May 13, 1959.

51. Spitzberg, *Racial Politics in Little Rock*, 23.

52. Spitzberg, *Racial Politics in Little Rock*, 19.

53. Spitzberg, *Racial Politics in Little Rock*, 19.

54. Jacoway, *Turn Away Thy Son*, 321–22.

55. Miller, *Fearless*, 45.

56. Huckaby journal, May 16, 17, 18, 1959.

57. Advertisement, *Arkansas Gazette*, May 20, 1959.

58. L. Adams, interview, Mar. 19, 1996, 36.

59. William Walker, interview with author, Mar. 23, 1996, 36.

60. H. M. Alexander, *Little Rock Recall Election*, 12. See also Reed, "Teacher Purge Begun."

61. Stancil, interview, Feb. 27, 1996, 44.

62. Stancil, interview, Feb. 27, 1996, 44.

63. Reed, "Teacher Purge Begun."

64. "Faubus Recalls School Board Fired Him, Too," *Arkansas Gazette*, May 7, 1959.

65. "Faubus Recalls School Board Fired Him."

66. See the appendix for a copy of this declaration by students in support of teachers.

67. Irving Spitzberg, video interview with author, Aug. 8, 2006. Spitzberg's involvement in high school colored his views on race, desegregation, and school closure to the point that he eventually wrote *Racial Politics in Little Rock: 1954–64* (1987).

68. Miller, *Fearless*, 47.

69. See the appendix for the May 23, 1959, speech.

70. H. M. Alexander, *Little Rock Recall Election*, 27.

71. H. M. Alexander, *Little Rock Recall Election*, 28.

72. "Negro Teachers Honored," *Arkansas Gazette*, May 20, 1959.

73. Spitzberg, *Racial Politics in Little Rock*, 23. Also see Jacoway, *Turn Away Thy Son*, 442 n.43, which explains that the suit was eventually dropped in 1962.

74. This lawsuit was abandoned in 1962. See reference in Jacoway, *Turn Away Thy Son*, 442 n43; Brewer, *Embattled Ladies of Little Rock*, 161.

75. Advertisement, *Arkansas Gazette*, May 20, 1959; Huckaby journal, May 16, 17, 18, 1959.

76. Huckaby journal, May 15–24, 1959.

77. "McKinley, Moser Named in Libel Suit," *Arkansas Gazette,* May 23, 1959.

78. "Teacher Gets Nod to See Firing Data," *Arkansas Gazette,* May 22, 1959.

79. "Teacher Gets Nod."

80. H. M. Alexander, *Little Rock Recall Election,* 22.

81. H. M. Alexander, *Little Rock Recall Election,* 22.

82. H. M. Alexander, *Little Rock Recall Election,* 31.

83. H. M. Alexander, *Little Rock Recall Election,* 28.

84. H. M. Alexander, *Little Rock Recall Election,* 28.

85. "Governor Comes Out for McKinley Slate," *Arkansas Gazette,* May 23, 1959.

86. Doris Glenn, an English teacher (Huckaby journal, May 8, 1959).

87. Huckaby journal, May 8, 1959.

88. "ALC's Probe May Be Source of Purge List," *Arkansas Gazette,* May 8, 1959.

89. "ALC's Probe May Be Source."

90. "Faubus Says He Didn't Give McKinley Data," *Arkansas Gazette,* May 22, 1959.

91. "3 Teachers Say McKinley Quoted without Authority," *Arkansas Gazette,* May 25, 1959.

92. Huckaby journal, May 21, 1959.

93. Huckaby journal, May 25, 1959.

94. Huckaby journal, May 25–26, 1959.

95. H. M. Alexander, *Little Rock Recall Election,* 31.

96. H. M. Alexander, *Little Rock Recall Election,* 2.

97. H. M. Alexander, *Little Rock Recall Election,* 1, 30; Bill Lewis, "Lease Plan Negotiations Are Started," *Arkansas Gazette,* Sept. 28, 1958.

98. Silverman, *Little Rock Story,* 31.

CHAPTER SEVEN: THE COMMUNITY RALLIES—SOME LEADERS DO NOT

1. Jerol Garrison, "STOP Worker Cheers Little Rock 'Awakening,'" *Arkansas Gazette,* May 26, 1959.

2. Silverman, *Little Rock Story,* 31; H. M. Alexander, *Little Rock Recall Election;* Murphy, *Breaking the Silence,* 160–80; Brewer, *Embattled Ladies of Little Rock,* 155–67; Spitzberg, *Racial Politics in Little Rock,* 12–30; Freyer, *Little Rock on Trial,* 207–11; Reed, *Faubus,* 252–55; Bartley, *Rise of Massive Resistance,* 328–31; Jacoway, *Turn Away Thy Son,* 318–29, 331–34.

3. "Faubus Puts Off Recall Comment," *Arkansas Gazette,* May 26, 1959.

4. Ernest Valachovic, "Governor Sees No Hands-off Warning for Him in Returns," *Arkansas Gazette,* May 28, 1959.

5. Brewer, *Embattled Ladies of Little Rock,* 169. See also Murphy, *Breaking the Silence,* 185.

6. George Bentley, "County Board Picks Three to Succeed Recalled Directors," *Arkansas Gazette,* June 12, 1959.

7. Huckaby journal, June 11, 1959.

8. "Arkansas," *Southern School News 6*, no. 1 (1959); Brewer, *Embattled Ladies of Little Rock,* 170.

9. "Teacher Purge Expunged; New Board Keeps Powell; Hubbard Gives Up Post," *Arkansas Gazette,* June 16, 1959.

10. "Arkansas," *Southern School News 6*, no. 1 (1959). Though the lower courts would soon rule Act 115 unconstitutional, they left Act 10 standing. It would be Dec. 12, 1960, before Act 10 was ruled unconstitutional in a 5–4 decision by the U.S. Supreme Court (*Shelton v. Tucker,* 1960).

11. Gephardt is listed in the LRSD personnel records for 1959–60 as continuing in his position as vocational and printing teacher at Central High School.

12. "Teacher Purge Expunged." Teachers who failed to sign Act 10 and were listed in the newspaper are included here. The following information was gained from interviews with the author regarding persons whose names were publicized for not complying with Act 10, most of whom had been purged:

J. O. Powell, the vice principal of Central High, left Arkansas for California.

Ernest Gephardt, the industrial education teacher at Central High, appears on the official list of school personnel issued by the LRSD for 1959–60 under "Vocational, and Printing."

Jennie Perkins, the social science teacher at Central High, was cited for failing to sign Act 10. Her name does not appear in the LRSD personnel directory for the 1959–60 school year.

Mary Gaines, the home economics teacher from Dunbar Junior High, left Arkansas to teach in Chicago.

Zerita Tate, the math teacher from Dunbar Junior High, left Arkansas to teach in Colorado.

B. T. Shelton, the trades teacher at Dunbar Junior High, lost his job but continued his lawsuit against the district, winning it in 1960 (*Shelton v. Tucker*).

L. M. Christophe, the principal of Horace Mann High, signed Act 10, but because of his purge, he left Arkansas and became the principal of Howard High in Wilmington, Delaware. Several other teachers from Mann accompanied him, and some later moved to work for him in Delaware.

13. Powell and Powell Collection.

14. A list of teachers from the three high schools who did not return in 1959–60 can be found in the appendix. The list in the appendix was compiled from LRSD personnel directories in the author's personal collection.

15. Huckaby journal, June 18, 1959.

16. Silverman, *Little Rock Story,* 33.

17. Spitzberg, *Racial Politics in Little Rock,* 110.

18. Jacoway, *Turn Away Thy Son,* 328, chap. 17 ("The New Elite Consensus").

19. B. F. Johnson, "After 1957," 270–71.

20. Jacoway, *Turn Away Thy Son,* 332.

21. Reed, *Faubus,* 255.

22. Brewer, *Embattled Ladies of Little Rock*, 165–66; Huckaby journal, June 3, 1959.

23. Almeta Lanum (Smith), interview with author, Oct. 18, 1998.

24. Mary Ragston (Dennis), interview with author, Jan. 14, 1999.

25. Bob Lawrence, telephone interview with author, Dec. 21, 2006.

26. Betty Douglas (Brumbelow), interview with author, Dec. 21, 2006.

27. "Arkansas," *Southern School News* 6, no 1 (1959).

28. Philip Moore, telephone interview with author, Dec. 20, 2006.

29. David Scruggs, video interview with author, July 27, 2005.

30. Elkins, "Secondary Education."

31. "Arkansas," *Southern School News* 5, no. 12 (1959): 2–3.

32. "Arkansas," *Southern School News* 5, no. 12 (1959): 2–3.

33. Elkins, "Secondary Education," 24–26.

34. Elkins, "Secondary Education," 28–29.

35. However, on Sept. 9, after all public high schools had operated for weeks, the Anthonys announced that all but ten students who had registered with them had enrolled in the public schools and that they would not operate facilities for high school students.

36. "Arkansas," *Southern School News* 6, no. 2 (1959): 6. See also Jacoway, *Turn Away Thy Son,* 307.

37. Murphy, *Breaking the Silence,* 187–89.

38. Brewer, *Embattled Ladies of Little Rock,* 144–46. See also Ben F. Johnson III, "Resisting Integration in Little Rock," *Arkansas Historical Quarterly* 65, no. 2 (2007): 258–83.

39. Jacoway, *Turn Away Thy Son,* 313, 335, 307; B. F. Johnson, "Resisting Integration in Little Rock," 270.

40. *Southern School News* 6, no. 2 (1959): 6.

41. *Southern School News* 6, no. 3 (1959): 1.

42. *Southern School News* 6, no. 2 (1959): 6. See the letter to Governor Faubus in Brewer, *Embattled Ladies of Little Rock,* 193–97.

43. Murphy, *Breaking the Silence,* 195.

44. Murphy, *Breaking the Silence,* 194.

45. Murphy, *Breaking the Silence,* 194.

46. Jacoway, *Turn Away Thy Son,* 338.

47. Brewer, *Embattled Ladies of Little Rock,* 186–87.

48. Well after the high schools opened, the LRSD began hearings of appeals on Sept. 8, 1959.

49. Melba Patillo Beals, *White Is a State of Mind: A Memoir* (New York: Penguin Putnam, 1999).

50. Biography of Thelma Mothershed, National Park Service, Little Rock Central High School National Historic Site Collection.

51. "3 Negroes Assigned to Hall, 3 to Central under '59 State Act," *Arkansas Gazette,* Aug. 1, 1959. On the first day of classes, because the high schools opened quite early, Carlotta Walls was still out of town attending summer school in

Chicago. For this reason, Elizabeth went with Jefferson to the Central High campus to support him. The remaining members of the Little Rock Nine had moved away and were enrolled out of state, except Ernest Green, who had graduated in May 1958 and was attending college in Michigan.

52. Jacoway, *Turn Away Thy Son*, 342.

53. Huckaby journal, June 24–July 20, 1959.

54. Huckaby journal, July 20, 1959

55. Huckaby journal, July 21, 1959.

56. *Southern School News 6*, no. 3 (1959): 1.

57. Elkins, "Secondary Education," 15–16. By mid-Sept., the LRPSC had officially closed the doors of Raney High, leaving only the disposition of property and transcripts. T. J. Raney said the school had been closed "for all practical purposes" since Aug. 15, when he released most of the staff. The building itself belonged to Vance Thompson of McCrory, from whom the property had been leased the previous Oct. ("Raney High Closes Door: Board to Meet," *Arkansas Gazette*, Sept. 17, 1959).

58. Reed, *Faubus*, 255–56; Jacoway, *Turn Away Thy Son*, 341; Brewer, *Embattled Ladies of Little Rock*, 197.

59. Brewer, *Embattled Ladies of Little Rock*, 193.

60. Brewer, *Embattled Ladies of Little Rock*, 197.

61. Huckaby journal, Aug. 4–14, 1959.

62. Jacoway, *Turn Away Thy Son*, 339.

63. Roy Reed, "Segregationists Cite Polio Fear," *Arkansas Gazette*, Aug. 6, 1959; "Dr. Salk, 36 Doctors See No Polio Danger in Early School Opening," *Arkansas Gazette*, Aug. 7, 1959.

64. "Dr. Salk, 36 Doctors."

65. Murphy, *Breaking the Silence*, 196.

66. Dougan, *Arkansas Odyssey*, 504. Lamb, by far the board member most open to full integration, would serve two terms on the board; would lose twenty-one of twenty-six of his advertising accounts in Arkansas, due to harassment by segregationists; and at midlife would retrain as a lawyer rather than an advertising executive. Such were the consequences of demonstrating the moral courage to publicly speak up for racial integration. Lamb later committed suicide.

67. Jerry Jones, "Rally at Capitol Got Paraders in Noisy Mood," *Arkansas Gazette*, Aug. 13, 1959.

68. Roy Reed, "Police Rout March on Central Arrest 24; Hall Opening Quiet," *Arkansas Gazette*, Aug. 13, 1959. See also Jerry Dhonau, "Soggy and Cursing Marchers Never Got Near Their Target," *Arkansas Gazette*, Aug. 13, 1959.

69. Brewer, *Embattled Ladies of Little Rock*, 199–200.

70. Roy Reed, "School Office, City Officials' Places Bombed," *Arkansas Gazette*, Sept. 8, 1959.

71. "Target; Office of Langford, City Director," *Arkansas Gazette*, Sept. 12, 1959.

72. "Target; Office of Langford."

73. Roy Reed, "Hearing Today: Police Question another Suspect," *Arkansas Gazette*, Sept. 10, 1959.

74. "Citizens' Council President Praises Bombing Suspect," *Arkansas Gazette,* Sept. 11, 1959.

75. B. F. Johnson, *Arkansas in Modern America,* 147. Also, Reed, *Faubus,* 257.

76. "School Board Hears Appeals of 9 Students," *Arkansas Gazette,* Sept. 9, 1959.

77. Reed, *Faubus,* 209. Lee Andrew Hill, telephone interview with author, Dec. 21, 2006.

78. "School Board Winds Up Pupil Transfer Hearings," *Arkansas Gazette,* Sept. 10, 1959.

79. "3 Negro Pupils Get Transfers," *Arkansas Gazette,* Sept. 16, 1959.

80. Sybil Jordan Hampton, telephone interview with author, Dec. 27, 2006. After admission to Central, Hampton found the teachers "excellent" and the environment fair and well run. She believes the setting benefited her learning. Her own mother was a teacher in the Little Rock school system, and she recalls that Ted Lamb later visited with her mother regarding that school interview. Hampton graduated from Central High and later attended Earlham College, a Quaker school in Richmond, Indiana. Later, Ted Lamb's son attended the same school.

81. "1959 School Board Tells of Two Dissenters on Transfer Vote," *Arkansas Gazette,* Sept. 17, 1959.

82. "1959 School Board Tells of Two Dissenters."

83. See footnote 66 above.

84. "Segregation-Desegregation Status," *Southern School News* 5, no. 12 (1959): 1.

85. Jacoway, *Turn Away Thy Son,* 352.

86. Kirk, *Redefining the Color Line,* 170–76; *LRSD v. PCSSD* (E.D. Ark. 2007); *Arkansas Democrat-Gazette,* Feb. 24, 2007, quoted in B. F. Johnson, "Resisting Integration in Little Rock," 283 n33. Historian John A. Kirk has written extensively of the pattern of resistance to desegregation in *Beyond Little Rock,* particularly the last three chapters: "White Opposition to the Civil Rights Struggle—Massive Resistance and Minimum Compliance" (94–115), "White Support for the Civil Rights Struggle" (116–38), and "City Planning and the Civil Rights Struggle" (139–58).

87. B. F. Johnson, *Arkansas in Modern America,* 153–54.

88. Ed Williams, email to author, Sept. 7, 2006; official LRSD records (http://quickfacts.census.gov/qfd/states/05/0541000.html).

89. Robert L. Brown, "The Second Crisis of Little Rock: A Report on Desegregation Within the Little Rock Public Schools" (Winthrop Rockefeller Foundation, June 1988); " The Third Crisis in Little Rock," *Arkansas Historical Quarterly* 65, no. 1 (2006): 39–45.

90. *LRSD v. PCSSD* (E.D. Ark. 2007); *Arkansas Democrat-Gazette,* Feb. 24, 2007, as quoted in B. F. Johnson, "Resisting Integration in Little Rock," 283 n.33. See entire article (258–83).

91. Williams, email, Sept. 7, 2006; official LRSD Records (http://quickfacts.census.gov/qfd/states/05/05119.html and http://quickfacts.census.gov/qud/states/05/0541000.html).

92. Irving Spitzberg, video interview with author, May 10, 2006.

AFTERWORD

1. D. Gardner, interview, Feb. 14, 2003.

2. Gilkey, interview, Mar. 29, 2003.

3. Margaret Martin-Hall, "Dreams Deferred: Students of the 1958–59 Little Rock School District Lost Year" (Ph.D. diss., University of Arkansas at Little Rock, 2001), 58.

4. Edie Garland (Barentine), video interview with author, July 22, 2005.

5. Gilkey, interview with author, Mar. 29, 2003.

6. Faye Perry (Russ), interview with author, Sept. 28, 1998.

7. See footnote 90 in chapter 7 and references within the text (295–96).

8. Robert L. Brown, personal communication with author, Apr. 2, 2008. *Lakeview v. Mike Huckabee and the State of Arkansas* demanded an overhaul of the state's school-funding mechanism. The Arkansas General Assembly met in special session in Jan. 2004 and obligated spending more than $400 million in additional money for adequacy and equity in the state's schools—an increase of 13.5 percent—to meet the needs of Arkansas's children.

INDEX

Sondra Gordy is professor of history at the University of Central Arkansas. She has received a number of awards, including University Educator of the Year from the Arkansas Council of the Social Studies, Teaching Excellence Award Winner from the University of Central Arkansas, and the Violet B. Gingles Award from the Arkansas Historical Association. She produced a documentary entitled *The Lost Year*. A copy of the DVD can be ordered at www.thelostyear.com.